英语专业系列教材

A COURSE OF ENGLISH AND AMERICAN POETRY

SECOND EDITION

国家精品资源共享课《英美诗歌欣赏》教材
国家精品课程《英美诗歌欣赏》教材

英美诗歌教程（第二版）

李正栓　主　编
吴晓梅　张青梅　白凤欣　副主编

清华大学出版社
北 京

内 容 简 介

本书共收英、美两国52位著名诗人的100首诗，在第一版的基础上修订而成。编写体例实用、注释详略得当、译文准确优雅。全书分英国诗歌和美国诗歌两大部分，按诗人出生年代排列，每位诗人为一章，每章均包含5大板块：作者生平简介、诗作原文、注释、参考译诗、思考题。

本书适用于英语专业学生作为文学教材，也可作报考英语专业研究生时的参考用书，还可用于非英语专业的学生作为选修课或自学教材。

图书在版编目（CIP）数据

英美诗歌教程 / 李正栓主编. —2版. —北京：清华大学出版社，2014（2021.1重印）
（英语专业系列教材）
ISBN 978-7-302-37600-2

Ⅰ. 英…　Ⅱ. ①李…　Ⅲ. ①英语—高等学校—教材 ②诗歌欣赏—英国 ③诗歌欣赏—美国　Ⅳ. ①H31

中国版本图书馆CIP数据核字（2014）第186511号

责任编辑：刘细珍
封面设计：覃一彪
责任校对：王凤芝
责任印制：丛怀宇

出版发行：清华大学出版社
网　址：http://www.tup.com.cn，http://www.wqbook.com
地　址：北京清华大学学研大厦A座　**邮　编：**100084
社总机：010-62770175　**邮　购：**010-62786544
投稿与读者服务：010-62776969，c-service@tup.tsinghua.edu.cn
质 量 反 馈：010-62772015，zhiliang@tup.tsinghua.edu.cn
印 装 者：三河市金元印装有限公司
经　销：全国新华书店
开　本：170mm×230mm　**印　张：**20.75　**字　数：**345千字
（附光盘1张）
版　次：2004年10月第1版　2014年9月第2版　**印　次：**2021年1月第5次印刷
定　价：69.00元

产品编号：060183-03

第二版前言
Foreword (2nd Edition)

《英美诗歌教程》自2004年出版以来，10年时间飞逝而过。这本教材连续多次印刷，获得了广泛好评。全国各高校广大教师使用这本教材为学生开设了精彩的英美诗歌欣赏课程，使这本小书长销不衰，给了我们极大的鼓舞。同时，在多年的使用过程中，这本教材也经受了考验，我们发现仍有不少需要完善之处。为了更好地为广大教师服务，并进一步完善教材、丰富内容，我们决定对第一版教材进行修订。

修订的基本原则是：保持第一版体例；适当增减内容；增加思考题。

这本教材最初是为非英语专业学生开设选修课而编写的，在使用过程中，帮助非英语专业学生增加文学和文化知识、进行文理渗透的目标实现了。但后来发现，许多学校使用这本教材为英语专业本科生讲授英美诗歌，并且还成为英语专业学生考研究生的复习和参考用书之一。因此，我们更需要审视教材内容并研究需要改进之处。我们发现，有如下几个问题需要解决：1. 第一版诗歌所选篇目略显不足，需要增加一定数量的诗。2. 第一版中，有些诗过长，有的表现了不合时宜的价值观，需要调整。3. 第一版中，当代诗歌较少。虽然公认的当代著名诗人不多，但也有鲜明特色，所以有必要收进一些读者和评论家比较认可的当代诗人及其代表诗作。4. 第一版中，为了给教师更大的主动权，没有设计练习。这样一来，学生学完诗歌后不知从何处进行思考。因此，需要设计一些思考题，以使学生巩固所学诗歌，进行分析、比较和思考。这些思考题对理解诗歌的主旨以及如何欣赏这些诗歌给出了提示和思考的角度，对学生的创造性学习以及发散性思维都很有指导意义。

在编写第二版时我们考虑了不同层次学生的需要。1. 为了使读者更全面地了解某位诗人的风貌，我们增加了一些一般诗集和教材很少选用的篇目。比如，大多数诗歌选集都会选录莎士比亚最经典的十四行诗第十八首、第二十九首等。提起这些名篇，很多学生耳熟能详，甚至倒背如流，但是如果问起莎士比亚十四行诗的第一首，很多学生会张口结舌，他们不知道莎士比亚的十四行诗第一首其实是一首完美的开篇诗，很值得学习和欣赏。2. 对于一些篇幅太长的诗歌，比如托马斯·格雷的《墓畔哀歌》，我们只选择了本诗的开头几节，使读者对此诗有一个基本的认识，感兴趣的同学课下可以再进一步学习研究。3. 很多学生学过彭斯的《一朵红红的玫瑰》，但是却不知道《友谊地久天长》这首永恒的歌曲同样也出自彭斯之手，所以我们在编写第二版时兼顾了所选作品的深度和广度。

本书第一版包括32位诗人的65首作品。大部分是经典的诗歌作品，近现代的作品偏少。随着时代的发展，读者越来越渴望能够更全面地了解英美诗歌的演变及发展，所以我们在第二版中进行了补充和调整。第二版包括52位诗人的100首作品。英国诗歌中，增加了托马斯·哈代、吉拉德·曼莱·霍普金斯、阿尔弗莱德·爱德华·霍斯曼、塔特·休斯和西默斯·希尼等诗人及其代表作。美国诗歌中增加了华莱士·史蒂文斯、朗斯顿·休斯、约翰·阿什贝利和大卫·莱曼等诗人及其代表作。现当代诗歌没有产生巨匠，但是多样性的风格及创作使英美诗坛五彩缤纷，尤其是涉及现代社会这一主题的诗歌很值得学习和研究。另外，美国诗坛曾经是白种诗人一统天下，在近现代则出现了多元化的局面，比如黑人“桂冠诗人”朗斯顿·休斯的作品表明：美国现代的主流文化不仅是白人的文化，还包括黑人以及其他少数族裔的文化。丰富多彩的诗人及作品为学生学习以及研究提供了多样性的选择。

当然，学无止境，在使用过程中如果读者有建设性的建议，欢迎不吝赐教，以便我们进一步完善。

李正栓

2014年5月

第一版前言
Foreword (1st Edition)

北京大学胡家峦教授在《英语诗歌精品》（北京大学出版社，1995）一书中，引用英国诗人Thomas Nash的话说："诗是百花之蜜，一切学问的精髓，智慧的本质，天使的词语。"胡家峦教授接着说道："纳什的名言，既是他本人对诗的高度概括的形象描述，又是他同时代的英国人对诗歌的极为普遍的传统认识。……这种认识来源于英国的诗歌沃土。……在英国文学史上，自民族史诗《贝奥武夫》直到18世纪现代小说兴起之前，'诗'几乎是'文学'的代名词。"

隋刚说："英语诗歌是一个充满活力、不断发展的有机体系，是一个色彩斑斓、意境深远的文学世界。……诗海无边，是全人类共有的文化风景的一部分。"（《英美诗歌意境漫游》，外文出版社，1998）

隋刚对于诗歌还有如下论述："人天生爱诗。……人珍惜诗意——自知必须靠自己在生活中发现诗意或创造诗意。……人生如诗，诗如人生。……诗意的生活是有情趣的生活，是有爱心的生活，是有信仰的生活。……诗意的生活是有安全感的生活。……人在，诗在。"（同上）

一位智者曾说道："人诗意地栖居于大地之上。"（同上）

颜学军如此说："诗歌犹如一盏盏古典的烛火，在苍凉的角落闪着温暖的光芒。这些光芒如一枚枚箭，刺痛着黑夜里跋涉的眼睛，让身虽疲惫的人不至于累倒。诗歌作为一种源远流长的艺术，它如阳光和水，浸透了我们脚下的这片土地。它是一种不死的鸟，在我们的灵魂深处飞翔、叫鸣，高高低低无所不在。诗歌滋润和喂养了一代一代人。"（《百年诗歌赏析》，江西文化音像出版社，2004）。

我们认为，诗，作为最古老、最高级的文学形式，具有很强的教育和娱乐功能，诗歌里的真善美使人知过去，识未来，净化灵魂，陶冶情操，能有效地提高人的修养和素质。

我们还认为，激昂产生诗情；恬然酝酿诗意；思与想的过程迸发诗的火花；感情世界里富含诗的温柔；痛苦能以诗的形式抒发；欢乐能以诗的形式高歌；动有动的诗，静有静的诗；生有生命的赞美诗，死有死亡的墓志铭。生活中，诗无时不在，无处不在。

实际上，中国人对诗并不陌生。关于中国诗词，中国古典诗词学会常务副会长兼秘书长一刀指出："世界上没有哪一个国家能像中国一样拥有多如繁星的诗人词家，浩如烟海的诗歌词作。……诗词里凝聚了历代勤劳聪慧、感情丰富的中国人民多姿多彩的生活：他们的劳动，他们的奋斗，他们的感触，……当然，'诗言志'、'词缘情'，诗词里表露着诗人词家们高尚的爱国情操，飞扬着他们的凌云壮志，记载着他们的悲欢离合，传达着他们的喜怒哀乐，也渗透了他们对人生的体验、对世界的思考。缠绵的爱情，真挚的友情，浓郁的乡情，情真意切、感人至深，感事、咏物、讽喻，意味深长、发人深省……诗词，具有征服人心的魔力。"（《中国古典诗词赏析》，内蒙古文化出版社，2002）

英语诗歌也不乏一刀先生对中国诗词所概括的内容。

许渊冲教授指出："21世纪是全球化的世纪。新世纪的新人不但应该了解全球的文化，而且应该使本国文化走向世界，成为全球文化的一部分，使世界文化更加灿烂辉煌。如果说20世纪是美国世纪的话，那么，19世纪可以说是英国世纪，18世纪则是法国世纪。再推上去，自7世纪至13世纪，则可以说是中国世纪或唐宋世纪，因为中国在唐宋六百年间，政治制度先进，经济繁荣，文化发达，是全世界其他国家难以企及的。"

本书的编写旨在帮助"新世纪的新人了解全球文化"的部分精华，也希望读者在了解了英美诗歌后对传播中国文化产生兴趣，积极温习中国诗歌，在合适的时间和场所向外国朋友推广我们的文化，以达到世界范围的文化沟通与思想融合，为实现世界的和平与共同繁荣做出自己的贡献。

英美诗歌是人类文明的一个重要组成部分，具有很高的艺术成就、思想价值和很强的教育功能，在英语国家以及学习英语的人群中，具有重要的启迪作用。多少人通过教授或学习英美诗歌了解了异域风情，解读了不同文化，丰厚了自己的思想，丰富了自己的语言，营养了自己的文化，加强了自己的素养，提高了自身的素质。其教育功能、娱乐功能、启迪作用是世人皆知的。

作为面向世界、面向未来、面向现代化大形势要求下成长起来的大学生，作为立志通过各种学习以提高自身素质为祖国建设服务的新型人才，作为愿意在国际化环境下、跨文化范围日益扩大的环境中高效工作的劳动者，虽不能完全做到“学贯中西”，也应当做到“略输”中西“文采”。因此，不少仁人志士和学者专家呼吁向英语专业和非英语专业的学生提供旨在提高修养和素养的各种课程，含中外诗歌必修课和选修课，并倡导文理渗透。这种倡导得到广大师生的认可和赞许。我们这本《英美诗歌教程》是这种思想支配下的一种努力。

《英美诗歌教程》编写体例是实用的。1. 分英国诗歌和美国诗歌两部分；2. 按诗人出生年代排列；3. 提供作者生平简介，供教师讲授或学生自己阅读；4. 诗作原文；5. 较为详尽的注解，主要由编者注释，部分由著名学者所注，也有编者与其他学者思想的结合，旨在帮助学生从英语注释中学到更多的英语，用英语解释原诗，以进一步提高读者英文水平；6. 参考译诗。译文是经过斟酌译出，也有著名翻译家的译作，旨在帮助学生加深对诗歌的理解并通过语言对比提高自己的鉴赏能力。

《英美诗歌教程》共收英、美两国32位诗人的65首诗。所选都是英国和美国文学史上的著名诗人。诗篇也大都是这些诗人的抒情力作，或讴歌大自然，或歌咏爱情，或赞颂祖国，或感叹人生，或激发希望，或尽情嬉戏于田园，或沉思城市尘嚣，或探索天庭神秘，或探讨人与人之间的关系，或抒发人对自然的深情。应当说，所选诗作给我们提供了一个过去丰富的世界，展示了人生的现实，描绘了人们向往的乐园般美景。这些诗作对一个人的成长会大有裨益。

编写之前，曾想过在诗作原文注释后设计一些思考题，供同学们思考。后来觉得应留给任课教师一些天地，让他们发挥自己的主观能动性，随讲课进程和内容设计自己的问题。让学生在不事先看已设问题的情况下思考教师自己设计的问题，让学生边学边欣赏，以达到更好的学习目的和效果。我们想让学生在教师讲解之时或之后去品味，按自己的理解去欣赏佳作。因此，本书也不提供赏析范例。

《英美诗歌教程》的读者对象主要包括非英语专业的大学生，适合于参加选修课或自学；对英语专业的大学生也有很大参考价值，可作为对已有文学教材的补充，也可作报考英语专业研究生时的重要复习和参考内容。实际上，只要有一定的英语基础并愿意使自己成为一个有情感有文化有修养的人，都应学习一些英语诗歌。诗歌本身没有英语专业和非英语专业之分。本书注释详细、译文优雅，因此也非常适合广大的英语和文学爱好者。

在编写过程中，我们参考过一些学者的研究成果，已在参考文献部分及译文后或注释中注明，在此一并表示感谢。在本书出版过程中，清华大学外文系吕中舌教授通读了书稿并提出宝贵意见。清华大学出版社宫力老师给予了大力支持，徐梦非老师极为认真仔细地编辑了本书，那种严谨治学的精神令人钦佩，我们对她的感谢之情难于言表。由于水平所限，不足之处仍在所难免，希望发现后指正。

编者

2002年12月

Contents

Part One
English Poetry

PART TWO
American Poetry

Part One

English Poetry

Edmund Spenser
埃德蒙·斯宾塞
（1552−1599）

Edmund Spenser, the greatest nondramatic poet of the English Renaissance, is called the "poet's poet". He was born in a merchant's family in London. He attended the Merchant Tailors' School, the headmaster of which was Richard Mulcaster, an enlightened scholar with advanced ideas of educating people. In 1596, he went to Cambridge. His reading of the classics and Italian poets at Cambridge laid a solid foundation for his later career as a poet. It was also at Cambridge that he began to write poems. In religion, he was much influenced by Puritanism. He even translated some poems for a volume of anti-Catholic propaganda. He got the degree of B.A. in 1573 and M.A. in 1576.

After graduation from Cambridge, he served some prominent men, including Dr. John Yong (Bishop of Rochester), the Earl of Leicester (the queen's favorite), and Lord Grey of Wilton (Lord Deputy of Ireland).

His friendship with Sir Philip Sidney and Sir Edward Dyer, and their common interest in reforming English poetry influenced his writing. Together, they made their effort to promote a new English poetry. Spenser's contribution to this movement is *The Shepheardes Calendar* (published in 1579), which he dedicated to Sir Philip Sidney.

From 1580 to his death he served first as secretary of Lord Grey, then worked as clerk and sheriff officer in Ireland. In 1599, his house on the estate of 3,000 acres was burned down in an uprising. He fled to London and died in poverty in the same year. He was buried just beside Geoffrey Chaucer in Westminster Abbey.

Both *The Faerie Queene* (1589, 1596) and *Amoretti* (1595) were written in Ireland. *Amoretti* is a sonnet sequence of 89 sonnets, making a record of his courtship of Elizabeth Boyle.

Amoretti[1]: Sonnet 34

Lyke as[2] a ship that through the Ocean wyde[3],
By conduct of[4] some star doth[5] make her way,
Whenas a storme hath dimd her trusty guyde,[6]
Out of her course doth wander far astray.
So I whose star, that wont with her bright ray,
Me to direct,[7] with cloudes is overcast,[8]
Doe[9] wander now in darknesse[10] and dismay,
Through hidden perils round about me plast[11].
Yet hope I well, that when this storme is past,
My Helice the lodestar of my lyfe,[12]
Will shine again, and looke on[13] me at last,
With lovely light to cleare[14] my cloudy grief.
Till then I wander carefull[15] comfortlesse[16],
In secret sorrow and sad pensivenesse[17].

注释

1. **Amoretti** an Italian word, meaning "little love poems". Spenser's *Amoretti* is a group of sonnets to a girl named Elizabeth—probably Elizabeth Boyle, who became Spenser's second wife.
2. **Lyke as** like
3. **wyde** wide
4. **By conduct of** guided by
5. **doth** （古用法）动词do的第三人称单数现在时，即does
6. **Whenas a storme hath dimd her trusty guyde** whenas: when; hath dimd: has dimmed; guyde: guide
7. **that wont with her bright ray / Me to direct** that wont to direct me with her bright ray. wont: used
8. **with cloudes is overcast** is overcast with cloudes. cloudes: clouds
9. **Doe** do
10. **darknesse** darkness
11. **round about me plast** plast round about me. plast: placed
12. **My Helice the lodestar of my lyfe** Helice 是大熊星座（Ursa Major）的又一名称，

也是文艺九女神的住地赫利孔山（Helicon）下一座城市的名称。the lodestar是Helice的同位语。lyfe: life

13. **looke on** look on, look at
14. **cleare** clear
15. **carefull** full of care
16. **comfortlesse** comfortless
17. **pensivenesse** pensiveness: 沉思

参考译诗

爱情小诗：第34首十四行诗

如同一只船驶在茫茫的海面，
全凭着一颗星辰来为它导航，
一旦风暴把可靠的向导遮暗，
它就会远离自己的航道漂荡。
我的星辰曾常常用它的亮光，
为我指路，现却被乌云笼罩，
我在深深的黑暗和苦闷中彷徨，
绕过我周围重重的险滩暗礁。
但是我希望，经过这一场风暴，
我的北斗呵，我那生命的北极星，
会再次闪现，最终把我来照耀，
用它的光辉驱除我忧郁的阴云。
在这以前，我忧心忡忡地徘徊，
独自暗暗地悲伤，愁思满怀。

（胡家峦　译）

思考题

1. What's the rhyme scheme of this poem?
2. What is the main idea of this sonnet? What are the related images?

Amoretti: Sonnet 75

One day I wrote her name upon the strand[1],
But came the waves and washéd it away:
Agayne[2] I wrote it with a second hand,
But came the tyde[3], and made my paynes his pray[4].
"Vayne[5] man," sayd[6] she, "that doest in vaine assay,
A mortall thing so to immortalize,[7]
For I my selve[8] shall lyke to this decay[9],
And eek my name bee wypéd out lykewize."[10]
"Not so," quod[11] I, "let baser things devize[12],
To dy[13] in dust, but you shall live by fame:
My verse your vertues[14] rare shall eternize,
And in the heavens wryte[15] your glorious name.
Where whenas[16] death shall all the world subdew[17],
Our love shall live, and later life renew[18]."

注释

1. **strand** seashore
2. **Agayne** again
3. **tyde** tide
4. **made my paynes his pray** paynes: pains; pray: prey
5. **Vayne** vain
6. **sayd** said
7. **that doest in vaine assay / A mortall thing so to immortalize** that doest assay in vain so to immortalize a mortall thing. 徒然地企图使一个终将死亡的东西变为不朽。doest: does; assay: try, attempt; mortall: mortal
8. **my selve** myself
9. **lyke to this decay** decay lyke to this. lyke to: like
10. **And eek my name bee wypéd out lykewise** eek: also; bee: be; wypéd out: wiped out
11. **quod** said
12. **devize** devise
13. **To dy** to die

14. **vertues** virtues
15. **wryte** write
16. **whenas** when
17. **subdew** subdue
18. **later life renew** renew later life

参考译诗

爱情小诗：第75首十四行诗

有一天，我把她名字写在沙滩，
但海浪来了，把那个名字冲跑：
我用手再一次把它写了一遍，
但潮水来了，把我的辛苦又吞掉。
“自负的人呵，”她说：“你这是徒劳，
妄想使世间凡俗的事物不朽；
我本身就会像这样云散烟消，
我的名字也同样会化为乌有。”
“不，”我说：“让低贱的东西去筹谋
死亡之路，但你将靠美名而永活：
我的诗将使你的美德长留，
并把你光辉的名字写在天国。
死亡可以征服整个的世界，
我们的爱将长存，生命永不灭。”

（胡家峦　译）

注释

1. Identify the rhyme scheme of this poem.
2. After a brief story-like narration in the first quatrain, the rest of the lines are written in a dialogue form. What do you think of this writing style?
3. What is the main idea of this sonnet?

Christopher Marlowe
克里斯托弗·马洛
(1564–1593)

Christopher Marlowe was born in a shoemaker's family in Canterbury, two months older than Shakespeare. Part of his early schooling at King's School in Canterbury, beginning from 1578, was a good experience to him. When he studied Latin at King's School, one of the methods in teaching speaking was to train the pupils and students to act in classical plays. Such training must have paved the way for him to become a playwright.

In 1580, he left Canterbury for Cambridge where he studied for six years and finally got his degree of M.A. in 1587. At Corpus Christi College, Cambridge, he spent a lot of time on divinity as required, but he refused to take holy orders. Instead, he began to write plays.

Marlowe was learned and knowledgeable. He commanded a good knowledge of astronomy, geography, medical science, history, Greek epics and Latin. His special interest in drama led him to London in 1587. In the same year, he took London by storm with his play *Tamburlaine*, perhaps in collaboration with Thomas Nashe when he was at Cambridge. In the years when he was in London, he wrote five more plays, including *The Jew of Malta* (1592) and *Dr. Faustus* (1588).

Marlowe's abnormal death is a matter of great pity. When Marlowe died, Shakespeare had just begun to write some minor plays. Nobody can exactly tell what the English drama would have been like if he had not died a sudden early death. History tells people that he died from a dagger thrust in an argument over the bill in an inn on May 30, 1593. There is also a saying that he was a victim of planned political murder. It is Thomas Kid, another playwright with whom Marlowe was living together in London who gave information to the Privy Council accusing him of writing against the *Bible* and treason. A bright star with a life of only 29 years old thus fell out of the heaven of English literature.

The Passionate Shepherd to His Love written by Marlowe is a much-quoted poem commented upon in different ways.

The Passionate Shepherd to His Love

Come live with me and be my love,
And we will all the pleasures prove[1]
That valleys, groves, hills, and fields,
Woods, or steepy mountain yields[2].

And we will sit upon the rocks,
Seeing the shepherds feed their flocks,
By shallow rivers to whose falls[3]
Melodious birds sing madrigals[4].

And I will make thee beds of roses
And a thousand fragrant posies,
A cap of flowers, and a kirtle[5]
Embroidered all with leaves of myrtle[6];

A gown made of the finest wool
Which from our pretty lambs we pull;
Fair lined slippers for the cold,
With buckles[7] of the purest gold;

A belt of straw and ivy[8] buds,
With coral clasps[9] and amber studs[10]:
And if these pleasures may thee move,
Come live with me, and be my love.

Thy silver dishes for thy meat[11]
As precious as the gods do eat,
Shall on an ivory table be

Prepared each day for thee and me.

The shepherds' swains[12] shall dance and sing
For thy delight each May morning:
If these delights thy mind may move,
Then live with me and be my love.

注释

1. **prove** （古用法）experience
2. **yields** gives
3. **falls** the sound of the stream
4. **madrigals** love songs
5. **kirtle** long gowns
6. **myrtle** 桃金娘，即爱神维纳斯（Venus）的圣物
7. **buckles** （鞋的）带扣
8. **ivy** 常春藤，酒神 Bacchus 的圣物
9. **clasps** 扣子
10. **amber studs** 琥珀饰钮
11. **meat** （古用法）food
12. **swains** （古用法）乡村情郎

参考译诗

痴情的牧羊人致意中人

来，与我同住，做我的爱人，
我们会体验各种乐趣与欢欣；
品尝所有颠连高山的俏丽，
还有山谷田野带来的乐趣。

在那里，我们将坐在山石上，
看牧羊人放牧他们的群羊。
在浅唱的小溪边，悦耳动听的
小鸟欢唱着恋人们爱唱的情歌。

在那里，我将用玫瑰给你铺床，
还伴有千朵花儿吐芬芳；
为你编做一顶花冠，还有一条长裙，
长裙上桃金娘绿叶散发香馨。

从美丽羔羊身上揪采最好的羊毛
为你做一件长袍；
用纯金为你制作鞋扣，
为御寒把鞋子也要精美地刺绣；

为你做一条腰带，用草和藤编织，
上边点缀着珊瑚扣和琥珀的钮饰：
如果这各样的乐趣能让你动心，
来，与我同住，做我的爱人。

你用银碟盛饭菜
其丰盛宝贵堪与各路神食竞赛，
每天为了我和你
象牙桌上摆美食。

牧羊少年群歌舞，
领略五月早晨的幸福。
如果这各种欣喜能让你动心，
那么就与我同住，做我的爱人。

（李正栓　译）

思考题

1. Do you think the shepherd could succeed in courtship by the way described in the poem? Why?
2. What can you learn from this poem? State your idea about love.
3. Learn the first stanza of this poem by heart.
4. Find more Chinese versions of this poem.

William Shakespeare
威廉·莎士比亚
(1564–1616)

William Shakespeare was born in Stratford-on-Avon, Warwickshire, in central England. He was baptized on April 26, 1564; his birth is commemorated on April 23. His father, John Shakespeare, was a merchant and held various municipal offices. His mother, Mary Arden, was the daughter of a well-to-do farmer. At the age of seven he attended the local grammar school and there he studied for six years and learned Latin and a little Greek. When he was fourteen, his father fell into debt, and he probably left school and went to work. At eighteen he married Anne Hathaway, who was eight years senior, and they had three children.

At about 1586 Shakespeare left his hometown for London. Shortly after his arrival in the great city, he went to work at odd jobs in a theater. Then he became an actor and later started to write for the stage. He revised old plays before writing his own, and so gained a practical knowledge and technique of dramatic art. By the closing years of the 16th century he had already won the popularity as a successful playwright. About 1611 he retired from London to his native town, though he continued to write. On April 23, 1616, he died at the age of fifty-two.

Shakespeare's complete works include 37 plays, 2 narrative poems and 154 sonnets. When he died, no collected edition of his plays had been published. In 1623, two members of his company, John Heminges and Henry Condell, published the great collection of all the plays they considered authentic; it is called the *First Folio*.

As a dramatist, Shakespeare's career is usually divided into three periods. The first period dates from 1590 to 1600. In this period he wrote most of his historical plays and comedies, and a few early tragedies, and these plays are imbued with an optimistic atmosphere of humanism. Among the best known plays of this period are *Romeo and Juliet* (1594) and *The Merchant of Venice* (1596). The second period, from 1601 to 1608, includes chiefly his great tragedies: *Hamlet* (1601), *Othello* (1604), *King Lear* (1605), *Macbeth* (1605) and *Timon of Athens* (1609). The outstanding tragic-comedy *Measure for Measure* (1604) also belongs to this period. The above-mentioned plays reflected the social contradictions of the age. The third period dates from 1609 to 1612. In this period Shakespeare chiefly wrote three tragic-comedies, of which *The Tempest* (1612) is the most significant. In these last plays we see Shakespeare's optimistic faith in the future of humanity, at the same time we also see the dramatist's Utopianism.

As one of the greatest giants of the Renaissance, Shakespeare holds, by general acclamation, the foremost place in the world's literature. His close friend, the playwright Ben Jonson, said of him that he was "not of an age, but for all time." According to Paul Lafarque, Karl Marx "had made an exhaustive study of Shakespeare, for whom he had an unbounded admiration, and whose most insignificant characters, even, were familiar to him."

He wrote 154 sonnets, which are a great treasure in English poetry.

Sonnet 1[1]

From fairest creatures we desire increase[2]
That thereby[3] beauty's rose might never die,
But as the riper should by time decease[4],
His tender heir might bear his memory:
But thou, contracted to thine own bright eyes,
Feed'st thy light's flame with self-substantial fuel[5],
Making a famine where abundance lies,
Thy self thy foe, to thy sweet self too cruel:
Thou that art now the world's fresh ornament
And only herald to the gaudy[6] spring,
Within thine own bud buriest thy content[7],
And, tender churl, mak'st waste in niggarding[8]:
    Pity the world, or else this glutton[9] be,
    To eat the world's due, by the grave and thee[10].

注释

1. 莎士比亚的十四行诗于1609年合成一集出版，共154首。诗的节律是五音步抑扬格，全诗包括三个四行组和一个两行组，韵脚按abab，cdcd，efef，gg排列，被称为“莎士比亚式”、“伊丽莎白式”或“英格兰式”。
2. **increase** procreation, reproduction
3. **thereby** in that way, by that means; by means of fairest creatures desiring multiplication
4. **decease** die. “Decease” is similar to “decrease” in spelling, which is a reminder of the “increase” in Line 1.
5. **with self-substantial fuel** with fuel from your own body, with your own substance. The poet seems to say that the fuel should be renewable. This implies the poet’s criticism of the young man, who is intent on devouring himself and his future hope.
6. **gaudy** joyous, luxurious, bright, showy
7. **content** what is contained in you, that is the possibility of being a father; what would make you contented, that is, marriage
8. **niggarding** hoarding, being miserly, stingy
9. **glutton** it suggests both extravagant waste and selfish hoarding.
10. **by the grave and thee** it contains two ideas in great conciseness—it refers both to Southampton’s dying and to his death leaving no child.

第1首十四行诗

我们渴望最美丽生灵世代繁衍，
以便玫瑰般美丽永远不会死去，
但是成熟的人或物会最终消减，
他柔嫩子嗣会承载对他的记忆。
但你却只与自己的明眸订婚约，
用自身作燃料来喂你生命之光，
在原本富饶的地方你制造饥饿，
你与自己为敌把甜蜜事情中伤。
你现在青春活力是世界的饰品，
你是主要使者把灿烂春天播报，
你含苞未放就埋葬了你的自身，
你温柔小气吝啬地把生命消耗。

可怜可怜这个世界吧，不然就极端浪费，
吞食世界该得之物，让它随你和坟墓自毁。
（李正栓，张青梅　译）

思考题

1. This sonnet introduces the first important theme of the whole sequence. What is it?
2. What is the rhyme scheme of Shakesperian sonnet?
3. How do you understand the image of the rose?

Sonnet 18

Shall I compare thee to a summer's day?
Thou art more lovely and more temperate:
Rough winds do shake the darling buds of May,
And summer's lease[1] hath all too short a date[2]:
Sometime[3] too hot the eye of heaven[4] shines
And often is his gold complexion dimmed;
And every fair from fair sometimes declines,[5]
By chance[6] or nature's changing course untrimmed[7];
But thy eternal summer shall not fade,
Nor lose possession of that fair thou ow'st[8];
Nor shall death brag thou wander'st[9] in his shade,
When in eternal lines to time thou grow'st[10]:
　　So long as men can breathe, or eyes can see,
　　So long lives this[11], and this gives life to thee.

注释

1. **lease**　（土地、房屋等的）租借期限
2. **date**　a limited period of time
3. **Sometime**　sometimes, from time to time.
4. **the eye of heaven**　the sun

5. **And every fair from fair sometimes declines** And every fair sometimes declines from fair. every fair: every beautiful thing or person. from fair: from beauty
6. **chance** accidental events
7. **untrimmed** stripped (of beauty). the correct sentence structure is: untrimmed by chance or nature's changing course.
8. **ow'st** owest, own
9. **wander'st** wander
10. **to time thou grow'st** thou grow'st to time. Thou: you（主格）; grow'st: growest, grow
11. **this** this poem

参考译诗

第18首十四行诗

能不能让我来把你比作夏日？
你可是更加可爱，更加温婉；
狂风会吹落五月里盛开的花朵，
夏季的日子又未免太短暂：
有时候苍天的巨眼照得太灼热，
他那金彩的脸色也会被遮暗；
每一样美呀，总会（离开美而）凋落，
被时机或者自然的代谢所摧残；
但是你永久的夏天绝不会凋枯，
你永远不会失去你美的形象；
死神夸不着你在他影子里踯躅，
你将在不朽的诗中与时间同长；
　　只要人类在呼吸，眼睛看得见，
　　我这诗就活着，使你的生命绵延。

（屠岸　译）

思考题

1. Why does the speaker think "Thou art more lovely and more temperate" than "a summer's day"?
2. What is the theme of this sonnet?

3. What is the function of literature as expressed in this sonnet? Find more poems expressing or displaying such an idea.
4. Learn this sonnet by heart.

Sonnet 29

When, in disgrace with[1] fortune and men's eyes,
I all alone beweep[2] my outcast state[3],
And trouble deaf heaven with my bootless[4] cries,
And look upon myself, and curse my fate,
Wishing me like to one[5] more rich in hope,
Featured like him, like him with friends possessed[6],
Desiring this man's art[7] and that man's scope[8],
With what I most enjoy contented least;[9]
Yet in these thoughts myself almost despising,
Haply[10] I think on thee—and then my state[11],
Like to the lark at break of day arising
From sullen earth, sings hymns at heaven's gate;
    For thy sweet love rememb'red such wealth brings
    That then I scorn[12] to change my state[13] with kings.

注释

1. **in disgrace with** out of favour with
2. **beweep** weep over
3. **outcast state** 被（人或社会）排斥的境况
4. **bootless** futile
5. **like to one** like to: like; one: someone
6. **with friends possessed** possessed with friends. possessed with: having
7. **art** skill
8. **scope** range, referring to wide scope of knowledge
9. **With what I most enjoy contented least** least contented with what I most enjoy. 本身最为擅长之事，恰好是自己最不稀罕之处。
10. **Haply** fortunately, luckily; by chance

11. **state** state of mind
12. **scorn** 不屑于（去做某事）
13. **state** chair of state; throne

参考译诗

第29首十四行诗

我一旦失去了幸福，又遭人白眼，
就独自哭泣，怨人家把我抛弃，
白白地用哭喊来麻烦聋耳的苍天，
又看看自己，只痛恨时运不济，
愿自己像人家那样：或前程远大，
或一表人才，或胜友如云广交谊，
想有这人的权威，那人的才华，
于自己平素最得意的，倒最不满意；
但在这几乎是看轻自己的思想里，
我偶尔想到你呵，——我的心怀
顿时像破晓的云雀从阴郁的大地
冲上了天门，歌唱起赞美诗来；
　　我记着你的甜爱，就是珍宝，
　　教我不屑把处境跟帝王对调。

（屠岸　译）

思考题

1. Explain the meaning of the word “state” in Lines 2, 10 and 14.
2. There are two moods contrasted in this sonnet. What are they?
3. What does “lark” stand for?

Sonnet 55

Not marble[1], nor the gilded monuments
Of princes, shall outlive this powerful rhyme;
But you shall shine more bright in these contents[2]
Than unswept stone[3], besmeared[4] with sluttish[5] time.
When wasteful[6] war shall statues overturn,
And broils[7] root out the work of masonry[8],
Nor Mars his sword nor war's quick fire[9] shall burn
The living record of your memory.
'Gainst[10] death and all-oblivious[11] enmity
Shall you pace forth; your praise shall still[12] find room[13]
Even in the eyes of all posterity[14]
That wear this world out[15] to the ending doom[16].
　　So, till the judgment that yourself arise,[17]
　　You live in this[18], and dwell in lovers' eyes.

注释

1. **marble** 大理石，大理石纪念碑
2. **contents** lines contained in the poem
3. **stone** tombstone
4. **besmeared** 被弄脏，被涂污
5. **sluttish** dirty; slovenly
6. **wasteful** destructive
7. **broils** 争论；内讧；火并。梁宗岱译为"内讧"，屠岸译为"火并"。
8. **masonry** 石工技艺
9. **Nor Mars his sword nor war's quick fire** Mars 是罗马神话中的战神。Nor...nor = neither...nor; his: Mars's
10. **'Gainst** against
11. **all-oblivious** 湮没一切的
12. **still** always
13. **room** 位置。但room 也有"空间"之义，即space。这就暗示战胜时间，也是战胜空间。
14. **posterity** offsprings

15. **wear this world out** 消耗完这个世界
16. **the ending doom** doomsday
17. **till the judgment that yourself arise** until the last judgment when you yourself shall rise from the dead. that: when
18. **in this** in this poem

参考译诗

第55首十四行诗

白石，或者帝王们镀金的纪念碑
都不能比这强有力的诗句更长寿；
你留在诗句里将放出永恒的光辉，
你留在碑石上就不免尘封而腐朽。
毁灭的战争是会把铜像推倒，
火并也会把巨厦连根儿烧光，
但是战神的利剑或烈火烧不掉
你刻在人们心头的鲜明印象。
对抗着湮灭一切的敌意和死，
你将前进；人类将永远歌颂你，
连那坚持到世界末日的人之子
也将用眼睛来称赞你不朽的美丽。
　　到最后审判你复活之前，你——
　　活在我诗中，住在恋人们眼睛里。

（屠岸　译）

思考题

1. What comparisons are displayed in this sonnet? What's the function of comparison here?
2. Compare the Spenserian sonnet with that of Shakespeare. Identify the similarity and difference of the rhyme scheme.
3. What is the theme of this sonnet?
4. Comment on the last line of this sonnet.

Ben Jonson
本·琼生
（1572–1637）

Though once a brick-layer when young, Ben Jonson was a very complex figure whom one can never easily take a whole perspective of.

His father died early. In his infancy he was adopted by a brick-layer from whom he learned the skill of building. But he was educated by a great classical scholar. He was complex because he was a man of diversity. He was a soldier, actor, playwright, poet, poet laureate, scholar, critic, man of letters, and head of a literary group. Around him was clustered a group of literary figures called "sons of Ben".

Ben Jonson was a man of wisdom. He could always make himself victorious in all matters. As a soldier in Flanders, he fought single-handedly with an enemy soldier and killed this man. As a person who was to be hanged for killing a fellow-actor, he got himself free by proving he could read and write. He came out of jail though he insulted the King's home country Scotland. He had literary wars with other playwrights. He rode out the troubles when he was much suspected after the Gunpowder Plot. He grew more and more mature as he grew older and older. He was so respected by his contemporary literary figures and the whole society that he became the uncrowned king of literature in London, the king's pensioned poet, a favorite of the court, a good friend of great statesmen and great poets like William Shakespeare, John Donne, Francis Beaumont, John Seldon, Francis Bacon and others. He also made good friends with dukes, diplomats, and distinguished folks. Younger poets like Robert Herrick, Thomas Carew, Sir John Suckling and the "Cavalier school" of English poets who called themselves "sons of Ben" showed their warmest affection and greatest respect toward Ben Jonson.

Ben Jonson was mainly remembered as the author who wrote comedies such as *Every Man in His Humour* (1598), *Volpone* (1606), and *The Alchemist* (1610). *Sejanus* (1603) is a tragedy.His short poems also display his unique ideas.

Song: To Celia

Drink to[1] me only with thine eyes,
And I will pledge[2] with mine;
Or leave a kiss but[3] in the cup,
And I'll not look for wine.
The thirst that from the soul doth rise,
Doth ask a drink divine:
But might I of Jove's nectar sup[4],
I would not change for thine.[5]

I sent thee late[6] a rosy wreath,
Not so much honoring thee,
As giving it a hope,[7] that there
It could not withered be.[8]
But thou thereon did'st only breathe,[9]
And sent'st[10] it back to me;
Since when[11] it grows, and smells, I swear,
Not of itself, but thee.[12]

注释

1. **Drink to** 向……祝酒
2. **pledge** 祝酒
3. **but** only
4. **might I of Jove's Nectar sup** might I sup of Jove's Nectar. 纵使我能饮到天神的美酒。might I: if I might; sup: sip; of: some of; Jove: Jupiter，即罗马神话中的主神朱庇特。Jove：朱庇特的别称，译为"朱威"。
5. **I would not change for thine** I would not change (Jove's Nectar) for thine (your wine).
6. **late** lately
7. **Not so much honoring thee / As giving it a hope** 与其说是尊敬你，不如说是用来给它一种希望。Not so much...as: 与其……不如；it: the rosy wreath
8. **that there / It could not withered be** there: with you; withered: 枯萎

9. **But thou thereon did'st only breathe** But if you merely breathe on it. did'st breathe: did breathe; thereon: on it
10. **sent'st** sent
11. **Since when** after which time
12. **Not of itself, but thee** Not of itself, but (of) thee

参考译诗

致西丽娅

用你的眼神为我祝酒，
我也用眼神为你祝福；
你留下一个吻在杯口，
我就不会把美酒当作口福。
灵魂深处升出的渴求
的确愿喝神圣的美酒：
但即使我能品尝朱威的甘醇，
我也不愿拿它与你这杯交换！

我最近赠你一玫瑰花环，
并非全是为了向你献媚，
也有为它祈福的心愿，
愿它永不凋谢枯萎。
但你只对它闻了闻，
之后又把它送回。
此后它茁壮成长，
散发出的只是你的芳香。

（李正栓　译）

思考题

1. What kind of love do you think was described in the poem?
2. What is the image of the rose used for?
3. Can you find other similar poems?

John Donne
约翰·邓恩
（1572–1631）

A more thoroughly characteristic figure of the early seventeenth century is John Donne. Born of a family with a strong Roman Catholic tradition, he attended the universities of Cambridge and Oxford, but got no degree because he was a Catholic. Later, as a member of Lincoln's Inn, he read voraciously. Neither could he find a job because he was a Catholic. Yet he did not forget to try to worm his favour into the court and the society. He went with Essex on the expedition to Cadiz in 1596, an enterprise that ranked for daring with the repulse of the Armada, and later became secretary to Lord Keeper Egerton. Before this he had written a body of poetry which, though not published until after his death, circulated in manuscript, and like Wyatt's and Surrey's, had an immense influence on younger poets. Part of this poetry is in such classical forms as satires, elegies, and epistles—though its style has anything but classical smoothness—and part is written in lyrical forms of extraordinary variety. Most of it purports to deal with life, descriptively or experimentally, and the first thing to strike the reader is Donne's extraordinary frankness and penetrating realism. The next is the cynicism which marks certain of the lighter poems and which represents a conscious reaction from the extreme idealization of woman encouraged by the Petrarchan tradition. In his serious love-poems, however, Donne, while not relaxing his grasp on the realities of the love-experience, suffuses it with an emotional intensity and a spiritualized ardor unique in English poetry.

This astonishing new poetry took the literary cliques of London by storm. But as striking as the novelty of subject matter and point of view is that of its form. Instead of the unvarying succession of sonnets, Donne gave nearly every theme a verse and stanza form peculiar to itself; and instead of decorating his theme by conventional comparisons, he illumined or emphasized his thought by fantastic metaphors and extravagant hyperboles. In moments of inspiration his style became wonderfully poignant and direct, heartsearching in its simple human accents, with an originality and force for which we look in vain among the clear and fluent melodies of Elizabethan lyrists. Sometimes the "conceits", as these extravagant figures are called, are so odd that we lose sight of the thing to be illustrated, in the startling nature of the illustration.

At about 1601 Donne fell passionately and seriously in love with the niece of the Lord Keeper, married her secretly, and was imprisoned for a time by his angry father-in-law. For several years after his release he and his growing family were dependent on friends and patrons; then, at the persuasion of influential admirers, he entered the church in 1615, where he rose rapidly to be Dean of Saint Paul's Cathedral in 1621, and the most famous preacher of his time. After the death of his wife in 1617 he fell more and more under the shadow of a terrible spiritual gloom.

As his life drew near its close, he had himself sculptured in his winding-sheet, standing upright in his coffin, and this monument was placed above his grave in Saint Paul's.

John Donne's poetry is very difficult to understand. But once understood, its influence on the reader's mind is everlasting. Only with great patience and intellect can a reader appreciate Donne's poems full of feeling, thought and wit.

Song

Go[1], and catch a falling star[2],
　　Get with child a mandrake root,[3]
Tell me, where all past years are[4],
　　Or who cleft the Devil's foot[5],
Teach me to hear mermaids[6] singing,
Or to keep off envy's stinging[7],
　　　　And find
　　　　What wind
Serves to advance an honest mind.[8]

If thou beest born to strange sights,[9]

Things invisible to see,
Ride ten thousand days and nights,
Till age snow white hairs on thee,[10]
Thou, when thou return'st, wilt[11] tell me
All strange wonders that befell thee[12],
And swear[13]
No where
Lives a woman true, and fair[14].

If thou find'st[15] one, let me know,
Such a pilgrimage[16] were[17] sweet;
Yet do not,[18] I would not go,
Though at next door we[19] might meet;
Though[20] she were true when you met her,
And last[21] till you write your letter,
Yet she
Will be
False, ere I come, to two, or three.[22]

注释

1. **Go** 诗以祈使句开始，如同对话，充满戏剧性，颇像戏剧独白。这首诗用了许多扬抑格，且不少地方用爆破音开始，充满语音暴力，彰显说话者心中的愤怒。
2. **catch a falling star** 抓住陨星，寓不可能之意
3. **Get with child a mandrake root** 使曼德拉草怀胎成孕。mandrake: 曼德拉草，其根部像人的两条腿，所以可译为“人形草”；with child: pregnant
4. **where all past years are** 时光无影无踪，昨日不可能重现
5. **who cleft the Devil's foot** 这是无法回答的问题。cleft 是 cleave（劈开）的过去时形式之一。据传，Devil凶残，无人能接近，更无人能将其脚面劈开。
6. **mermaids** 美人鱼，此处指希腊神话中半人半鸟的海妖（Sirens），其声优美，任何被其声音吸引并接近的人都会被它们吃掉。
7. **envy's stinging** envy: envious people; stinging: biting
8. **What wind / Serves to advance an honest mind** wind [waind]; advance: promote
9. **If thou beest born to strange sights** beest: be的第二人称单数现在时的古用法，即 are; sights: power of seeing

10. **Till age snow white hairs on thee** 直到年岁使你白发苍苍。snow:（动词）下雪
11. **wilt** will
12. **that befell thee** that happened to you
13. **And swear** And (wilt) swear
14. **a woman true, and fair** a fair (beautiful) woman who is true (faithful), too
15. **find'st** find
16. **pilgrimage** 朝圣。去见忠实美丽的女人就像朝圣一样，说明此种女人很难找到。
17. **were** would be
18. **Yet do not** Yet do not (let me know)
19. **we** 指"我"和那个女子
20. **Though** suppose
21. **last** (will) last, continue to be true
22. **False, ere I come, to two, or three** False to two or three (men) ere I come. ere: before

参考译诗

歌

去，去抓住一颗陨星，
　　让人形草也怀孕胚胎，
告诉我，过去的岁月哪里去找寻，
　　是谁把魔鬼的脚劈开，
教教我如何听美人鱼歌唱，
或如何躲开嫉妒的刺伤，
　　　去弄清
　　　什么风
能将老实人提升。

如果你天生长有奇特视力，
　　能把无形的东西看见，
那你就骑马奔驰一万个夜与日，
　　直到你头发如雪成老年，
你归来时就会给我讲
你遇到的奇事一桩又一桩，
　　　你会咒骂恶语

天下无一地
住着女人，忠实又美丽。

假如你真的找到，就让我晓知，
　　这样的朝圣还算甜蜜；
但你还是别说，反正我不会去，
　　尽管我们会在隔壁相遇；
假如初遇时她还有真情，
忠实到你把情书写成，
　　　她却已
　　　还没等我送过去
就将两三个人抛弃。

（李正栓　译）

思考题

1. What kind of love do you think was described in the poem?
2. Point out the rhyme scheme of this poem.
3. What is the tone of the speaker?
4. Do you think it is fair to describe women in this way? What is Donne's real purpose of writing this poem?

The Flea[1]

Mark[2] but this flea, and mark in this,
How little that which thou deniest me is;
Me it sucked first, and now sucks thee,
And in this flea our two bloods mingled[3] be;
Thou know'st that this cannot be said
A sin, or shame, or loss of maidenhead,
　　Yet this enjoys before it woo,

And pampered swells with one blood made of two,
And this, alas, is more than we would do.

Oh stay[4], three lives in one flea spare,
Where we almost, nay more than married, are.
This flea is you and I, and this
Our marriage bed and marriage temple is;
Though parents grudge[5], and you, we are met,
And cloistered in these living walls of jet,
Though use make you apt to kill me
Let not to that, self-murder added be,
And sacrilege, three sins in killing three.

Cruel and sudden, hast thou since
Purpled thy nail,[6] in blood of innocence?
Wherein could this flea guilty be,
Except in that drop which it sucked from thee?
Yet thou triumph'st, and say'st that thou
Find'st not thy self nor me the weaker now;
'Tis true, then learn how false fears be;
Just so much honor, when thou yield'st to me,
Will waste, as this flea's death took life from thee.

注释

1. 这首诗以跳蚤入诗，极富推理，充满了奇想妙喻。该诗以戏剧独白写成，也叙述了戏剧行动，全诗三节犹如戏剧三幕。
2. **Mark** look at
3. **mingled** mixed
4. **stay** stop: 住手，颇有“刀下留人”之意，此处为“指下留蚤”。
5. **grudge** are unwilling
6. **Purpled thy nail** make your nail purple by killing

参考译诗

跳　蚤

你看吧，你看看这跳蚤，
你否认我的成分能有多少？
它先咬了我，此刻又咬你，
我俩的血已在它里边融为一体；
要承认，这件事不能被说成是羞耻
或罪过，也算不上你贞操的损失，
　　而它却未求婚就先得快意，
　　合我俩的血为一体，涨大它的腹肌，
　　唉，它做得远远超过我们自己。

啊，住手，饶过这跳蚤里的三个生命。
在它体内，我们不止是结了婚，
它是你是我，是我们的花烛温床，
是我们婚姻的殿堂；
尽管父母和你都不愿意，我们还是聚在一起。
同居于这乌黑的活墙里。
　　尽管习俗使你轻易杀我，
　　但不要把三个生命剥夺，
　　不要再加上自杀和渎圣的罪过。

你突然狠心地把毒手下，
用无辜者的血染紫了你的指甲？
这跳蚤只吸过你一口血，
这怎能算作一种罪过？
而你却得意扬扬地说：
你和我都不比从前弱；

不错，我因此全知：说你害怕是多么虚假！
你此时同意我，但跳蚤之死已把你生命夺下。
多少的道义或矜持都浪费。说你害怕也白搭。

（李正栓　译）

思考题

1. What is the flea compared to? In what way is this poem full of dramatic quality?
2. How is this love poem different from that of others? Make comparisons if you can.
3. Choose the lines that you like best. Tell why you like them.
4. Learn one of the stanzas by heart.

Robert Herrick
罗伯特·赫里克
（1591–1674）

Robert Herrick was born in a rich goldsmith's family. Though slow in taking his degrees and finding a career, he was, as a follower of Ben Jonson, the happiest English poet.

When social pressures were too great, he took orders in the church and reluctantly moved to a parish at Dean Prior in Devonshire in the west of the country. There he was keen on writing poems, as someone put it, "secreting poems as a hen lays eggs." He invented dozens of imaginary mistresses in his poems, but Prudence (his housekeeping maid) was a main figure.

In *Corinna's Going a-Maying*, the product of Herrick at the top of his poetic bent, Herrick produced a truly major lyric on the central theme of his life, the happy reconciliation of nature and nature's god. However, most of his poems were casual, even trivial.

Herrick did not advertise his beliefs, but when the Puritans came to power, he was dismissed from his post and went back to London. Back in London, he published his poems in 1648. There were altogether 1,200 poems, including secular poems in *Hesperides* and sacred poems in *Noble Numbers*. When Charles II was restored in 1660, Herrick went back to Dean Prior, where he lived in peace.

To the Virgins, to Make Much of Time

Gather ye rose-buds while ye may[1],
　Old time is still a-flying[2];
And this same flower that smiles today,
　Tomorrow will be dying.

The glorious lamp of heaven, the sun[3],
  The higher he's a-getting[4],
The sooner will his race be run[5],
  And nearer he's to setting.

That age is best which is the first,[6]
  When youth and blood are warmer;
But being spent, the worse, and worst
  Times still succeed the former.

Then be not coy[7], but use your time[8],
  And, while ye may, go marry;
For, having lost but once[9] your prime[10],
  You may forever tarry[11].

注释

1. **while ye may**　趁你有可能。ye: 第二人称代词thou（= you）的复数形式。此行有两解。一是有花了，可以采摘。二是趁你有能力，抓紧采摘。有人把这个主题解释成“及时行乐”，即 Carpe diem，英语叫“seize the day”或 “seize the hour”。我们称它为 “只争朝夕”主题，英译为“seize each eve and morn”。
2. **a-flying**　flying
3. **the sun**　The glorious lamp of heaven 的同位语。这是一个暗喻，太阳被比作“华灯”。
4. **a-getting**　getting
5. **his race be run**　跑完他的路程。race 指太阳的运行。
6. **That age is best which is the first**　that age which is the first is best.
7. **coy**　羞怯的
8. **use your time**　抓住时间
9. **but once**　just once
10. **prime**　youth
11. **tarry**　耽搁，迟延

参考译诗

劝少女们珍惜好时光

花开堪折直须折，
光阴总是在飞驰；
今日花笑同一朵，
明日笑容会消逝。

太阳华灯天上悬，
越近高处路越短；
太阳越是向西沉，
路程终点越临近。

青春年华最美好，
血气方刚热情高；
青春年华若虚度，
一天不如一天好。

抓紧时间别羞怯，
能得悦时及时悦；
一旦错过好年华，
千古遗憾悔成河。

（李正栓　译）

思考题

1. Do you know the "Carpe Diem" theme?
2. Are you familiar with the central idea of this poem? Please name some poems with the similar idea either in English or Chinese poetry.
3. Identify the rhyme scheme of the poem.
4. Learn the first stanza by heart.

George Herbert
乔治·赫伯特
(1593–1633)

George Herbert was born in an ancient and distinguished Welsh family. His father died early. His mother, Magdalen Herbert, a lady of piety with a deep love of letters and a large circle of friends including the then famous poet John Donne, brought him up.

Herbert attended the University of Cambridge. When he graduated, he was elected Public Orator of the University, an important post of dignity and some authority, a post that easily helped people climb higher in politics. The task at this post was to express the sentiments of the university on public occasions. But the death of his patrons and the bent of his own temper drew him to another direction in which he did very well. In 1626, he took a minor office in the church. In 1630, he accepted the living of Bemerton in Salisbury and took orders.

He married Jane Danvers in 1629. He only had four years of married life when he died in 1633.

George Herbert was different from other young people of that time who took holy orders but did not perform their duties except accepting the pay. He won the respect of the people. He was recognized by the public as "a learned, godly, and painful divine." He preached to the public and prayed to God both in practice and his writing. He rebuilt the church even with money from his own pocket. He visited the poor, consoled the sick and the dying. He showed his love for the poor and the rich alike. During his ministry at Bemerton, apart from his mission, he wrote poems which were published in the volume known as *The Temple* shortly after his death of consumption in 1633.

George Herbert was a quiet, inward, subtle, graceful and neat poet. He followed the tradition of Christian types and imagery, delighting in using quaint devices and homely images. But his feeling was so pure, fresh, and free that the reader thinks Herbert had only one feeling, i.e., his profound piety to God. That is why some people describe him as a poet of religious faith, of submission, and of acceptance. Usually, Herbert was not flashy, nor strongly dramatic. He was devoted to the quiet middle way. Yet his emotion is rich. His moods changed quickly. But his prayer can be heard and felt in each of his poems. His poetry was never void of "freshness", rich in traditional designs, which was open for the humblest and simplest person to enter.

Virtue[1]

Sweet day, so cool, so calm, so bright,
The bridal of the earth and sky:
The dew shall weep thy fall tonight;
　For thou must die.

Sweet rose, whose hue, angry[2] and brave,
Bids the rash gazer wipe his eye:[3]
Thy root is ever in its grave,
　And thou must die.

Sweet spring, full of sweet days and roses,
A box where sweets[4] compacted lie;
My music[5] shows ye have your closes[6],
　And all must die.

Only a sweet and virtuous soul,
Like seasoned timber[7], never gives[8];
But though the whole world turn to coal[9],
　Then chiefly lives[10].

注释

1. 这首诗语言浅显，寓意却非常深刻：世俗万物，均难免亡，唯美德永存。每节诗有四行，三长一短，很像三句半。此种形式的使用者古有希腊女诗人萨福，后有苏格兰诗人彭斯。

2. **angry** red，像人发怒时面色通红那样
3. **Bids the rash gazer wipe his eye** 引得性急的观望者也拭目细看。bids: invites
4. **sweets** perfumes
5. **My music** my poem
6. **closes** 音乐术语，意为乐章的终止
7. **seasoned timber** 干燥的木料。seasoned: dried
8. **gives** bends
9. **turn to coal** 化为灰烬。coal: ashes, cinders
10. **chiefly lives** 其主语是 a sweet and virtuous soul（Line 13）

参考译诗

美　　德

可爱的白日，这么凉爽、明朗、静谧，
你把天和地婚配成双。
露珠会为你今夜坠落而哭泣，
　　因为你注定要消亡。

芬芳的玫瑰，你红艳似怒，
使急性子观者也拭目凝望。
但你总植根于坟墓，
　　这注定你要消亡。

可爱的春天，你充满良辰和玫瑰，
你是一只匣，里边凝藏芳香。
我的音乐显示你也有终有尾，
　　世间一切都会死亡。

只有美好有德的灵魂
像焙干的木材永不变形；
纵然是整个世界化为灰烬，
　　美德仍然长存永生。

（李正栓　译）

思考题

1. Analyze the structure of this poem. Where is the climax of this poem?
2. Explain how the poet reaches his goal by a successful use of the four images "day", "rose", "spring" and "seasoned timber". Which one of them do you think is the most vivid and amazing? Why?
3. Choose one stanza to learn by heart.
4. What is virtue? Why is virtue important in one's life? Read some of the well-known essay on virtue and list their main points.

John Milton
约翰·弥尔顿
（1608–1674）

On a December day in 1608, while Shakespeare was still writing his great plays, another future great English poet was born in London. He was John Milton.

Milton's father made a business of preparing law papers, and was a prosperous man. He was a Puritan, but not so harsh as most of the Puritans of his day, for he loved music and taught his boy to love it. He also loved books, and young John Milton began to show, when a very small boy, that he loved them, too. His father had a private teacher for him, and when scarcely more than ten years old the boy wrote good verses and sat up later than was good for him over his studies.

When about twelve years old, young Milton was sent to a famous boys' school in London called St. Paul's and from there, at fifteen, he went to Cambridge University. He was handsome, but somewhat proud and independent in his ways of thinking. He was said to be the finest scholar in the university.

Milton had planned to be a clergyman of the English Church, but strife arose between the Puritans and the Church. It was about this time that the Pilgrims went to Plymouth, and a few years later colonies of Puritans settled at Salem and Boston in New England.

After finishing the university course and deciding not to be a clergyman of the English Church, Milton was for a time in some doubt about what he should do, but the more he thought of it, the more clear it seemed to him that he was born to be a poet. So for five years he lived at home in his father's country house at Horton, about twenty miles from London, writing poems and studying hard, in order to better fit himself for his work.

It was during these years at Horton that he wrote his shorter poems: *L'Allegro* describing happiness; *Il Penseroso*, describing meditation; *Lycidas*, praising a dear friend who had been drowned; and *Comus*, presenting a masque or play.

But Milton was soon tired of this quiet country life. He longed to see more of the world, and at last, with money which his father gave him, he set out to travel through France, Switzerland and Italy. While he was in Italy, news came that trouble had sprung up in England between the king and the people, and that war might break out. He immediately gave up his plans for traveling and writing poetry, and went back to England.

On his return to London, Milton opposed the monarchic party and gave all his energies to the writing of pamphlets dedicated to the people's liberty. His principal pamphlets are: *Areopagitica,* or *Speech for the Liberty of Unlicensed Printing* (1614), a bold attack on the censorship of the press; *Eikonoklastes* (1649), a pamphlet in which the author justified the execution of the Commonwealth and Revolution.

Paradise Lost won him great honour. Famous scholars and statesmen came from far away to visit him. After finishing this poem, he wrote *Paradise Regained*.

Surrounded by a few devoted friends, John Milton, the great English poet, died on November 8, 1674. His greatest work *Paradise Lost* presents the author's views in an allegoric religious form, and readers will easily discern its basic idea—the exposure of reactionary forces of his time and passionate appeal for freedom.

When I Consider How My Light Is Spent[1]

When I consider how my light is spent
    Ere half my days,[2] in this dark world and wide[3],
    And that one talent[4] which is death to hide,[5]
    Lodged[6] with me useless, though my soul more bent[7]
To serve therewith my Maker,[8] and present
    My true account, lest he returning chide;
    "Doth God exact day-labour, light denied?"[9]
    I fondly[10] ask; but Patience to prevent
That murmur,[11] soon[12] replies, "God doth not need
    Either man's work or his own gifts; who best
    Bear his mild yoke, they serve him best.[13]

His state is kingly. Thousands[14] at his bidding speed
And post[15] o'er[16] land and ocean without rest:
They also serve who only stand and wait."[17]

注释

1. 弥尔顿于1651年左眼失明，1652年因写《为英国人民声辩》，劳累过度，右眼也失明。
2. **Ere half my days** before half of my days
3. **dark world and wide** dark and wide world
4. **And that one talent** And (when I consider how) that one talent. talent 是古希伯来人计算银子的单位，此处暗指自己的文学才能（literary talent)。
5. **which is death to hide** to hide which is death
6. **Lodged** (is) lodged
7. **though my soul more bent** though my soul (be) more bent. Though 后省略了be，用虚拟语气；bent: eager
8. **To serve therewith my Maker** 用它来为我的造物主服务。therewith: with which（指talent）
9. **Doth God exact day-labour, light denied** 上帝要我做日工，又不给我光？ light denied：独立结构，if light is denied
10. **fondly** foolishly
11. **To prevent / That murmur** 预先阻止那种抱怨。murmur: complaint
12. **soon** quickly
13. **who best / Bear his mild yoke, they serve him best** 以who 引导的从句用作定语，修饰they。The normal sentence structure is: They who best bear his mild yoke serve him best. mild yoke: 温和的羁轭，指上帝加在人肩上的责任和义务。
14. **Thousands** thousands (of angels)
15. **post** hasten, hurry up
16. **o'er** over
17. **They also serve who only stand and wait** They who only stand and wait also serve.

哀 失 明

想到了在这茫茫黑暗的世界里，
还未到半生这两眼就已失明，
想到了我这个泰伦特，要是埋起来，

会招致死亡，却放在我手里无用，
虽然我一心想用它服务造物主，
免得报账时，得不到他的宽容；
想到这里，我就愚蠢地自问，
“神不给我光明，还要我做日工？”
但“忍耐”看我在抱怨，立刻止住我：
“神并不要你工作，或还他礼物。
谁最能服从他，谁就是忠于职守，
他君临万方，只要他一声吩咐，
万千个天使就赶忙在海陆奔驰，
但侍立左右的，也还是为他服务。”

（殷宝书　译）

思考题

1. How is the word “talent” used?
2. How do you understand “wait”, the last word of the whole sonnet?
3. What is Milton’s feeling about his blindness?
4. What is the function of Patience’s words?
5. In what way is this sonnet dramatic?

Methought I Saw My Late Espouséd Saint[1]

Methought[2] I saw my late espouséd saint[3]
Brought to me like Alcestis[4] from the grave,
Whom Jove’s great son[5] to her glad husband gave,
Rescued from death by force though pale and faint.
Mine,[6] as whom[7] washed from spot of childbed taint[8],
Purification in the old law[9] did save[10],
And such, as yet once more I trust to have
Full sight of her[11] in Heaven without restraint[12],

Came vested all in white, pure as her mind.
　　Her face was veiled,[13] yet to my fancied sight[14],
　　Love, sweetness, goodness, in her person shined[15]
So clear, as in no face with more delight[16].
　　But O, as to embrace me she inclined[17],
　　I waked, she fled, and day brought back my night.

注释

1. 此诗可能写于1658年。多数评论家认为，诗中写的是弥尔顿的第二个妻子卡瑟琳·伍德科克，她于1656年11月与弥尔顿结婚，在产下一女三个多月后，于1658年2月去世，女儿也不久夭亡。此诗表达了诗人对亡妻的深刻怀念，其情之深堪比苏东坡的《江城子》（十年生死两茫茫）。
2. **Methought** It seemed to me
3. **my late espouséd saint** the woman whom I lately married, now one of the blessed in heaven
4. **Alcestis** 阿尔塞斯蒂
5. **Jove's great son** 指赫拉克勒斯（Heracles）
6. **Mine** my wife
7. **as whom** as (one) whom
8. **washed from spot of childbed taint** 洗清了产床上的血污。taint: blood taint
9. **Purification in the old law** 古律法中的洁净礼。the old law: 指摩西律法
10. **save** 拯救
11. **such, as yet once more I trust to have / Full sight of her** such as I trust yet once more to have full sight of
12. **without restraint** 此语有两种解释，一是她解除了古律法中的禁律；二是诗人将来到天国后可以无拘无束、自由自在地看到妻子。
13. **Her face was veiled** 她的脸上蒙着面纱，实际上是失明的诗人看不清她的面孔
14. **my fancied sight** the eye of my fancy, my imagination
15. **shined** shone
16. **as in no face with more delight** with more delight in her face than in any other
17. **inclined** bent over me

参考译诗

梦亡妻

我仿佛看见婚后不久便进入天堂的妻
回到了我身边，像阿尔塞斯蒂从坟墓

被朱庇特伟大的儿子从死亡中抢救出，
交还她欣喜的丈夫，虽然她苍白无力。
我的妻，如同古戒律规定的净身礼
拯救的女子，洗清了产褥上的血污，
这样的她，我相信我必能再度
在天堂里无拘无束地细细瞻视，
她穿着和她心灵一样洁白的衣袍，
脸上蒙着面纱，但我好像看得真切，
爱、温柔、善良在她身上闪耀，
任何人脸上显不出这样的喜悦。
但是，唉，正当她俯身要和我拥抱，
我醒了，她逃了，白昼带回了我的黑夜。

（胡家峦　译）

思考题

1. How do you understand the last line of the poem?
2. What is the paradox used in this poetry?
3. Please compare this poem with Su Shi's poem:
   十年生死两茫茫。不思量。自难忘。千里孤坟，无处话凄凉。纵使相逢应不识，尘满面，鬓如霜。
   夜来幽梦忽还乡。小轩窗。正梳妆。相顾无言，唯有泪千行。料得年年肠断处，明月夜，短松冈。
4 Learn this sonnet by heart.

Thomas Gray
托马斯·格雷
(1716–1771)

Thomas Gray is the author of the famous *Elegy Written in a Country Churchyard*, the most scholarly and well-balanced of all the poets prior to the Romantic poets. In his youth he was a weakling, the only one of twelve children who survived infancy; and his unhappy childhood, the tyranny of his father, and the separation from his loved mother, gave to his whole life the stamp of melancholy which is noticeable in all his poems. At the famous Eton School, and again at Cambridge, he seemed to have followed his own scholarly tastes rather than the curriculum. One happy result of his school life was his friendship with Horace Walpole, who took him abroad for a three years' tour of the Continent.

On his return to England, Gray lived for a short time at Stoke Pogis, where he wrote his *Ode* to Eton, and probably sketched his *Elegy*, which however, was not finished till 1750, eight years later. During the later years of his shy and scholarly life he was a professor of Modern History and Languages at Cambridge. Here he gave himself up to study and to poetry, varying his work by "prowlings" among the manuscripts of the New British Museum, and by his "Lilliputian" travels in England and Scotland. He died in his room at Pembroke College in 1771, and was buried in the little churchyard of Stoke Pogis.

Elegy Written in a Country Churchyard[1]

The curfew[2] tolls the knell of parting day,
    The lowing[3] herd[4] wind slowly o'er the lea[5],
The plowman homeward plods his weary way,
    And leaves[6] the world to darkness and to me.

Now fades the glimmering landscape on the sight[7],
　　And all the air a solemn stillness holds[8],
Save[9] where the beetle[10] wheels[11] his droning flight[12],
　　And drowsy tinklings[13] lull the distant folds[14];

Save that from yonder ivy-mantled tower[15]
　　The moping[16] owl does to the moon complain
Of such[17], as wandering near her secret bower[18],
　　Molest[19] her ancient solitary reign.

注释

1. 这三节诗选自《墓畔哀歌》。全诗共32节。所选诗节中的所有注解为杨周翰教授原注。Elegy: 在古希腊，原意是箫歌，逐渐也用来纪念战争中的阵亡者，而成为哀歌、挽歌。这种格律在罗马常有诗人用来写爱情诗。邓恩写的elegies 是爱情诗。在近代欧洲文学中，elegy 往往只作哀歌解。
   全诗用所谓iambic pentameter诗行写成，每行五步（foot），每步一轻音，一重音；但有时，尤其在开始，可以一重一轻。四行成一段（stanza），按a b a b押韵。
   Country Churchyard 指 Buckinghamshire 的 Stoke Pogis的乡村墓地，诗人的母亲住在Stoke Pogis，诗人常从剑桥大学到此度假。诗人及其母葬于此地。
2. **curfew** 宵禁钟声，晚八点钟敲，是中世纪遗留下来的风俗。读者可以注意这行的诗的五个重音有四个是长音；在整首诗里，诗人用长音的时候极频繁；而且全诗长短重音间隔有致。这首诗是英国文学里最著名的诗歌中的一首，本诗作者很少在一行的中间断句。
3. **lowing** 牛鸣
4. **herd** 牛群
5. **lea** 草地
6. **leaves** 主语为plowman，这行诗的内容和意境并非作者所独创，诗人William Collins（1721–1759）1746年发表Ode to Evening，以及其他诗人写的诗，已创造过这样的意境，说明这种孤独情绪已成一种风气。在表达方式方面古典主义诗人遵循罗马贺拉斯的论调，认为内容固然重要，而表达方式即使不更重要，至少也同等重要，对内容往往人同此感，但只有真正的诗人才能表达得好，即蒲柏（Pope）所说What oft was thought, but ne'er so well expressed，因此他们刻意在表达方式上用功，争相竞胜。
7. **sight** 眼睛，视线，指眼睛已看不清昏暗中的景色了
8. **holds** 统治。主语为stillness，宾语为air。诗中往往因音节排列的关系，动词放在最后，同时动词前主语、宾语位置往往先后不一致，或主语在先，或宾语在先。
9. **Save** 除了
10. **beetle** 甲虫。Collins在Ode to Evening 中有句云："Now air is hushed, save where the wead-eyed bat... / Or where the beetle winds / His small but sullen horn." 而Collins又脱胎于Milton，Lycidas 28: "What time the grey-fly [即beetle] winds her sultry, horn." Gray和18世纪许多英国诗人一样，特别服膺Milton, Shakespeare等作家，常套引他们的诗句，"寻章摘句"。

11. **wheels** 旋转飞翔
12. **droning flight** 飞翔时嗡嗡作响
13. **tinklings** 羊颈上的铃声
14. **folds** 羊圈
15. **ivy-mantled tower** 为常春藤所缠绕的教堂塔楼
16. **moping** 烦躁不安
17. **such** 可以指人，但更可能指其他动物，如飞禽、昆虫之类
18. **bower** 指闺房，绣房，不可随意闯入
19. **Molest** 损害

参考译诗

墓畔哀歌

晚钟响起来一阵阵给白昼报丧，
牛群在草原上迂回，吼声起落，
耕地人累了，回家走，脚步踉跄，
把整个世界留给了黄昏与我。

苍茫的景色逐渐从眼前消退，
一片肃穆的寂静盖遍了尘寰，
只听见嗡嗡的甲虫转圈子纷飞，
昏沉的铃声催眠着远处的羊栏。

只听见常春藤披裹的塔顶底下，
一只阴郁的鸱枭向月亮诉苦，
怪人家无端走近它秘密的住家，
搅扰它这个悠久而僻静的领土。

（卞之琳　译）

思考题

1. Have you ever read other elegies? Compare the elegies you know.
2. What is the striking feature of this elegy reflected in the first stanza?
3. Learn these stanzas by heart.

William Blake
威廉·布莱克
（1757–1827）

Of all the romantic poets of the eighteenth century, William Blake is the most independent and the most original.

Blake, born on November 28, 1757, son of a London haberdasher, was a strange, imaginative child, whose soul was more at home with brooks and flowers and fairies than with the crowd of the city streets. He received little education. His only formal education was in art: At the age of 10 he entered a drawing school and later studied for a time at the school of the Royal Academy of Arts. At 14 he apprenticed for seven years to a well-known engraver, James Basire, read widely in his free time, and began to try his hand at poetry. At 24 he married Catherine Boucher, daughter of a market gardener. She was then illiterate, but Blake taught her to read and to help him in his engraving and printing. In the early and somewhat sentimentalized biographies, Catherine is represented as an ideal wife for an unorthodox and penniless genius. Blake, however, must have been a trying domestic partner, and his vehement attacks on the torment caused by a possessive, jealous female will, which reached their height in 1793, and remained prominent in his writings for another decade, probably reflect a troubled period at home. The couple had no children.

In 1800, he moved to Felpham in Sussex, where he had a patron who wanted to transform Blake into a conventional artist and bread earner. But Blake had his ideals and wanted to pursue his spiritual life. He rebelled.

After three years at Felpham, Blake moved back to London, determined to follow his "Divine Vision" though it meant a life of isolation, misunderstanding and poverty. He had a one-man show put on in 1809, which proved a total failure. Blake passed into almost complete obscurity. Only when he was in his 60's did he finally attract a small but devoted group of young painters who served as an audience for his work and his talk. Blake's old age was serene, self-confident and joyous, largely free from the bursts of irascibility with which he had earlier responded to the shallowness and blindness of the English public. He died in his seventieth year in 1827.

Blake was a very important poet in the history of English literature. His poems seem easy, but difficult to understand on account of his use of mysterious images and symbols. And one cannot really understand him if not versed in religious knowledge.

He was strongly influenced by the French Revolution, the ideas of Thomas Paine, William Godwin, Mary Wollstonecraft and others.

His main works include *Songs of Innocence* (1789), *Songs of Experience* (1794) and *The Marriage of Heaven and Hell* (1790).

London[1]

I wander thro'[2] each charter'd[3] street,
Near where the charter'd Thames[4] does flow,
And mark[5] in every face I meet
Marks of weakness, marks of woe.

In every[6] cry of every Man,
In every Infant's cry of fear,
In every voice, in every ban[7],
The mind-forg'd manacles[8] I hear.

How the chimney-sweeper's[9] cry
Every blackning[10] church appalls[11];
And the hapless Soldier's sigh
Runs in blood down Palace walls.[12]

But most[13] thro' midnight streets I hear
How the youthful Harlot's curse
Blasts[14] the new-born Infant's tear,
And blights[15] with plagues[16] the Marriage hearse[17].

注释

1. This poem is taken from *Songs of Experience.*
2. **thro'** through
3. **charter'd** chartered，指享有专利权的大商人或大公司所独占的
4. **Thames** 泰晤士河
5. **mark** notice
6. **every** 具体地从成人和婴儿、话语和法令的角度描绘伦敦的苦难
7. **ban** 禁令
8. **mind-forg'd manacles** 指用英国统治阶级思想铸成的镣铐。-forg'd: -forged
9. **chimney-sweeper** 扫烟囱者
10. **blackning** blackening
11. **appalls** be surprised
12. **And the hapless Soldier's sigh / Runs in blood down Palace walls** 诗人听到不幸士兵的叹息，仿佛看到他们的鲜血正从王宫的墙壁上流下来。hapless: unfortunate
13. **most** most of all
14. **Blasts** 使干枯，指吓得婴儿不敢哭泣
15. **blights** destroy
16. **plagues** 指包括性病在内的各种疫病
17. **the Marriage hearse** 婚姻的柩车

参考译诗

伦　敦

我徘徊在每条被独占的街上，
靠近那也被霸占的泰晤士河，
注意到所遇的每个行人脸上
都把衰弱和痛苦的烙印铭刻。

从每个男女的每一声呼喊中，
从每个婴孩害怕的哭叫，
从每个声音里，从每一条禁令
都能听到思想铸成的镣铐。

听扫烟囱孩子的叫喊
震惊着每座熏黑的教堂。
不幸士兵的悲叹
像鲜血冲下堵堵宫墙。

但我常听见在深夜的街边
年轻妓女不停地诅咒。
它吓得新生儿不敢哭喊，
妓女带来瘟疫，使婚车变成灵柩。

（李正栓　译）

思考题

1. Which image strikes you the most? Why?
2. Why does the poet use "every" many times? What effect can it produce?
3. Learn the first two stanzas by heart.

The Tyger[1]

Tyger! Tyger! burning bright[2]
In the forests of the night,
What immortal hand or eye
Could frame thy fearful symmetry[3]?

In what distant deeps[4] or skies
Burnt the fire of thine eyes?
On what wings dare he[5] aspire[6]?
What the hand, dare seize the fire[7]?

And what shoulder[8], and what art[9],
Could twist the sinews of thy heart[10]?
And when thy heart began to beat,
What dread[11] hand? and what dread feet?

What the hammer[12]? what the chain?
In what furnace was thy brain?
What the anvil? what dread grasp[13]
Dare its deadly terrors clasp?

When the stars threw down their spears[14],
And water'd heaven with their tears,
Did he smile his work to see?
Did he who made the Lamb[15] make thee?

Tyger! Tyger! burning bright
In the forests of the night,
What immortal hand or eye
Dare frame thy fearful symmetry?

注释

1. **Tyger** This poem is taken from *Songs of Experience*. Tyger: tiger
2. **burning bright** 指老虎的眼睛在黑暗中发出炽烈的光
3. **thy fearful symmetry** 可怕的匀称
4. **deeps** seas
5. **he** God，指造物者
6. **aspire** rise high
7. **seize the fire** （敢）抓住这样的火
8. **shoulder** 指肩臂的力量
9. **art** skills
10. **twist the sinews of thy heart** 拧制在你心脏的筋肉。sinews: 筋，腱
11. **dread** dreadful
12. **the hammar** 诗人用铁匠的形象喻老虎的创造者
13. **grasp** 指手臂
14. **spears** tears
15. **the Lamb** 指耶稣基督

参考译诗

老　虎

老虎！老虎！炯炯发亮，
燃烧在黑夜的林莽。
是什么脱俗的手和眼睛
塑造了你这可怕的匀称？

眼睛的火光来自什么地方？
是来自远处的深海还是高处的天堂？
凭什么翅膀他胆敢高翔？
敢抓这火的是什么样的手掌？

什么样的肩膀，什么样的技艺
能把你心脏的肌肉拧制？
当你心胸开始搏跳，
制造你的是多么可怕的手与脚？

是什么样的铁锤？是什么样的铁链？
是什么样的熔炉把你的头脑冶炼？
是什么样的铁砧？是什么可怕的手臂？
敢把这死的恐怖握得结结实实？

当群星洒泪做成长矛若干，
用泪水把整个天宇来浇灌，
他可曾因见到自己的创作而微笑？
莫非是创造了羔羊的人也同样把你创造？

老虎！老虎！炯炯发亮，
燃烧在黑夜的林莽。
是什么脱俗的手和眼睛
敢塑造你这可怕的匀称？

（李正栓　译）

思考题

1. What is the tiger like? Describe its appearance in your own words.
2. What is the image of God?
3. Whom did the poet give praise to? The tiger or God?
4. What is the rhyme scheme of this poem?
5. Learn the first two stanzas by heart.

Robert Burns
罗伯特·彭斯
(1759–1796)

The greatest of Scottish poets, Robert Burns, is regarded as a national hero by Scottish people. He was born in a peasant's clay-built cottage, a mile and a half south of Ayrshire. His father was a man whose morality, industry and zeal for education made him an admirable parent. The poet had little formal schooling, but under paternal influence he learned how to teach himself.

Until his twenty-eighth year, Robert Burns was an ordinary labourer on one or another of the Ayrshire tenant farms which his father or brothers leased. At the age of fifteen, he did a man's full labour. He called his life on the Ayrshire farms "the unceasing toil of a galley slave." All his life he fought a hand-to-hand fight with poverty.

In 1786, when he was twenty-seven years old, he resolved to abandon the struggle and seek position in the far-off island of Jamaica. In order to secure money for his passage, he published some poems which he had thought out while following the plough or resting after the day's toil. Six hundred copies were printed at three shillings each. All were sold a little over a month. At the end of the nineteenth century a copy of this edition was sold in Edinburgh for 572 pounds. His fame from that little volume has grown as much as its monetary value.

Some Edinburgh critics praised the poems very highly and suggested a second edition. He abandoned the idea of going to Jamaica and went to Edinburgh to arrange a new edition. Here he was entertained by the foremost men of the town, some of whom wished to see how a plowman would behave in polite society, while others desired to gaze on what they regarded as a freak of nature. The new volume appeared in 1787. The following winter he again went to Edinburgh, but he was almost totally neglected by the leaders in literature and society.

In 1788 Burns married Jean Armour and took her to a farm which he leased in Dumfriesshire. The first part of this new period was the happiest in his life. This farm proved unprofitable. He appealed to influential persons for some position that would enable him to support his family and write poetry. This was an age of pensions, but not a farthing of pension did he ever get. He was made an exciseman or gauger, at a salary of 50 pounds a year, and he followed that occupation for the few remaining years of his life. He died miserably in 1796, when he was only thirty-seven years old. He was buried in Dumfries, mourned by all honest people of his country.

Burns is often referred to as a poet of the labouring people for he pours out the sentiment of them. In his poems, he sings of his hometown, his people, friendship, love, nature, etc. Burns' poems seem easy, but they exert far-reaching influence on readers. Many of his poems are sung or recited even now.

My Heart's in the Highlands[1]

My heart's in the Highlands, my heart is not here;
My heart's in the Highlands a-chasing[2] the deer;
Chasing the wild deer, and following the roe,
My heart's in the Highlands, wherever I go.

Farewell to the Highlands, farewell to the North[3],
The birth-place of valor[4], the country of worth[5];
Wherever I wander, wherever I rove,
The hills of the Highlands for ever I love.

Farewell to the mountains high cover'd with snow;
Farewell to the straths[6] and green valleys below;
Farewell to the forests and wild-hanging woods[7];
Farewell to the torrents and loud-pouring floods.

My heart's in the Highlands, my heart is not here;
My heart's in the Highlands a-chasing the deer;
Chasing the wild deer, and following the roe,
My heart's in the Highlands, wherever I go.

Robert Burns
罗伯特·彭斯

注释

1. **the Highlands** 苏格兰高地
2. **a-chasing** chasing
3. **the North** 北方，指苏格兰
4. **valor** 英勇
5. **worth** 高尚品德
6. **straths** 平底河谷
7. **wild-hanging woods** 位于高处或斜坡上的丛林野树

参考译诗

我的心在高原

我的心在高原，我的心不在这里；
我的心在高原，追逐着鹿群，
追逐着野鹿，跟踪着野狍，
我的心在高原，不管我在何处飘摇。

再见吧，高原！再见吧，北方！
你是品德的家园，是勇士的故乡；
不管我流浪何处，不管我何处浪迹，
高原的群山永远在我心底。

再见吧，银装素裹的高山；
再见吧，绿色山谷与河滩；
再见吧，参天的森林和丛生的野树；
再见吧，汹涌的激流和轰鸣的流瀑。

我的心在高原，我的心不在这里；
我的心在高原，追逐着鹿群，
追逐着野鹿，跟踪着野狍，
我的心在高原，不管我在何处飘摇。

（李正栓 译）

思考题

1. What's the main idea of this poem?
2. Identify the rhyme scheme of the poem.
3. List some poems or songs that sing praise of a person's hometown.
4. Write a poem by imitating this one.
5. Which stanza do you like best? Why? Learn it by heart.

A Red, Red Rose[1]

O My luve's[2] like a red, red rose,
　　That's newly sprung in June;
O My luve's like the melodie[3]
　　That's sweetly play'd[4] in tune.

As fair art thou[5], my bonie lass[6].
　　So deep in luve am I;
And I will luve thee still, my dear,
　　Till a'[7] the seas gang dry[8].

Till a' the seas gang dry, my dear,
　　And the rocks melt wi'[9] the sun:
O I will luve thee still, my dear,
　　While the sands o' life[10] shall run.

And fare thee weel[11], my only luve,
　　And fare thee weel awhile[12]!
And I will come again, my luve,
　　Tho' it were ten thousand mile.

注释

1. 全诗形容了姑娘之可爱，表明了诗人的心迹。诗人以海枯石烂作比，向爱人表示永不变心，不管远行千里万里，终要回到爱人的身旁。第一节形容姑娘长得像玫瑰，音如乐曲，这里朦朦胧胧地描绘了姑娘的音容笑貌。第二节表达他对姑娘的爱。第三节和第四节表达了诗人的决心：不管远行千里万里，最终要回到她身旁。
2. **luve's** love is
3. **melodie** melody
4. **play'd** played
5. **art thou** are you
6. **bonie lass** good maid; pretty girl
7. **a'** all
8. **gang dry** go dry
9. **wi'** with
10. **sands o'life** sands of life. 古代以沙漏计时，沙漏中沙子流动，表示时间不止，生命尚存。
11. **fare thee weel** bid you farewell; goodbye
12. **awhile** for a while

参考译诗

一朵红红的玫瑰

呵，我的爱人像一朵红红的玫瑰，
　　六月里迎风初开；
呵，我的爱人像一支甜甜的乐曲，
　　演奏得合弦又合拍。

我的好姑娘，你是这么美，
　　我的爱是这么深；
亲爱的，我要永远地爱你，
　　直到大海干枯水流尽。

直到大海干枯水流尽，
　　直到太阳把岩石化作灰尘：
呵，亲爱的，我将会永远地爱你，
　　只要我一息犹存。

再见吧，我唯一的真爱，
　　让我们暂时分离！
亲爱的，我一定要回来，
　　哪怕是远行千里万里。

（李正栓　译）

思考题

1. Identify the rhyme scheme of this verse.
2. What's the main idea of the poem?
3. Compare this poem with some Chinese love poems that express similar ideas on love.
4. To what do people usually compare love? List some, either from English poems and songs or Chinese ones.
5. Learn the whole poem by heart.
6. Find the tune of this poem and learn the song.

Scots, Wha Hae[1]

Scots, wha hae wi' Wallace[2] bled,
Scots, wham[3] Bruce[4] has aften led,
Welcome tae[5] your gory bed[6],
　　Or tae Victorie!

Now's the day, and now's the hour:
See the front o' battle lour[7],
See approach proud Edward's power[8] —
　　Chains and Slaverie!

Wha will be a traitor knave?
Wha can fill a coward's grave?

Wha sae base as be a slave?[9]
Let him turn and flee!

Wha, for Scotland's king and law,
Freedom's sword will strongly draw,
Freeman stand, or Freeman fa',[10]
Let him follow me!

By[11] Oppression's woes and pains!
By your sons in servile chains!
We will drain your dearest veins,
But they shall be free!

Lay the proud usurpers low![12]
Tyrants fall in every foe!
Liberty's in every blow!
Let us do, or die!

注释

1. **Scots, Wha Hae** Scots, who have. 原题为Robert Bruce's Address at Bannockburn。
2. **Wallace** Sir William Wallace（1272–1305），威廉・华莱士爵士，苏格兰民族英雄
3. **wham** whom
4. **Bruce** Robert Bruce（1274–1329），罗伯特・布鲁斯
5. **tae** to
6. **gory bed** bloody bed
7. **lour** lower, look dark or threatening
8. **Edward's power** 爱德华的军队。Edward指爱德华二世（Edward II，1284–1327），在Battle of Bannockburn一战中被苏格兰军队击败。
9. **Wha sae base as be a slave** Who is so mean as to be a slave? sae: so
10. **Freeman stand, or Freeman fa'** As freeman we live, as freeman we die. fa': fall
11. **By** we swear by
12. **Lay the proud usurpers low** 打倒傲慢的篡位者

参考译诗

苏格兰人

随华莱士浴血奋战的苏格兰人，
布鲁斯经常统率的苏格兰人，
欢迎你战死成仁，
　　要么就大获全胜。

现在就是这一天，现在就是这一刻，
看吧，战斗一步步近逼，
看啊，爱德华大军咄咄逼人——
　　要带来枷锁和奴役！

谁愿做可耻的叛徒？
谁愿钻进懦夫的坟墓？
谁愿当低贱的农奴？
　　那他就掉头逃跑！

谁捍卫苏格兰国王和法律的尊严，
谁为自由而勇敢地亮剑，
谁愿生做自由人死做自由仙，
　　那就随我冲杀！

凭着受压迫的苦难发誓！
为子孙不受奴役而发誓！
我们将血战到底，
　　这样他们才能自由！

打倒傲慢侵略我们的人，
每杀一个敌人就少一个暴君！

每一次痛击都铸就自由之魂！——
要么去奋战，要么就死去！
（李正栓，白凤欣 译）

思考题

1. Read the poem and comment on the fourth line of each stanza.
2. What is the strategy used in this address? How does the speaker effectively call on his followers?
3. Find some other poems calling on people to fight for a purpose.
4. Which stanza do you like best? Why?
5. Learn the first stanza by heart.

Auld Lang Syne[1]

Should auld acquaintance be forgot
And never brought to mind?
Should auld acquaintance be forgot,
And auld lang syne?

For auld lang syne, my dear,
For auld lang syne.
We'll tak a cup o' kindness[2] yet,
For auld lang syne.

And surely ye'll be your pint-stowp[3],
And surely I'll be mine;
And we'll tak' a cup o' kindness yet,
For auld lang syne.

We twa hae run about the braes, [4]

And pou'd the gowans fine;[5]
But we've wander'd mony a weary fitt[6],
Sin' auld lang syne.

We twa hae paidl'd in the burn[7],
Frae morning sun till dine[8];
But seas between us braid[9] hae roar'd.
Sin' auld lang syne.

And there's a hand, my trusty fiere[10]!
And gie's[11] a hand o' thine!
And we'll tak' a right gud-wellie waught[12],
For auld lang syne.

For auld lang syne, my dear,
For auld lang syne.
We'll tak a cup o' kindness yet,
For auld lang syne.

注释

1. **Auld Lang Syne** long ago, old long since
2. **tak a cup o' kindness** take a cup of friendship wine
3. **pint-stowp** 能装一品特酒的容器
4. **We twa hae run about the braes** We two have run about the slopes.
5. **And pou'd the gowans fine** And pulled the daisies fine.
6. **mony a weary fitt** many a weary foot
7. **paidl'd in the burn** paddled in the stream
8. **dine** 吃晚饭的时候
9. **braid** broad
10. **fiere** friend; comrade
11. **gie's** give us
12. **tak' a right gud-wellie waught** 干上一杯美酒，举起酒杯痛饮。gud-wellie: good will; waught: a big draught

参考译诗

过去的好时光

老朋友怎能遗忘掉，
　　永不再放心上？
老朋友怎能遗忘掉，
　　还有过去的好时光？

为了过去的好时光，亲爱的，
　　为了过去的好时光，
让我们干一杯友谊的酒，
　　为了过去的好时光。

请你干尽这杯酒，
　　我也把这一杯喝光。
让我们干一杯友谊的酒，
　　为了过去的好时光。

我们俩曾游遍山岗，
　　并把野菊来采摘；
我们已历尽苦与辛，
　　远离过去的好时光！

我们俩曾趟溪又过河，
　　从早到日悬中央；
如今大海将我们分离，
　　远离过去的好时光！

老朋友，我已伸出我的手，
　　请你也伸手相握！
让我们干一杯友谊的酒，

为了过去的好时光。

为了过去的好时光，亲爱的，
为了过去的好时光，
让我们干一杯友谊的酒，
为了过去的好时光。

（李正栓　译）

思考题

1. What is the theme of this poem?
2. Learn the first two stanzas by heart.
3. Learn to sing this song.

William Wordsworth
威廉·华兹华斯
(1770–1850)

William Wordsworth was born in Cockermouth, West Cumberland, in 1770. He came from a family sound and healthy in its moral tone, and vigorous physically. He lost his parents early in life, and was left to the care of uncles who discharged their trust in a praiseworthy manner.

He went to school in his ninth year at Hawkshead, a village on the banks of Esthwaite Water. His school days were happy. He boarded in the village with a kindly old dame, whom he has fondly described in his *Prelude*, and, out of school hours, he was free from the supervision of tutors. He wrote: "I was left at liberty then, and in the vacation, to read whatever books I liked." He was free also to go about as he pleased, and he roamed early and late over the mountains.

The healthy out-of-door life hardened the fibers of his sturdy frame and kept him vigorous, and the constant sight of nature in the wondrous beauty of the Lake District awoke love and reverence in him. He enjoyed the sports of hunting, skating and rowing. Little by little, the glories of Nature grew upon him, until his soul seemed flooded with unutterable delight. This profound passion was fostered by his life in these early years, and grew steadily with his youth. At seventeen, he went to Cambridge and, for a time, was dazzled by the intercourse with town-bred people, but the infatuation was of short duration, and his four years at college were the least congenial of his life.

His travels on the Continent in his last vacation and after his graduation brought him in contact with the French Revolution, and he came under its spell, as did most of the enthusiastic young people of the time. His hopes were stirred and his imagination fired with dreams of an ideal republic, which he fancied would arise from the Revolution.

He was prepared to throw himself personally into the struggle, when his relatives called him back to England to face the ugly specter of poverty. The rude shock came too suddenly upon his ardent aspirations, and, following closely upon it, came the failure of the revolutionists, the period of anarchy and imperialism in France. He sank into a dejection as deep as his hopes had been high, and, as he slowly recovered from his disappointment, he became more and more conservative in his politics, and less in sympathy with any violent reactions. For this he was censured by Byron, Shelley, and other strong adherents of liberty, but such moderation was more natural to Wordsworth than the excitement of his early years. To the end of his days, he never failed to utter for genuine liberty a hopeful, though calm and tempered note.

He returned from France in 1792. In 1795 a bequest of 900 pounds relieved the financial strain which had caused his anxiety, and secured for him and his sister Dorothy a modest maintenance. They went back to the Lake District, in which, save for an occasional tour, they passed the rest of their lives. The two places most associated with the poet were Grasmere, where he wrote the best of his poetry between the years 1798 and 1808, and Ryday Mount, where he lived in his later years. Dorothy was his lifelong companion. She won him back from his hopelessness over the Revolution and urged upon him the duty of devoting himself to poetry. Their favorite pastime was walking.

In 1797 he made friends with S.T. Coleridge and a year later they jointly published the *Lyrical Ballads*. The majority of poems in this collection were written by Wordsworth. Coleridge's chief contribution was his masterpiece *The Rime of the Ancient Mariner*.

Wordsworth's principal poems include: *Lines Composed a Few Miles above Tintern Abbey* (1798), *The Prelude* (1805–1806), *The Excursion* (1814), miscellaneous sonnets (written at different periods of his life).

Wordsworth is quite popular with the readers. His poems are clear in imagery, deep in feeling yet is to read aloud and recite. He advocated writing the language of common people and writing about the common people and nature.

In the preface to the *Lyrical Ballads*, he wrote, "All good poetry is the spontaneous overflow of powerful feelings: it takes its origin from emotion recollected in tranquility."

The Solitary Reaper

Behold her, single in the field,
Yon[1] solitary Highland Lass!
Reaping and singing by herself;
Stop here, or gently pass!
Alone she cuts and binds the grain,
And sings a melancholy strain[2];
O listen! for the Vale profound
Is overflowing with the sound.

No Nightingale did ever chaunt[3]
More welcome notes[4] to weary bands
Of travelers[5] in some shady haunt,
Among Arabian sands[6];
A voice so thrilling ne'er[7] was heard
In springtime from the Cuckoo bird,
Breaking the silence of the seas
Among the farthest Hebrides[8].

Will no one tell me what she sings?[9]—
Perhaps the plaintive numbers[10] flow
For old, unhappy, far-off things,
And battles long ago;
Or is it some more humble lay[11],
Familiar matter of today?
Some natural sorrow, loss, or pain,
That has been, and may be again?

Whate'er[12] the theme, the Maiden sang

As if her song could have no ending;
I saw her singing at her work,
And o'er the sickle bending[13] —
I listened, motionless and still;
And, as I mounted up the hill,
The music in my heart I bore,
Long after it was heard no more.

注释

1. **Yon** yonder
2. **strain** melody
3. **chaunt** chant
4. **welcome notes** 令人快乐的音调
5. **weary bands / Of travelers** 一队队疲乏的旅行者，指商旅
6. **Arabian sands** 阿拉伯沙漠
7. **ne'er** never
8. **Hebrides** 赫布里底群岛，在苏格兰西北部的大西洋中
9. **Will no one tell me what she sings** 那姑娘是用苏格兰高地的盖尔语（Erse）歌唱的，诗人听不懂。
10. **the plaintive numbers** sad songs. numbers: songs
11. **lay** （唱的）短抒情诗或短叙事诗
12. **Whate'er** whatever
13. **o'er the sickle bending** bending over the sickle

参考译诗

孤独的刈麦女

你看，那边高原上孤独的少女，
独自个儿在这田野里！
她自己一人，边收割边哼着小曲；
停下吧，要么就悄悄地绕过去！
她孤独一人，又收割又绑捆，
唱出的曲调有些哀婉伤心；
啊，听！那深深的峡谷
也把她的歌声洒布。

在阿拉伯沙漠
偶见的绿荫，对疲惫的旅人，
夜莺会唱出甜美的歌，
但怎么也超不过这少女的唱吟；
在遥远的赫伯利群岛，
听到啼叫报春的布谷鸟
打破辽阔海域的沉寂，
却也赶不上少女的歌声醉人心迷。

就没人告诉我她唱的是什么？——
也许只是些伤感事，
也许是些遥远过去不幸的生活，
也许是古老的战场怨曲。
也许唱的是更普通的曲子，
唱的是当今的生活琐事。
也许诉说着自然的伤感、损失和痛苦，
这些事曾经发生，以后也许会反复。

不管这少女唱的主题是什么，
仿佛这歌声无头无尽远流长；
我见她边唱歌儿边工作，
我见她弯腰运镰收割忙。
我凝神贯注静静地听，
我登高侧耳仍听见那歌声。
那乐声在我这儿长存，
久未听见，却仍留于心。

（李正栓　译）

思考题

1. Why does the speaker say “Will no one tell me what she sings”?
2. What is the most vivid image of the reaper and why is the speaker carried away?
3. What does the poet want to say through the poem?
4. Which stanza do you like best? Why? Learn it by heart.

I Wandered Lonely as a Cloud[1]

I wandered lonely as a cloud[2]
That floats on high[3] o'er vales and hills,
When all at once I saw a crowd,
A host, of golden daffodils;
Beside the lake, beneath the trees,
Fluttering and dancing in the breeze.

Continuous as the stars that shine
And twinkle on the milky way,[4]
They stretched in never-ending line
Along the margin of a bay:
Ten thousand saw I at a glance,
Tossing their heads in sprightly dance.

The waves beside them danced; but they
Outdid the sparkling waves in glee;
A poet could not but be gay,
In such a jocund company;
I gazed—and gazed—but little thought
What wealth the show to me had brought:

For oft, when on my couch I lie
In vacant or in pensive mood,
They flash upon that inward eye
Which is the bliss of solitude;
And then my heart with pleasure fills,
And dances with the daffodils.

注释

1. 在这首诗里，诗人表达了对大自然的热爱以及大自然对人类心理的积极影响。即便是孤独的人，只要与美好的大自然合一，他也会幸福无比，孤意全消。
2. **I wandered lonely as a cloud** wander: 徘徊；lonely: 孤独，无伴；as a cloud: 像一片云. 这些都是“孤独”的形象。
3. **on high** in the sky
4. **Continuous as the stars that shine / And twinkle on the milky way** 指湖边的水仙花数不胜数，犹如银河系闪烁的繁星，连绵不断。这个意象扩大了想象的空间，把人从地上带到天上。给人一种不知“湖边与水仙”是“天空与繁星”，还是“天空与繁星”是“湖边与水仙”的感觉，妙不可言。

参考译诗

我独自漫游像一朵浮云

我独自漫游像一朵浮云，
高高地漂浮在山与谷之上，
突然我看见一簇簇一群群
金色的水仙在开放：
靠湖边，在树下，
随风起舞乐开花。

它们连绵不断，像银河中的
群星闪烁、眨眼，
它们展延无限成远景，
沿着湖湾的边沿：
一瞥眼我看见成千上万，
它们欢快摇首舞翩翩。

近旁的波浪跳着舞；但水仙
欢快的舞姿远远胜过闪光的波浪；
有这样欢乐的侣伴，
诗人怎能不心花怒放？
我凝视着——凝视着——当时并未领悟
这景色给我带来的是何等财富：

常常是，当我独卧榻上，
或是沉思，或是茫然，
它们在我心田闪光，
这是我独处时的欢乐无限；
我的心就充满欢乐，
随着那些水仙起舞婀娜。

（李正栓　译）

思考题

1. From what images can you figure out the meaning of loneliness?
2. What is the function of nature in driving away the speaker's loneliness?
3. The speaker used the third person to represent himself in the line "A poet could not but be gay." Why? Can you find such a phenomenon in other poems either English or Chinese?
4. What is the rhyme scheme of this poem?
5. Learn the first stanza by heart.

She Dwelt among the Untrodden Ways[1]

She dwelt among the untrodden ways
　　Beside the springs of Dove,
A Maid whom there were none to praise
　　And very few to love;

A violet by a mossy stone
　　Half hidden from the eye! —
Fair as a star, when only one
　　Is shining in the sky.

She lived unknown, and few could know

When Lucy ceased to be[2];
But she is in her grave, and, oh,
The difference to me!

注释

1. 这首诗写于1799年，写于德国，后寄给柯尔律治。初稿原有五节，1800年出版时改为现在的三节。
2. **ceased to be** died

参考译诗

她住在人迹罕至的地方

她住在人迹罕至的地方，
　　就在多佛小溪旁，
无人曾将这少女称赞，
　　也没几人把她放在心上。

青苔石旁紫罗兰，
　　怀抱苔石半遮面！——
她美丽得像一颗孤星
　　独自个儿在夜空中闪现。

她活着，无人知晓，
　　她死了，没几人知道；
但她现在孤坟之中，
　　对我，就不同了。

（李正栓　译）

思考题

1. What do the comparisons in the second stanza suggest about Lucy?
2. What's the main idea of this poem?
3. Find more Chinese versions of this poem.
4. Learn the whole poem by heart.

My Heart Leaps Up

My heart leaps up when I behold
  A rainbow in the sky:
So was it when my life began;
So is it now I am a man;
So be it when I shall grow old,
  Or let me die!
The Child is father of the Man;
And I could wish my days to be
Bound each to each by natural piety.

参考译诗

我的心剧烈地跳动

每当我看到天挂彩虹，
  我的心就剧烈地跳动。
我生命之初就是这样；
我成年后它仍是如此，
但愿我年老后它仍然如是，
  要不，就让我现在死去！
童年乃成年之父；
但愿我的一生
贯穿我天然的爱与敬。

（李正栓　译）

思考题

1. Explain Line 7 and find and compare the different translators of the same line.
2. What's the central idea of the poem?
3. Learn this poem by heart.

London, 1802[1]

Milton! thou should'st be living at this hour:
England hath need of thee: she is a fen[2]
Of stagnant[3] waters: altar, sword, and pen[4],
Fireside, the heroic wealth of hall and bower,
Have forefeited their ancient English dower
Of inward happiness.[5] We are selfish men;
Oh! raise us up, return to us again;
And give us manners[6], virtue, freedom, power.
Thy soul was like a Star, and dwelt apart;[7]
Thou hadst a voice whose sound was like the sea:[8]
Pure as the naked heavens[9], majestic, free,
So didst thou travel on life's common way,
In cheerful godliness[10]; and yet thy heart
The lowliest duties on herself did lay.[11]

注释

1. 这首诗是意大利十四行体诗，每行五音步，韵律为abba abba cdd ece。
2. **fen** marsh
3. **stagnant** not running or flowing
4. **altar, sword, pen** these words represent the three professions: the church, the Army and literature.
5. **Fireside, the heroic wealth of hall and bower/Have forefeited their ancient English dower/Of inward happiness** hall: 客厅；bower: 卧室；forefeited: 丧失；Fireside 指家庭。家庭生活（男人客厅，主妇卧室）内外纵然豪华，却丧失了（充满内心快乐）的旧有英国之室。
6. **manners** 良好的生活方式；礼节；行为方式
7. **Thy soul was like a Star, and dwelt apart** Milton is compared to the star, dwelling apart.
8. **Thou hadst a voice whose sound was like the sea** Milton's verse is extremely grand and the mighty roll of this verse is thus appropriately compared to the thunder of the ocean.
9. **naked heavens** bare heavens. This is the favorite image of Wordsworth.

10. **cheerful godliness** 愉快而虔诚。godly: religious, devout, loving and obeying God
11. **The lowliest duties on herself did lay** and yet thy heart did lay the lowliest duties on herself. Milton, though a great poet, did not despise the hard, unpleasant work of routine duties. He was Latin secretary to the Commonwealth, and (before that) had been engaged in teaching.

参考译诗

伦敦，一八零二年

弥尔顿！你应该活在这一时代：
英国需要你：她是一池浊水。
那尊贵的祭坛、军人的剑与文人的笔，
家庭、客厅、内室、英雄的气概，
已丧失它们古昔英国的内在
幸福的天禀。我们自私又自卑。
啊，振奋我们，再次予以转回；
给我们风尚、德行、自由与天才。
你的灵魂像颗星，闪烁在天空：
你的诗音似大海的波涛激荡，
纯洁如赤裸的碧空，自由与端庄；
因而你走过了人生平凡的路程
似神般的欢快；但是你的心胸
为自己担负着人世低微的责任。

（吴伟仁　译）

思考题

1. What was the condition of London in 1802?
2. Identify the figures of speech used in this poem.

Samuel Taylor Coleridge
塞缪尔·泰勒·柯尔律治
（1772—1834）

Being a poet, literary critic and philosopher, Samuel Taylor Coleridge was born in Ottery St. Mary, Devonshire on October 21, 1772. After his father John Coleridge, a pastor and the headmaster of Henry Ⅷ's Free Grammar School, died in 1781, Samuel was sent to Christ's Hospital, a charity school in London, where he spent his childhood, where he established friendship with Charles Lamb and Leigh Hunt, where he read Virgil, William Lisle Bowles, Greek tragedies, William Shakespeare and John Milton, where he began writing poetry. Very young, Samuel developed great enthusiasm for reading and devoured books which aroused his imagination. But he felt lonely at school since his mother rarely allowed him to go back home during the school term. This made him feel estranged with his family. However, he appreciated his teacher, a severe master from whom he learnt that "poetry had a logic of its own" and that "the sense of poetry might have been conveyed with equal force and dignity in plainer words." From 1791 to 1794, he studied at Jesus College, Cambridge, but he never received a degree.

In 1794 Coleridge met Robert Southey, future poet laureate. Under the influence of Southey, he accepted some radical and philosophical ideas. Then they planned to establish in Pennsylvania, a utopian community named Pantisocracy (equal government by and for all). Both of them envisioned that people in that community shared the workload, library, philosophical ideas, and freedom of religious and political beliefs. Due to disagreements about money and politics between them, the plan failed in the end. In 1795, they married sisters Sarah and Edith Fricker, but Coleridge's marriage with Sara was not happy and he eventually separated from her.

In 1795 Coleridge met William Wordsworth. Thus began the most fruitful and happiest time of Coleridge's life. In 1796, Coleridge published his first volume of poetry *Poems on Various Subjects*. In 1798 they collaborately published *Lyrical Ballads*, which opened with Coleridge's *The Rime of the Ancient Mariner,* generally regarded as his masterpiece. The publication of *Lyrical Ballads* marked the break with classicism and the beginning of English romantic period. They set a different style for poetic writing by the use of common people's language and new ways of examing nature. From 1797 to 1798 Coleridge lived nearby with Wordsworth in the Lake District. Disillusioned with politics in England and France, Coleridge, together with Wordsworth and Dorothy in 1798, travelled to Germany. He became interested in Immanuel Kant, Friedrich von Schiller and Joseph Scheling. After his return to England, he translated some German works into English. In 1810 he quarreled bitterly with Wordsworth and the two poets never entirely regained their former intimacy.

After traveling in Italy, Coleridge came back to England and settled at Keswick. Over the next two decades he lectured on literature and philosophy. He became a successful lecturer. His philosophical works, such as *On Method* (1818), *Aids to Reflection* (1825), *On the Constitution of Church and State* (1830), *Confessions of an Inquiring Mind* (1840), influenced American transcendentalists. In 1816 and 1817 he published the following poems *Christabel*, *Kubla Khan* and *Sibylline Leaves*. His notable work of lietary criticism *Biographia Literaria* (1817) afforded the new Romantic poetry a new principle of criticism, whose task was not to judge but to appreciate and interpret. He discussed the relationship between poet and critic. To him the poet was a creator and the critic an assistant in the work of creation. The poet, as a man endowed with imaginative genius and fine perception, must be allowed to present the truth in his own without regard to rules or models. And the critic must enter into the poet's purpose and art, and interpret ideas and beauty for the benefit of the reader.

The Rime of the Ancient Mariner relates the experiences of a sailor who has returned from a long sea voyage. The mariner stops a man who is on the way to a wedding ceremony and begins to narrate a story. The wedding-guest's reaction turns from bemusement to impatience to fear to fascination as the mariner's story progresses, as can be seen in the language style: Coleridge uses narrative techniques such as personification and repetition to create a sense of danger, the supernatural, or serenity, depending on the mood in different parts of the poem.

Suffering from neuralgic and rheumatic pains, Coleridge had been addicted to opium. Then he moved in Highgate with Dr. James Gillman until his death on July 25, 1834 at the age of 61. He was buried in the aisele of St. Michael's Church.

The Rime of the Ancient Mariner[1]

It is an ancient[2] Mariner,
And he stoppeth[3] one of three.
"By thy long grey beard and glittering eye,
Now wherefore[4] stopp'st thou me?

The Bridegroom's doors are opened wide,
And I am next of kin[5];
The guests are met, the feast is set:
May'st[6] hear the merry din."

He holds him with his skinny hand,
"There was a ship, "quoth he.
"Hold off[7]! unhand me[8], grey-beard loon[9]!"
Eftsoons[10] his hand dropt he.

He holds him with his glittering eye[11]—
The Wedding-Guest stood still,
And listens like a three years' child:
The Mariner hath his will.

注释

1. 这四节诗选自《古舟子咏》第一部分的前四节。第一部分共二十节。全诗共七部分。
2. **ancient** 年长且经验丰富的
3. **stoppeth** (古用法) stops
4. **wherefore** (古用法) why
5. **next of kin** relative
6. **May'st** You may
7. **Hold off** get away
8. **unhand me** take your hands off me
9. **loon** rascal

10. **Eftsoons** quickly, at once
11. **his glittering eye** 他（指老水手）那炯炯目光

参考译诗

古 舟 子 咏

那是一位年长的水手，
他拦住了三个行人中的一人。
“凭你的花须和炯炯的眼睛，
你为什么阻挡我的前行？

“新郎家的门已开敞，
而我是他的至亲好友；
宾客已到，宴席摆好，
笑语欢声在耳边响。

他用枯瘦的手将他紧抓，
开始讲述：“曾有一艘船。”
“走开，撒手，你这老疯头！”
他即刻放手不磨缠。

他那炯炯目光盯着他——
使赴宴宾客驻足不前，
俨如三岁孩童听他讲述：
老水手终遂了心愿。

（白凤欣　译）

思考题

1. Describe the ancient mariner’s manner when he stopped the guests at the wedding.
2. Identify the rhyme scheme of the poem.
3. Learn the first stanza by heart.

George Gordon, Lord Byron

乔治·戈登·拜伦

(1788–1824)

George Gordon, Lord Byron was born in 1788 of a noble family notorious for their passionate temper, their amatory adventures, and their thriftlessness. To his extraordinary physical beauty, his lameness added a touch of pathos. Personal fascination was his from the first. He mastered his little world of school-fellows at Harrow with the same power of personality which later took captive the imagination of Europe. His first volume of poems, *Hours of Idleness* (1807), an immature little book, was mercilessly ridiculed in the *Edinburgh Review*. Byron nursed his revenge, and in 1809 he published a vigorous onslaught upon his critics, entitled *English Bards and Scotch Reviewers*. This poem is written in the manner of Pope, for whom Byron always professed admiration, and is not unworthy of his school, either in mastery of the heroic couplet or in energy of satire. It is significant that Byron's first performance should have been conceived in a satiric vein, and educed by a blow to his personal pride.

In the same year the poet set off upon his travels, which he was to recount in the first two cantos of *Childe Harold Pilgrimage* (1812). Not content with the conventional Grand Tour, he pushed on into Albania, Greece and the islands of the Aegean: dining in the tents of robber chieftains, rescuing distressed beauties from death at the hand of harem slaves, and doing many other romantic things. The public, at any rate, was eager to ascribe all these adventures to him, incited thereto by the lurid verse-romances, *The Giaour* (1813), *The Corsair* (1814), *Lara* (1814), and others, which he now poured out with prodigal swiftness. These Oriental tales were crude and melodramatic, but they appealed enormously to the popular taste, and quite eclipsed Scott's saner and healthier muse.

On Byron's return to England, he was lionized by corrupt Regency society, and plunged into a series of notorious love affairs. His marriage was quickly followed by a separation from his wife and by his final departure from his native country. The next years he spent in Switzerland and Italy, part of the time in company with Shelley.

To this period belong his most important works, the later cantos of *Childe Harold Pilgrimage* (1816–1818), the dramas *Manfred* (1817) and *Cain* (1821), and his satiric masterpiece *Don Juan* (1819–1824). The romance of his life was crowned by a romantic and generous death. In 1824 he went to Greece, to put himself at the head of the revolutionary forces gathered to liberate that country from the tyranny of the Sultan. He was seized with fever in the swamps of Missolonghi, and died before he had had time to prove his ability as a leader.

Byron's poems are full of revolutionary enthusiasm. When translated into Chinese in the early days of the 20th century, they produced tremendous influence on the Chinese people in their spirit of breaking with the old and creating the new. *The Isle of Greece* is one of such examples.

When We Two Parted

When we two parted
　In silence and tears,
Half broken-hearted
　To sever[1] for years,
Pale grew thy cheek and cold,
　Colder thy kiss;
Truly that hour foretold
　Sorrow to this[2].

The dew of the morning
　Sunk[3] chill on my brow—
It felt[4] like the warning
　Of what I feel now.
Thy vows are all broken,
　And light is thy fame;
I hear thy name spoken,

And share in its shame.

They name thee before me,
A knell to mine ear;
A shudder comes o'er me—
Why wert[5] thou so dear?
They know not I know thee,
Who knew thee too well—
Long, long shall I rue thee,
Too deeply to tell.

In secret we met—
In silence I grieve,
That thy heart could forget,
Thy spirit deceive.[6]
If I should meet thee
After long years,
How should I greet thee?—
With silence and tears.

注释

1. **To sever** to part
2. **this** this condition
3. **Sunk** sank
4. **It felt** 它给人以……感觉
5. **wert** （古用法）were
6. **Thy spirit deceive** Your spirit (could) deceive (me).

当初我们分别

当初我们分别，
沉默无语泪纵流，

心几乎要碎裂，
　要分离多少个年头！
当时你的脸发白又发冷，
　你的吻更是发凉；
的确，那一小时的光景
　预告了今日的悲伤。

清晨的露珠
　滴落眉头眉发冷——
当初我的感触
　似与今日的相同。
你把誓言全背弃，
　你的名声浪荡轻浮；
听别人提起你的名字，
　我暗中分担你的耻辱。

他们在我面前提起你，
　像丧钟在我耳边回荡
我不禁浑身战栗——
　我对你怎么就那么意深情长？
他们不知我对你熟悉，
　其实我对你熟悉过度——
我会久久地把你惋惜，
　深深地惋惜，语言难以表述。

当初你我幽会密约——
　如今我无声地哀惋，
你的心竟会忘却，
　你的灵魂竟会欺骗！
长长数年之后，
　假若我再与你相会，

我该如何把你问候？
　只能用沉默和眼泪。

（李正栓　译）

思考题

1. Find other poems describing breakup between lovers.
2. What's the tone of the poem?
3. Which stanza do you like best? Why? Learn it by heart.

She Walks in Beauty

1

She walks in beauty, like the night
　Of cloudless climes[1] and starry skies;
And all that's best of dark and bright
　Meet in her aspect[2] and her eyes:
Thus mellowed to that tender light
　Which heaven to gaudy day denies[3].

2

One shade the more, one ray the less,[4]
　Had half impaired the nameless[5] grace
Which waves in every raven tress[6],
　Or softly lightens o'er her face;
Where thoughts serenely sweet express
　How pure, how dear their dwelling place[7].

3

And on that cheek, and o'er that brow,
　So soft, so calm, yet eloquent[8],
The smiles that win[9], the tints that glow,

But[10] tell of days in goodness spent,
A mind at peace with all below[11],
A heart whose love is innocent!

注释

1. **cloudless climes** 晴朗无云
2. **aspect** appearance
3. **to gaudy day denies** denies to gaudy day
4. **One shade the more, one ray the less** 多一丝阴影则太多，少一丝光亮则太少，指正好合适。shade 指色调的浓淡
5. **nameless** 不可名状的
6. **every raven tress** 每一绺乌黑油亮的长发
7. **their dwelling place** 思想的寓所，指心灵。their: thoughts'
8. **eloquent** 意味深长的
9. **win** attract
10. **But** only
11. **below** 在人世

参考译诗

她走在美的光彩中

1

她走在美的光彩中，像夜晚
　皎洁无云而且繁星满天。
明与暗底最美妙的色泽
　在她的仪容和秋波里呈现，
仿佛是晨露映出的阳光，
　但比那光亮柔和而幽暗。

2

增加或减少一分色泽
　就会损害这难言的美，
美波动在她乌黑的发上
　或者散布淡淡的光辉

在那脸庞，恬静的思绪
　指明它的来处纯洁而珍贵。

3

啊，那额际，那鲜艳的面颊，
　如此温和、平静，而又脉脉含情，
那迷人的微笑，那明眸的顾盼，
　都在说明一个善良的生命：
她和蔼地对待世间的一切，
　她的心流溢着纯真的爱情！

（查良铮　译）

思考题

1. What is the lady like as described in the poem?
2. Find other poems describing women's beauty.
3. Which lines do you like best? Why?

Percy Bysshe Shelley
波希·比希·雪莱
(1792–1822)

Percy Bysshe Shelley was born in 1792, just when the eyes of all Europe were fixed in hope and fear upon France, and the stars fought in their courses for the triumph of a new order. At Eton, among the tyrannies and conventions of a great public school, his sensitive nature was thrown into a fever of rebellion from which he never quite worked out into spiritual sanity and health. His schoolmates called him "mad Shelley", and in the judgment of the world he remained "mad Shelley" to the end of his life. At Oxford, whither he proceeded in 1810, he read the skeptical French philosophers, and deemed it his duty to publish his religious views in a pamphlet entitled *The Necessity of Atheism*, for which he was expelled. An ill-starred marriage with Harriet Westbrook followed, and after that came a quixotic attempt to arouse Ireland to seek redress for her national wrongs. The young couple carried on their mission by throwing from the windows of their lodging in Dublin copies of Shelley's *Address to the Irish People*, "to every passer-by who seemed likely." The curious mixture in Shelley of the visionary and the serious thinker is sharply brought out by the fact that the writings thus fantastically put in circulation are often of grave and simple eloquence, wise in counsel and temperate in tone, and that most of the reforms which they advocate have since been enacted into law.

An acquaintance with William Godwin, the revolutionary philosopher and novelist, author of the *Inquiry Concerning Political Justice*, and Caleb Williams, led Shelley to write *Queen Mab*, a crude poem attacking dogmatic religion, government, industrial tyranny, and war. He separated from Harriet Westbrook in 1814, and united himself with Godwin's daughter Mary, who after Harriet's suicide became his wife. In 1818 the Shelleys went to Italy, where his powers developed rapidly. At Rome amid the tangle of flowers and vines which at that time covered the mountainous ruins of the Baths of Caracalla, he wrote his lyrical drama *Prometheus Unbound*. In the same year (1819) he finished *The Cenci*, a drama intended for the stage, and written in much more simple and everyday language than his other works. The short remainder of his life is marked by many great poems, some of considerable length, like the *Sensitive Plant and Adonais*; others shorter, among them the wonderful *Ode to the West Wind*, and the best known of all Shelley's lyrics *To a Skylark*. In 1822 the poet was drowned off Leghorn, in one of those swift storms which sweep the Mediterranean during the summer heats. His body was burned on the beach, and his ashes were placed in the Protestant cemetery at Rome, near the grave where, a few months before, Keats had been laid.

Shelley has always been popular with the Chinese readers. The sentence "If Winter comes, can Spring be far behind?" has encouraged countless people with an uttermost of optimism.

Ode to the West Wind

1

O wild West Wind, thou breath of Autumn's being[1],
Thou, from whose unseen presence the leaves dead
Are driven, like ghosts from an enchanter fleeing,

Yellow, and black, and pale, and hectic[2] red,
Pestilence-stricken multitudes[3]: O Thou,
Who chariotest[4] to their dark wintry bed

The winged seeds[5], where they lie cold and low,
Each like a corpse within its grave, until
Thine azure sister of the Spring[6] shall blow

Her clarion[7] o'er the dreaming earth, and fill
(Driving sweet buds like flocks to feed in air[8])
With living hues and odours plain and hill:

Wild Spirit, which art[9] moving everywhere;
Destroyer and Preserver[10]; hear, O hear!

2

Thou on whose stream[11], 'mid[12] the steep sky's commotion,
Loose clouds like Earth's decaying leaves are shed,
Shook from the tangled boughs of Heaven and Ocean,[13]

Angels of rain and lightning:[14] there are spread
On the blue surface of thine aery surge,
Like the bright hair uplifted from the head

Of some fierce Mænad[15], even[16] from the dim verge
Of the horizon to the zenith's height,
The locks of the approaching storm.[17] Thou Dirge

Of the dying year,[18] to which this closing night
Will be the dome of a vast sepulcher,
Vaulted with all thy congregated might

Of vapours,[19] from whose solid atmosphere[20]
Black rain and fire and hail will burst: O hear!

3

Thou who didst waken from his summer dreams
The blue Mediterranean,[21] where he[22] lay,
Lulled by the coil[23] of his chrystalline streams,

Beside a pumice Isle[24] in Baiæ's bay[25],
And saw in sleep old palaces and towers
Quivering within the wave's intenser day[26],

All overgrown with azure moss and flowers
So sweet, the sense faints picturing them[27]! Thou
For whose path the Atlantic's level powers[28]

Cleave themselves into chasms,[29] while far below
The sea-blooms and the oozy woods[30] which wear
The sapless foliage of the ocean, know

Thy voice, and suddenly grow grey with fear,
And tremble and despoil[31] themselves: O, hear!

4

If I were a dead leaf thou mightest bear[32];
If I were a swift cloud to fly with thee;
A wave to pant beneath thy power, and share

The impulse of thy strength, only less free
Than thou, O Uncontrollable! If even
I were as in my boyhood, and could be

The comrade of thy wanderings over Heaven,[33]
As then,[34] when to outstrip thy skiey speed[35]
Scarce seemed a vision; I would ne'er have striven

As thus with thee in prayer in my sore need.[36]
Oh! lift me as a wave, a leaf, a cloud!
I fall upon the thorns of life! I bleed!

A heavy weight of hours[37] has chained and bowed
One too like thee:[38] tameless, and swift, and proud.

5

Make me thy lyre, even as the forest is[39]:
What if my leaves are falling like its own[40]!
The tumult of thy mighty harmonies[41]

Will take from both[42] a deep, autumnal tone,
Sweet though in sadness. Be thou, Spirit fierce,
My spirit! Be thou me, impetuous one!

Drive my dead thoughts over the universe
Like withered leaves to quicken a new birth!
And, by the incantation of this verse[43],

Scatter, as from an unextinguished hearth
Ashes and sparks, my works among mankind!
Be through my lips to unawakened Earth

The trumpet of a prophecy![44] O Wind,
If Winter comes, can Spring be far behind?

注释

1. **being** life
2. **hectic** feverish
3. **Pestilence-stricken multitudes** 像患上瘟疫的一大群（枯叶）
4. **chariotest** （古用法）chariot 的第二人称单数现在时，用车载送
5. **winged seeds** 种子随风扬起
6. **Thine azure sister of the Spring** 指春季的西风。azure: 蔚蓝的
7. **clarion** horn
8. **to feed in air** 如同牧人赶着羊群上山吃草，春风也赶着嫩芽食用空气。
9. **art** （古用法）be的第二人称单数现在时
10. **Destroyer and Preserver** 西风是破坏者（Destroyer），因为它摧毁了树上最后的生命迹象；它又是保护者（Preserver），因为它把种子吹撒到各地，到春天又会复活。
11. **stream** 气流
12. **'mid** amid

13. **Loose clouds like Earth's decaying leaves are shed / Shook from the tangled boughs of Heaven and Ocean** 流云像陆上的枯叶，从天与海相互缠结的枝条上摇落下来。
14. **Angels of rain and lightening** 雨和闪电的使者，指流云（loose clouds）
15. **Mænad** 希腊神话中的狂女，酒神（Bacchus）的女祭司
16. **even** just
17. **The locks of the approaching storm** 指流云
18. **Dirge / Of the dying year** 残年的挽歌，指秋风（之声）
19. **with all thy congregated might / Of vapour** 以你凝聚的全部蒸气的力量
20. **solid atmosphere** 浓密的大气
21. **The blue Mediteranean** 蓝色的地中海
22. **he** referring to Meditearanean
23. **coil** 回旋，指潮声
24. **pumice Isle** 意大利那不勒斯（Naples）附近的浮石岛
25. **Baiæ's bay** 意大利那不勒斯湾西端，在Campania 沿岸。古罗马帝王常去之处。
26. **intenser day** 海水透明闪亮。day: daylight
27. **the sense faints picturing them** 感官无力描绘它们
28. **the Atlantic's level powers** 大西洋海面上横流的（level）有力的波浪（powers）
29. **Cleave themselves into chasms** 把自己劈成了深渊巨壑
30. **oozy woods** 沾满淤泥的藻林
31. **despoil** strip (themselves) of (their leaves)
32. **bear** carry
33. **The comrade of thy wandering over Heaven** 做你漫游在天空的伴侣
34. **As then** 像那时
35. **to outstrip thy skiey speed** 超过你在空中的迅速飞奔。skiey是诗歌语言，即skyey, 天空的
36. **I would ne'er have striven / As thus with thee in prayer in my sore need** 我就不会像这样在我急需帮助时和你争着来祈祷。striven...with: contended...with
37. **A heavy weight of hours** 时间的沉重负担
38. **One too like thee** 指诗人自己
39. **even as the forest is** just as the forest is (thy lyre)
40. **like its own** like the forest's own (leaves)
41. **thy mighty harmonies** mighty: 强有力的; harmonies: music
42. **both** 指lyre和the forest
43. **by the incantation of this verse** 凭着这诗韵做符咒
44. **The trumpet of a prophecy** 预言的号角

西　风　颂

1

哦，狂暴的西风，秋之生命的呼吸！
你无形，但枯死的落叶被你横扫，

有如鬼魅碰上了巫师，纷纷逃避：

黄的，黑的，灰的，红的像患肺痨，
呵，重染疫疠的一群：西风呵，
是你以车驾把有翼的种子催送到

黑暗的冬床上，它们就躺在那里，
像是墓中的死尸，冰冷，深藏，低贱，
直等到春天，你碧空的姊妹吹起

她的喇叭，在沉睡的大地上响遍，
（唤出嫩芽，像羊群一样，觅食空中）
将色和香充满了山峰和平原：

不羁的精灵呵，你无处不运行；
破坏者兼保护者：听吧，你且聆听！

2

没入你的激流，当高空一片混乱，
流云像大地的枯叶一样被撕扯
脱离天空和海洋的纠缠的枝干，

成为雨和电的使者：它们飘落
在你的磅礴之气的蔚蓝的波面，
有如狂女的飘扬的头发在闪烁，

从天穹最遥远而模糊的边沿
直抵九霄的中天，到处都在摇曳
欲来雷雨的卷发。对濒死的一年

你唱出了葬歌，而这密集的黑夜
将成为它广大墓陵的一座圆顶，

里面正有你的万钧之力在凝结；

那是你的浑然之气，从它会迸涌
黑色的雨、冰雹和火焰：哦，你听：

3

是你，你将蓝色的地中海唤醒，
而它曾经昏睡了一整个夏天，
被澄澈水流的回旋催眠入梦，

就在巴亚海湾的一个浮石岛边，
它梦见了古老的宫殿和楼阁
在水天映辉的波影里抖颤，

而且都生满青苔，开满花朵，
那芬芳真迷人欲醉！呵，为了给你
让一条路，大西洋的汹涌的浪波

把自己向两边劈开，而深在渊底
那海洋中的花草和泥污的树林
虽然枝叶扶疏，却没有精力；

听到你的声音，它们已吓得发青：
一边颤栗，一边自动萎缩：哦，你听！

4

唉，假如我是一片枯叶被你浮起，
假如我是能和你飞跑的云雾，
是一个波浪，和你的威力同喘息，

假如我分有你的脉搏，仅仅不如
你那么自由，哦，无法约束的生命！

假如我能像在少年时，凌风而舞
便成了你的伴侣，悠游于太空
（因为呵，那时候，要想追你上云霄，
似乎并非梦幻），我就不敢像如今

这样焦躁地要和你争相祈祷。
哦，举起我吧，当我是水波、树叶、浮云！
我跌在生活的荆棘上，我流血了！

这被岁月的重轭所制伏的生命
原是和你一样的：骄傲、轻捷而不驯。

5

把我当作你的竖琴吧，有如树林：
尽管我的叶落了，那有什么关系！
你巨大的合奏所振起的乐音

将染有树林和我的深邃的秋意：
虽忧伤而甜蜜。呵，但愿你给予我
狂暴的精神！奋勇者呵，让我们合一。

请把我枯死的思想向世界吹落，
让它像枯叶一样促成新的生命！
哦，请听从这一篇符咒似的诗歌，

就把我的话语，像是灰烬和火星
从还未熄灭的炉火向人间播散！
让预言的喇叭通过我的嘴唇

把昏睡的大地唤醒吧！要是冬天
已经来了，西风呵，春日怎能遥远？

（查良铮　译）

思考题

1. In what way is the West Wind both a destroyer and a preserver?
2. What's the relationship between the West Wind and the poet?
3. Identify the rhyme scheme of the poem.
4. Find as many as possible Chinese versions of the line "If Winter comes, can Spring be far behind?"
4. Summarize the meaning of each division of the whole poem.
5. Learn the first stanza by heart.

To a Skylark[1]

Hail to thee, blithe Spirit!
  Bird thou never wert—
That from Heaven, or near it,
  Pourest thy full heart
In profuse strains of unpremeditated art.

Higher still and higher
  From the earth thou springst
Like a cloud of fire;
  The blue deep thou wingest,
And singing still dost soar, and soaring ever singest.

注释

1. 这两节诗选自《致云雀》。全诗共21节。

参考译诗

致 云 雀

我为你欢呼，快乐的精灵！
  你根本不是鸟——

你从天堂或它附近
　将全部心思倾倒，
唱着不需要思索就优美无比的曲调。

像一团火云
　你从地面上升腾，
越飞越高；
　你翱翔在蓝蓝的天空，
边唱边飞，歌声总在翱翔中。

（李正栓　译）

思考题

1. What does Shelley compare the sky lark to?
2. Learn these two stanzas by heart.

A Song[1]

A widow bird[2] sat mourning[3] for her love
　Upon a wintry bough[4];
The frozen wind[5] crept on above
　The freezing stream[6] below[7].

There was no leaf upon the forest bare,
　No flower upon her ground,
And little motion in the air
　Except the mill-wheel's sound.[8]

注释

1. 这是雪莱的一首很少被人注意的小诗。
2. **A widow bird** 失去伴侣的鸟
3. **mourning** 哀悼
4. **wintry bough** 冬季里的树枝，指没有树叶的树枝。枝无叶，鸟无伴，两相呼应，均写哀境。
5. **frozen wind** 已凝固了的风，形容很冷
6. **freezing stream** 结冰的溪流
7. below与上行的above形成对仗。第一节前两行描写从孤鸟到枯枝，孤枯相映的场景；第三、四行从高处到低处，均是寒冷意象，真是无处不凄凉。
8. 整个第二节从视觉和听觉两个角度描写，充分道出孤、苦、枯、静的凄凉景象。

参考译诗

歌

孤鸟栖枯树，
失伴多凄苦；
头上寒风爬，
脚下溪凝固。

树林叶落尽，
地上花不存。
空中无声响，
唯闻水车吟。

（李正栓　译）

思考题

1. How is the mournful scene displayed both from the visual and acoustic angles?
2. Can you find similar poems in Chinese literature?
3. How are the images of coldness and quietude presented?
4. Read the translation by Guo Moruo and make a comparative study with that of Li Zhengshuan.
5. Learn this poem by heart.

John Keats
约翰·济慈
(1795–1821)

John Keats was born in London in 1795, the son of a livery-stable keeper. He was apprenticed at fifteen to learn surgery, but after studying medicine in hospitals in London and passing his medical examinations, he gave up the profession for poetry. Leigh Hunt introduced him to a literary circle where his dawning talents found encouragement. In 1817 he published a little volume of verse, most of it crude and immature enough, but containing the magnificent sonnet *On First Looking into Chapman's Homer*, which reveals one source of his inspiration.

Before the 1820 volume was published, Keats was attacked by consumption, and had warned that another winter in England would prove fatal. In September of that year he sailed for Italy under the care of his faithful friend, Joseph Severn. Early in the spring of 1821 he died in Rome, and was buried in the Protestant cemetery by the Aurelian wall, where Shelley, also, was soon to be laid. On his tomb are carved, according to his own request, the words: "Here lies one whose name was writ in water." In a hopeful time and in a mood of noble simplicity, he had said: "I think, I shall be among the English poets after my death."

Keats' poems reveal a great extent of art and intense feeling. His poems are highly praised by crtics for both their poetic value and artistic value.

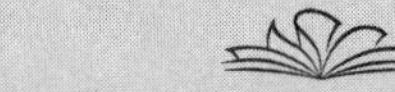

On First Looking Into Chapman's Homer

Much have I travell'd in the realms of gold[1],
　　And many goodly[2] states and kingdoms seen;
　　Round many western islands have I been[3]
Which bards in fealty to Apollo hold.[4]
Oft[5] of one wide expanse had I been told

That deep-brow'd Homer ruled as his demesne;[6]
Yet did I never breathe its pure serene[7]
Till I heard Chapman speak out loud and bold:
Then felt I like some watcher of the skies[8]
When a new planet swims into his ken[9];
Or like stout Cortez[10] when with eagle eyes
He star'd at the Pacific—and all his men
Look'd at each other with a wild surmise[11] —
Silent, upon a peak in Darien[12].

注释

1. **realms of gold** 黄金的国度，指伟大的文学领域
2. **goodly** 美丽的
3. **Round many western islands have I been** 我曾到许多西方岛屿上去漫游。此处指的是思想的漫游，并非真的去过。western islands 此处指 Greece
4. **Which bards in fealty to Apollo hold** 那些岛屿为臣服于阿波罗的诗人们所拥有。Bards: 古代抒情诗人；in fealty to: be loyal to; Apollo: 阿波罗，希腊神话中的诗神
5. **Oft** often
6. **That deep-brow'd Homer ruled as his demesne** 荷马在他的领地统治着。deep-brow'd: 眉额深邃的；demesne: 领地
7. **pure serene** 清纯的空气，指荷马的风格。serene: a clear and bright sky
8. **watcher of the skies** 观星者，即天文学家
9. **swims into his ken** 进入他的视野
10. **Cortez** Hernand Cortez（1485–1547），征服墨西哥的西班牙探险家。济慈记忆有误，实际上发现太平洋的是另一位西班牙航海家Vasco Balboa (1475–1519）。但无论怎样，济慈用探险家地理大发现后的惊喜来表达自己的心情。
11. **with a wild surmise** （因惊讶而）作出狂乱奇特的猜测
12. **Darien** 指巴拿马地岬中部城镇达利安（可译达连）和哥伦比亚之间巴拿马运河东部和南部的荒凉地区。

参考译诗

初读查普曼译荷马史诗有感

我游历过许多黄金的国度，
见过不少美好的城邦和王国，
还去过许多西方的岛屿，

那是诗人膜拜阿波罗的圣地。
我常听说有一片广阔无垠的地域，
浓眉的荷马在那里称王；
可我却从未领略过它纯净的空气，
直到我听见查普曼的声音无畏而高昂：
于是我的情感犹如一位观象家，
当他发现一颗新星游入视野；
或像考蒂兹用锐利如鹰的双眼
凝视着太平洋，而他的队员
在惊讶的揣测中面面相觑，
沉默无言——呆立在达利安山巅。

（查良铮　译）

思考题

1. Which kind of sonnet does this poem belong to, Italian form or English form?
2. How is the metaphor of travel used in this poem?
3. What are the two images that display Keats' great delight in being able to read Homer's poetry?
4 Learn the sonnet by heart.

Ode to a Nightingale

1

My heart aches, and a drowsy numbness pains
　　My sense, as though of hemlock[1] I had drunk,
Or emptied some dull opiate[2] to the drains[3]
　　One minute past,[4] and Lethe-wards[5] had sunk:
'Tis not[6] through envy of thy happy lot,
　　But being too happy in thine happiness, —
　　　That thou, light-winged Dryad[7] of the trees,
　　　　In some melodious plot

Of beechen green,[8] and shadows numberless,
Singest of summer in full-throated ease[9].

2

O, for a draught of vintage[10]! that hath been
Cool'd a long age in the deep-delved[11] earth,
Tasting of Flora[12] and the country green,
Dance, and Provençal song[13], and sunburnt mirth[14]!
O for a beaker full of the warm South[15],
Full of the true, the blushful Hippocrene[16],
With beaded bubbles[17] winking at the brim,
And purple-stained mouth;
That I might drink, and leave the world unseen,
And with thee fade away into the forest dim:

3

Fade far away, dissolve, and quite forget
What thou among the leaves hast never known,
The weariness, the fever, and the fret
Here, where men sit and hear each other groan;
Where palsy shakes a few, sad, last gray hairs,
Where youth grows pale, and spectre[18]-thin, and dies;
Where but to think is to be full of sorrow
And leaden-eyed[19] despairs,
Where Beauty cannot keep her lustrous eyes,
Or new Love pine at them[20] beyond to-morrow.

4

Away! away! for I will fly to thee,
Not charioted by Bacchus and his pards[21],
But on the viewless wings of Poesy,
Though the dull brain perplexes and retards:

Already with thee! tender is the night,
And haply[22] the Queen-Moon is on her throne,
Cluster'd around by all her starry Fays[23];
But here there is no light,
Save what from heaven is with the breezes blown
Through verdurous glooms and winding mossy ways.

5

I cannot see what flowers are at my feet,
Nor what soft incense hangs upon the boughs,
But, in embalmed darkness, guess each sweet[24]
Where with[25] the seasonable month[26] endows
The grass, the thicket, and the fruit-tree wild;
White hawthorn, and the pastoral eglantine;
Fast fading violets cover'd up in leaves;
And mid-May's eldest child[27],
The coming musk-rose, full of dewy wine,
The murmurous haunt of flies on summer eves.[28]

6

Darkling[29] I listen: and, for many a time
I have been half in love with easeful Death,
Call'd him soft names in many a mused rhyme[30],
To take into the air my quiet breath[31];
Now more than ever seems it rich to die,
To cease upon the midnight with no pain,
While thou art pouring forth thy soul abroad[32]
In such an ecstasy!
Still wouldst thou sing, and I have ears in vain—
To thy high requiem[33] become a sod.

7

Thou wast[34] not born for death, immortal Bird[35]!
No hungry generations[36] tread thee down;
The voice I hear this passing night was heard
In ancient days by emperor and clown[37]:
Perhaps the self-same song that found a path
Through the sad heart of Ruth[38], when, sick for home,
She stood in tears amid the alien corn[39];
The same that oft-times[40] hath
Charm'd magic casements[41], opening on the foam
Of perilous seas, in faery[42] lands forlorn[43].

8

Forlorn! the very word is like a bell
To toll me back from thee to my sole self[44]!
Adieu! the fancy cannot cheat so well
As she is fam'd[45] to do, deceiving elf[46].
Adieu ! adieu! thy plaintive anthem[47] fades
Past the near meadows, over the still stream,
Up the hill-side; and now 'tis buried deep
In the next valley-glades[48]:
Was it a vision, or a waking dream?
Fled is that music:—Do I wake or sleep?

注释

1. **hemlock** 毒胡萝卜精，一种毒药，人服后，将全身麻木而死亡。
2. **opiate** 鸦片剂
3. **to the drains** to the last dregs
4. **One minute past** One minute ago
5. **Lethe-wards** Lethe 是希腊神话中冥府的一条河，死者的灵魂喝了这条河的水就忘记生前的事。Lethe-wards: toward Lethe
6. **'Tis not** It is not
7. **Dryad** 林中仙女，指夜莺

8. **Of beechen green** green with beech trees
9. **in full-throated ease** 自由自在地放开歌喉
10. **for a draught of vintage** 但愿有一口酒。for 表示愿望；vintage: (in poetry) wine
11. **delved** dug
12. **Flora** 罗马神话中的花神，此处指花香
13. **Provencal song** 指12世纪普鲁旺斯（Provence）地方行吟诗人的爱情诗歌
14. **sun-burnt mirth** 指欧洲南部温暖地带常有太阳照射的人们的欢乐
15. **the warm South** 指欧洲南部温暖气候下酿出的美酒
16. **the blushful Hippocrene** Hippocrene 是阿波罗和九缪斯的圣地赫利孔山（Helicon）上的灵泉；blushful: red
17. **beaded bubbles** 串珠般的泡沫
18. **spectre** ghost
19. **leaden-eyed** 目光滞呆无神的
20. **them** 指上一行中的her lustrous eyes
21. **pards** （古用法）leonards
22. **haply** perhaps; by chance
23. **Fays** fairies
24. **each sweet** 每一种香味
25. **Where with** with which
26. **the seasonable month** the month of the season
27. **mid-May's eldest child** 五月中旬最早开放的花
28. **The murmerous haunt of flies on summer eves** referring to the sound of flies on summer eves.
29. **Darkling** (adv) in the dark
30. **mused rhyme** 沉思冥想的诗句
31. **breath** life
32. **abroad** out
33. **requiem** 安灵曲
34. **wast** （古用法）be 的第二人称单数过去时were
35. **immortal Bird** 不朽的鸟，指夜莺
36. **hungry generations** 此处为devouring time
37. **emperor and clown** 皇帝和农夫，此处指不管出身于皇家还是平民百姓家庭。
38. **Ruth** 据《圣经·路得记》所说，路得是摩押女子，大卫王族的女祖先。
39. **corn** wheat
40. **oft-times** often
41. **Charm'd magic casements** 迷住了被魔法镇住的城堡窗前的人。casement 此处不是指某一城堡，而是指被幽禁在城堡中的公主。
42. **faery** fairy
43. **forlorn** remote and far away
44. **my sole self** my whole lonely self
45. **fam'd** famed; widely known
46. **deceiving elf** 骗人的小精灵，指fancy

47. **anthem** song
48. **valley-glades** 山谷林间

参考译诗

夜莺颂

1

我的心在痛，困盹和麻木
　刺进了感官，有如饮过毒鸩，
又像是刚刚把鸦片吞服，
　于是向着列斯忘川下沉：
并不是我嫉妒你的好运，
　而是你的快乐使我太欢欣——
　　因为在林间嘹亮的天地里，
　　　你呵，轻翅的仙灵，
你躲进山毛榉的葱绿和阴影，
　放开了歌喉，歌唱着夏季。

2

唉，要是有一口酒！那冷藏在
　地下多年的清醇饮料，
一尝就令人想起绿色之邦，
　想起花神，恋歌，阳光和舞蹈！
要是有一杯南国的温暖
　充满了鲜红的灵感之泉，
　　杯沿明灭着珍珠的泡沫，
　　　给嘴唇染上紫斑：
　哦，我要一饮而悄然离开尘寰，
　　和你同去阴暗的林中隐没：

3

远远地、远远地隐没，让我忘掉
　你的树林中从不知道的一切，

忘记这疲劳、热病和焦躁，
　这使人对坐而悲叹的世界；
在这里，青春苍白、消瘦、死亡，
　而“瘫痪”有几根白发在摇摆；
　　在这里，稍一思索就充满了
　　　忧伤和灰眼的绝望，
　而“美”保持不住明眸的光彩，
　　新生的爱情活不到明天就枯凋。

4

去吧！去吧！我要朝你飞去，
　不用和酒神坐文豹的车驾，
我要展开诗歌的无形羽翼，
　尽管这头脑已经困顿、疲乏；
去了！呵，我已经和你同往！
　夜这般温柔，月后正登上宝座，
　　周围是侍卫她的一群星星；
　　　但这儿却不甚明亮，
　除了有一线天光，被微风带过
　　葱绿的幽暗，和苔藓的曲径。

5

我看不出是哪些花草在脚旁，
　什么清香的花挂在树枝上；
在温馨的幽暗里，我只能猜想
　这个时令该把哪种芬芳
赋予这棵树，林莽，和草丛，
　这白枳花，和田野的玫瑰，
　　这绿叶堆中易谢的紫罗兰，
　　　还有五月中旬的娇宠，
　这缀满了露酒的麝香蔷薇，
　　它成了夏夜蚊蚋的嗡吟的港湾。

6

我在黑暗里倾听；呵，多少次
　我几乎爱上了静谧的死亡，
我在诗里用尽了好的言辞，
　求他把我的一息散入空茫；
而现在，哦，死是多么富丽：
　在午夜里溘然魂离人间，
　　当你正倾写着你的心怀
　　　发出这般的狂喜！
　你仍将歌唱，但我却不再听见——
　　你的葬歌只能唱给泥土一块。

7

永生的鸟呵，你不会死去！
　饥饿的时代无法将你蹂躏；
今夜，我偶然听到的歌曲
　曾使古代的帝王和村夫喜悦。
或许这同样的歌也会激荡
　露丝忧郁的心，使她不禁落泪，
　　站在异邦的谷田里想着家；
　　　就是这声音常常
　在失掉了的仙城里引动窗扉：
　　一个美女望着大海险恶的浪花。

8

呵，失掉了！这句话好比一声钟
　使我猛省到我站脚的地方！
别了！幻想，这骗人的妖童，
　不能老耍弄它盛传的伎俩。
别了！别了！你怨诉的歌声
　流过草坪，越过幽静的溪水，

溜上山坡；而此时，它正深深
　埋在附近的峪谷中：
噫，这是个幻觉，还是梦寐？
那歌声去了：——我是睡？是醒？

（查良铮　译）

思考题

1. What is the speaker's mental and emotional state at the beginning of the poem? Why is he in this state?
2. What is the implied meaning of "forlorn" in this poem?
3. Which line or lines do you like best? Why?
4. Learn the first stanza by heart.

To Autumn[1]

1

Season of mists and mellow fruitfulness,
　Close bosom-friend of the maturing sun[2];
Conspiring[3] with him how to load and bless
　With fruit the vines that round the thatch-eves run;
To bend[4] with apples the moss'd cottage-trees[5],
　And fill all fruit with ripeness to the core;
　　To swell[6] the gourd, and plump[7] the hazel shells
　With a sweet kernel; to set budding more,
And still more, later flowers for the bees,
Until they think warm days will never cease,
　　For summer has o'er-brimm'd their clammy cells.

2

Who hath not seen thee oft amid thy store[8]?
　Sometimes whoever seeks abroad[9] may find

Thee sitting careless[10] on a granary floor,
Thy hair soft-lifted by the winnowing wind[11];
Or on half-reap'd furrow sound asleep,
Drows'd[12] with the fume of poppies, while thy hook[13]
Spares[14] the next swath and all its twined flowers:
And sometimes like a gleaner thou dost keep
Steady thy laden head across a brook;
Or by a cyder-press, with patient look,
Thou watchest the last oozings[15] hours by hours.

3

Where are the songs of spring? Ay, where are they?
Think not of them, thou hast thy music too, —
While barred clouds bloom the soft-dying day,
And touch the stubble-plains with rosy hue[16];
Then in a wailful choir the small gnats mourn
Among the river sallows[17], borne aloft
Or sinking as the light wind lives or dies[18];
And full-grown lambs loud bleat from hilly bourn;
Hedge-crickets sing; and now with treble soft
The red-breast whistles from a garden-croft;
And gathering swallows[19] twitter in the skies.

注释

1. 这首诗是约翰·济慈的代表作之一。《秋颂》共三节。第一节从秋色这一角度讲了秋季是个雾气霭霭、果实香醇的季节这一主题。第二节写秋人，通过描写丰收季节劳动中的人这一形象描绘秋季的收获与温暖。第三节写秋声，通过描写收获季各种鸟虫的鸣声，描绘了丰硕和温暖。诗人从秋色到秋人，再到秋声，给读者提供了丰富的视觉和听觉意象，充分表达了他的乐观主义精神。
2. **the maturing sun** the sun that makes things mature
3. **Conspire** plot, plan secretly
4. **To bend** to make...bend
5. **moss'd cottage-trees** The trees are covered with moss, showing the trees are old.
6. **To swell** to make...swell

7. **plump** to make...plump or swell
8. **store** the things she harvested
9. **seeks abroad** goes to the fields
10. **careless** carefree
11. **winnowing wind** wind that fans the chaff from the grain
12. **Drows'd** made sleepy
13. **hook** sickle
14. **Spares** leaves...uncut
15. **oozings** juice oozed from fruit
16. **hue** colour
17. **sallows** willows
18. **lives or dies** rises or falls
19. **gathering swallows** swallows that are returning home

参考译诗

秋　颂

1

雾气霭霭、果实香醇的季节，
　你是令万物成熟的太阳的密友；
你与他密谋策划如何将茅屋檐下的一切
　葡萄藤蔓挂上累累的珠球；
使屋前长满青苔的树弯腰挂果，
　所有果实填满熟味，直到心里；
　　让葫芦涨大；让榛子鼓壳，
　把甜核塞进；为蜜蜂一次又一次
催放晚开的花朵，
直到它们认为日子会永远暖和，
　　因为夏日早已填满它们的粘巢。

2

谁不常见你伴着谷仓？
　有时人们出门便能发现
你无忧无虑坐在打谷场上，
　簸谷的微风把你的发丝轻掀；

或见你酣睡于收割一半的田垄，
　罂粟花香使你沉迷，
　　你镰刀停歇在下一畦及其萦绕的花旁；
有时你像拾穗人头顶
　谷穗袋趟过小溪；
　有时见你在榨果机旁耐心凝视，
　一连几小时地瞧着徐徐榨出的汁浆。

3

春天的歌曲安在？它们安在？
　还是不去想它们，你也有自己的音乐，
慢慢逝去的白日被波云斜照回来，
　用胭脂红涂抹残梗仍存的田野，
此时，河柳下群群飞虫哀音同奏，
　一会儿高飞于空，
　　一会儿低落，随着微风的起与灭；
群羊在山圈里大声咩叫；
　篱下的蟋蟀竞相争雄；
　从园中传出知更鸟柔尖的叫声；
　　还有那归巢的群燕在天空呢喃不歇。

（李正栓　译）

思考题

1. What is autumn like?
2. What is the person in autumn like?
3. What does the autumn sound like?
4. How do the three stanzas help create the image of autumn?
5. Find images and tones expressed in Chinese poems about autumn.

On the Grasshopper and Cricket[1]

The poetry of earth is never dead:
  When all the birds are faint with the hot sun[2],
  And hide in cooling trees[3], a voice will run
From hedge to hedge about the new-mown mead[4];
That is the Grasshopper's —he takes the lead
  In summer luxury, —he has never done
  With his delights; for when tired out with fun[5]
He rests at ease beneath some pleasant weed.
The poetry of earth is ceasing never:
  On a lone winter evening, when the frost
  Has wrought a silence, from the stove there shrills
The Cricket's song, in warmth increasing ever,
  And seems to one in drowsiness half lost,
    The Grasshopper's among some grassy hills.

注释

1. 这首诗是济慈的早期诗作，写于1816年12月。本诗用grasshopper和cricket这两个意象把夏天与冬天连接起来，描写了“大地的诗歌永不死亡”这一主题，充分表达了多灾多难的济慈的乐观主义思想。这首诗可以与写于1819年的《秋颂》一起构成“春夏秋冬，欢歌不停”的催人奋发的意象。
2. **faint with the sun** lazy because of the sun
3. **hide in cooling trees** hide themselves in trees for coolness
4. **mead** meadow
5. **tired out with fun** exhausted because of playing

参考译诗

蝈蝈与蟋蟀

大地的诗歌永不间断；
  当鸟儿因酷日而懒洋洋

　在树上藏身乘凉，新刈的草地上
另一种声音便飘荡在篱笆之间；
那是蝈蝈在唱，它率先
　享受盛夏的喜悦，不停地唱，
　喜不自禁；直到耍累了不能再唱，
便心里舒适，憩息在欢乐的草丛间。
大地的诗歌永远不停；
　当孤寂冬夜里，冰霜冻结，
　万籁俱寂，炉边却响起了
蟋蟀的歌声，音量随室温而升，
　对醺醺欲睡者
仿佛是蝈蝈在草坡上鸣叫。

（李正栓　译）

思考题

1. What is the main idea of this sonnet?
2. What is the relationship between Line 9 and Line 1?
3. What is the tone of this sonnet?
4. Learn this sonnet by heart.

Elizabeth Barrett Browning
伊丽莎白·巴蕾特·布朗宁
（1806–1861）

Elizabeth Barrett's early life was shadowed by illness and affliction; and her early poetries *The Seraphim* (1838) and *Poems* (1844) show in many places the defects of unreality and of overwrought emotion natural to work produced in the loneliness of a sick-chamber. The best known of these early poems are perhaps *Lady Geraldine's Courtship*, where she workd under the influence of Tennyson's idylls, and *The Cry of the Children*, where she voiced the humanitarian protest against the practice of employing child labour in mines and factories. After her marriage to Robert Browning and removal to Italy, her health improved, and her art greatly strengthened. Mrs. Browning was deeply interested in the struggle of Italy to shake off her bondage to Austria, as is shown by her *Casa Guidi Windows* published in 1851. In 1857 appeared her most ambitious work *Aurora Leigh*, a kind of versified novel of modern English life, with a social reformer and humanitarian of aristocratic lineage, for hero, and a young poetess, in large part a reflection of Mrs Browning's own personality, for heroine.

Her characteristic note is that of intimate, personal feeling; even *Casa Guidi Windows* has been aptly called "a woman's love making with a nation."

Elizabeth Barrett Browning is more frequently called Mrs Browning, remembered mostly for many of her soul-touching love poems written to show the progress of her loving soul and the depth of her love for Browning who was younger than she was and whose power of love even once helped her recover from her paralysis.

Sonnets from the Portuguese: Sonnet 43

How do I love thee? Let me count the ways.
I love thee to the depth and breadth and height
My soul can reach, when feeling[1] out of sight[2]

For the ends of Being[3] and ideal Grace.
I love thee to the level of everyday's
Most quiet need, by sun and candlelight[4].
I love thee freely, as men strive for Right;
I love thee purely, as they turn from Praise.
I love thee with the passion[5] put to use
In my old griefs, and with my childhood's faith.
I love thee with a love I seemed to lose
With my lost saints—I love thee with the breath,
Smiles, tears, of all my life!—and, if God choose,
I shall but love thee better after death.

注释

1. **feeling** search by feeling with hands
2. **out of sight** beyond the scope of sight
3. **Being** existence
4. **by sun and candlelight** with sunlight or candlelight
5. **passion** suffering

参考译诗

葡萄牙的十四行诗：第43首十四行诗

我究竟怎样爱你？让我细数端详。
我爱你直到我灵魂所及的深度、
广度和高度，我在视力不及之处
摸索着存在的极致和美的理想。
我爱你像最朴素的日常需要一样，
就像不自觉地需要阳光和蜡烛。
我自由地爱你，像人们选择正义之路，
我纯洁地爱你，像人们躲避称赞颂扬。
我爱你用的是我在昔日的悲痛里
用过的那种激情，以及童年的忠诚。

我爱你用的爱，我本以为早已失去
（与我失去的圣徒一同）；我爱你用笑容、
眼泪、呼吸和生命！只要上帝允许，
在死后我爱你将只会更加深情。

（飞白　译）

思考题

1. How many ways does the poetess love her husband?
2. What is the rhyme scheme of this sonnet?
3. Do you know other poems with such a feeling?

Alfred Tennyson
阿尔弗雷德·丁尼生
(1809–1892)

Alfred Tennyson was born in 1809, at Somersby Rectory, Lincolnshire. His father was a vicar of the Church of England, holding several livings by gift from landed proprietors; so that Tennyson was from birth in close connection with the main conservative interests of England, ecclesiastical and economic. In 1830, while an undergraduate at Cambridge, he published his first independent volume, a group of little verse-studies in word-melody and word-picture. Two years later appeared a second volume, showing, in such poems as *The Lady of Shalott* and *The Lotus-Eaters*, a control of both medieval and classical story, and in certain others, like *The Palace of Art*, giving indication of his ambition to be not merely a singer, but also a teacher. In *The Miller's Daughter* and *The May Queen*, he began his long series of idylls of English life, short narratives richly pictured and melodiously tuned, with which he was destined to win the public all the more easily perhaps because of their touches of sentimentality and unreality.

In 1836 Tennyson went to live near London, where he came into contact with Carlyle, and was stirred by his spirit of social protest. He also found in the latter's spiritual view of the universe a support for his religious faith, which was to be sorely tried by doubt. For ten years he published nothing, but brooded and worded away in his London lodgings until, in 1842, he came forth with two volumes which took the critics and the world by storm. In these two volumes the range and variety of work was remarkable. Almost every province of poetry was touched upon, from the lyric simplicity of *Break, Break, Break* to the largely moulded epic narrative *Morte d' Arthur*. In one of these poems *Locksley Hall*, he uttered the protest which young men like himself, of good though not noble birth, were feeling in the presence of class distinctions which subordinated love to rank, and of an industrial civilization which made gold the supreme test of success.

Five years later, in 1847, appeared *The Princess*. It was Tennyson's contribution to the question, then beginning to be widely discussed, of the higher education of women. The subtitle is *A Medley*, and no description could be more just.

In 1850, Wordsworth, who had been poet-laureate after Southey, died; and Tennyson took the laurel. A government pension enabled him to get married and to settle in the Isle of Wight. From this time until his death, forty-two years later, in 1892, he stood as the spokesman of his people in times of national sorrow or rejoicing.

Break, Break, Break[1]

Break, break, break,
　　On thy cold gray stones, O Sea!
And I would[2] that my tongue could utter
　　The thoughts that arise in me.

O, well for[3] the fisherman's boy,
　　That he shouts with his sister at play!
O, well for the sailor lad,
　　That he sings in his boat on the bay!

And the stately ships go on[4]
　　To their haven under the hill;
But O for[5] the touch of a vanished hand[6],
　　And the sound of a voice[7] that is still[8]!

Break, break, break,
　　At the foot of thy crags, O Sea!
But the tender grace of a day that is dead[9]
　　Will never come back to me.

注释

1. **Break, Break, Break** the waves break on the cold rocks.
2. **I would** I wish
3. **O, well for** it would be well for
4. **the stately ships go on** 人们照常进行日常活动。stately: 庄严的
5. **O for** how I wish for
6. **a vanished hand** the hand of his dead friend
7. **a voice** the sound of his dead friend
8. **still** silent
9. **the tender grace of a day that is dead** gone are the days when he and his friend stayed together.

参考译诗

冲激，冲激，冲激

冲激，冲激，冲激，
　　大海呀，冲激你灰冷的石岩！
但愿我的舌端能道出
　　我内心涌起的思念。

若像那渔家儿童该多好，
　　他在和妹妹一起玩耍喊叫！
若像那青年水手该多好！
　　他在海湾里荡桨歌唱多美妙！

还有，一艘艘庄严的船舶
　　朝它们山下的港口驶近；
多么想得到那只消逝了的手的触摸，
　　还有那已不作声响的嗓音。

冲激，冲激，冲激，
　　大海呀，冲激你悬崖的脚下！
但那逝去的温文尔雅
　　将永远回不到我这里。

（李正栓　译）

思考题

1. What's the theme of this poem?
2. How does the poet develop the central idea of the poem?

Crossing the Bar[1]

Sunset and evening star,
  And one clear call for me!
And may there be no moaning of the bar,
  When I put out to sea,

But such a tide as moving seems asleep,
  Too full for sound and foam,
When that which drew from out the boundless deep[2]
  Turns again home.

Twilight and evening bell,
  And after that the dark!
And may there be no sadness of farewell,
  When I embark;

For tho' from out our bourne[3] of Time and Place
  The flood may bear me far,
I hope to see my Pilot[4] face to face
  When I have crost the bar.

注释

1. Although not the last poem written by Tennyson, *Crossing the Bar* appears, at his request, as the final poem in all collections of his work. bar: a long pile of sand or stones under the water at the entrance to a harbour
2. **deep** the sea

3. **bourne** boundary
4. **Pilot** a person who steers a ship through a difficult stretch of water, for example, at the entrance to a harbour

参考译诗

渡 沙 洲

落日，晚星，
一个清晰的声音把我召唤！
但愿不再有沙洲的悲吟，
当我出海扬帆。

流动的海潮好似入眠，
太满反无声息和浪花，
原本来自无限的深渊，
如今又回到家。

暮光，晚钟，
接下来便是一片黑暗！
但愿不再有告别的悲痛，
当我乘船离岸。

即使潮水把我带走，
将时空的疆界超越，
我希望面对我的舵手，
当我渡过沙洲。

（白凤欣　译）

思考题

1. What an overall mood does the poet create in this poem?
2. Pick out the images that contribute to the creation of that mood.
3. Learn the poem by heart.

Robert Browning
罗伯特·布朗宁
(1812–1889)

Robert Browning was born in London in 1812. Mingled with the English and Scottish blood in his veins was a more distant strain of German and Creole, a fact of value in considering the cosmopolitan range of his imagination. He passed his boyhood and youth in the suburb of Camberwell, close enough to London to make the great smoky city on the horizon a constant reminder of the complex human life he was to interpret as subtly and deeply as any poet had done since the Elizabethan age.

In 1846, Browning eloped with Elizabeth Barrett, whose poetic reputation was then far greater than his, and went to live in Italy. The pair settled in Florence, in the house called "Casa Guidi", from which was taken the title of Mrs. Browning's poem on the Italian Liberation, *Casa Guidi Windows*. Here Browning continued his great series of dramatic monologues. Here, also, after Mrs. Browning's death in 1861, he began *The Ring and the Book*. This is the crowning effort of his genius for the vastness of its scope and its grasp of human nature, though it lacks the spontaneous grace and charm which the best of his shorter pieces share with *Pippa Passes*, that perfect fruit of his youthful imagination. After the death of his wife, Browning spent most of his time in England. He wrote much, with a steady gain in intellectual subtlety, but with a corresponding loss of poetic beauty. He made a more and more deliberate sacrifice of form to matter, wrenching and straining the verse-fabric in order to pack into it all the secondary meanings of the theme. To the last, however, his genius continued to throw out bursts and jets of exquisite music, colour and feeling. Such, for instance, are the little pieces called *Wanting Is—What?* and *Never the Time and Place*, written in his seventy-first year. When he died, in 1889, he was buried in Westminster Abby.

Robert Bowning is very well-known for his use of dramatic monologue, a technique he learned from the Renaissance poets.

Home-Thoughts, from Abroad

1

Oh, to be in England
Now that April's there,[1]
And whoever wakes in England
Sees, some morning, unaware[2],
That the lowest boughs and the brushwood sheaf [3]
Round the elm-tree bole[4] are in tiny leaf,
While the chaffinch sings on the orchard bough
In England—now!

2

And after April, when May follows,
And the whitethroat builds, and all the swallows!
Hark[5], where my blossomed peartree in the hedge
Leans to the field and scatters on the clover
Blossoms and dewdrops—at the bent spray's edge—
That's the wise thrush; he sings each song twice over,
Lest you should think he never could recapture
The first fine careless rapture!
And though the fields look rough with hoary dew,
All will be gay when noontide wakes anew
The buttercups, the little children's dower[6]—
Far brighter than this gaudy melon-flower[7]!

注释

1. **Oh, to be in England / Now that April's there** Oh, how wonderful it is to be in England now that April is there!
2. **unaware** without knowing
3. **sheaf** denoting that the bunch is very dense
4. **bole** trunk

5. **Hark** listen
6. **dower** dowery
7. **melon-flower** flower of sweet melon

参考译诗

异域乡思

1

呵，要在英格兰该多好！
那里正是四月，
一朝早醒就会不知不觉看见
英格兰春天的风景：
连最矮的树枝和灌木林丛
在榆树周围也已嫩芽葱葱，
果园枝头的苍头燕
正欢唱鸣叫在英格兰！

2

四月去后五月随，
白喉筑巢燕子回！
听，我围篱内开花的梨树
俯向田野，洒香于苜蓿与朝露，
就在弯曲枝桠的顶头——
是机灵的画眉在唱：每首歌他连唱两遍，
唯恐你以为他不能再次
捕捉初次美妙无忧的欢娱！
尽管田野因白露显得不齐整，
一切会欢闹，当正午再次唤醒金凤花，
小孩子们喜用这花弄成嫁妆——
比炫丽甜瓜花还鲜亮！

（李正栓　译）

思考题

1. How is England like in April?
2. What happens in England in May?
3. What is the mood of the speaker in this description?
4. Find some poems or songs that sing praise of one's hometown.
5. Learn the first stanza by heart.

Meeting at Night

1

The gray sea and the long black land;
And the yellow half-moon large and low;
And the startled little waves that leap
In fiery ringlets[1] from their sleep,
As I gain the cove with pushing prow,
And quench its speed I'the slushy sand[2].

2

Then a mile of warm sea-scented beach;
Three fields to cross till a farm appears;
A tap at the pane[3], the quick sharp scratch
And blue spurt of a lighted match,
And a voice[4] less loud, through joys and fears,
Than the two hearts beating each to each!

注释

1. **In fiery ringlet** small ringlets like fire
2. **quench its speed I' the slushy sand** 船头在泥沙中一下刹住。I': in
3. **pane** 窗户上的单块玻璃
4. **a voice** 指窗内的人轻声的欣喜叫声

参考译诗

深夜幽会

1

海，灰暗；地，漫长、漆黑；
半轮黄月，大而低垂；
细浪从梦中惊醒，
在火一般的涟漪中闪动。
我驾急行的小舟抵达海湾，
船头扎进充满泥沙的海滩。

2

之后，走过一里散发温暖海香的沙滩，
又穿过三块田地，直到一农庄出现；
轻扣窗户；急速的哧啦声响，
蓝光闪过，火柴点亮。
柔声细语，透露出惊与喜。
两颗心怦怦地惊跳在一起。

（李正栓　译）

思考题

1. Find other poems that describe lovers' private meeting at night.
2. What's the theme of the poem?
3. Find other Chinese versions of this poem.

Parting at Morning

Round the cape of a sudden came the sea,[1]
And the sun looked over the mountain's rim[2]:
And straight was a path of gold for him[3],
And the need of a world of men for me.

注释

1. **Round the cape of a sudden came the sea** 转过海岬，忽见大海
2. **rim** a raised edge; mountain's rim
3. **for him** for the sun

参考译诗

清 晨 离 别

绕过海角，忽现大海一片，
太阳俯瞰着群山的边缘：
等待他的是笔直的金光大道，
我仍需与世人周旋。

（白凤欣 译）

思考题

1. What's the tone of the poem?
2. What's the main idea of the poem?
3. Learn the poem by heart.

Matthew Arnold
马修·阿诺德
(1822–1888)

Matthew Arnold was born in a village in the valley of the Thames. Such a birthplace left its trace in his memory and he later wrote good poems on water. Clear-flowing streams were later to appear in his poems as symbols of serenity. At six, Arnold was moved to Rugby School, where his father, Dr. Thomas Arnold, had become headmaster, who as a clergyman and leader of the liberal or Broad Church, was also a famous educational reformer, and a teacher who instilled into his pupils an earnest preoccupation with moral and social issues and also an awareness of the connection between liberal studies and modern life.

At Rugby Matthew Arnold was directly exposed to the powerful force of the father's mind and character. His attitude towards this force was a mixture of attraction and repulsion. His permanent influence he received from his father is evident in his poems and in his writings on religion and politics, but he made a determined effort in his youth to be different. At Oxford he behaved in a strange way. Elegantly and colorfully dressed, alternately languid or merry in manner, he attracted attention as a dandy whose irreverent jokes irritated his more solemn undergraduate friends and acquaintances.

Arnold did much of his writing and reading in his spare time. In 1847, he became private secretary to Lord Lansdowne, and in 1851, the year when he got married, he became an inspector of schools, a position which he held for 35 years. The post as inspector reduced his production as a writer, yet it had several advantages. First, his extensive traveling in England took him to the homes of the more ardently Protestant middle classes, and when he criticized the dullness of middle class life (as he often did), Arnold knew his subject intimately. Second, his position also led him to travel on the Continent to study the schools of Europe. As a critic of English education he was thus able to make helpful comparisons and to draw on a stock of fresh ideas in the same way as in his literary criticism he used his knowledge of French, German, Italian, and classical literatures to measure the achievements of English writers. Third, though his job as inspector was dull and monotonous, Arnold became convinced of its importance. He tried to develop a satisfactory system of education for the middle classes.

In 1849, Arnold published *The Strayed Reveler*, the first of his volumes of poetry. Eight years later, as a tribute to his poetic achievement, he was elected to the Professorship of Poetry at Oxford, a part-time position which he held for ten years. Later, Arnold toured America in order to make money by lecturing. For his two visits (1883 and 1886) there was the further inducement of seeing his daughter Lucy, who had married an American. Two years after his second visit to the United States, Arnold died of a sudden heart attack in 1888.

Arnold was a great poet and critic. His *Dover Beach* is a much studied poem which is full of beauty in meaning and sound.

Dover Beach

The sea is calm tonight.
The tide is full, the moon lies fair
Upon the straits[1] —on the French coast the light
Gleams and is gone; the cliffs of England[2] stand,
Glimmering and vast, out in the tranquil bay.
Come to the window, sweet is the night air!
Only, from the long line of spray
Where the sea meets the moon-blanched land[3],
Listen! you hear the grating roar
Of pebbles which the waves draw back, and fling,
At their return,[4] up the high strand,
Begin, and cease, and then again begin,
With tremulous cadence slow, and bring
The eternal note of sadness in.

Sophocles[5] long ago
Heard it[6] on the Aegean[7], and it brought

Into his mind the turbid ebb and flow
Of human misery; we
Find also in the sound a thought,
Hearing it[8] by this distant[9] northern sea.

The Sea of Faith[10]
Was once, too, at the full, and round earth's shore
Lay like the folds of a bright girdle furled.[11]
But now I only hear
Its melancholy, long, withdrawing roar,
Retreating, to the breath
Of the night wind, down the vast edges drear[12]
And naked shingles of the world.
Ah, love, let us be true
To one another![13] for the world, which seems
To lie before us like a land of dreams,
So various, so beautiful, so new,
Hath really neither joy, nor love, nor light,
Nor certitude, nor peace, nor help for pain;
And we are here as on a darkling plain
Swept with confused alarms of struggle and flight,
Where ignorant armies clash by night.

注释

1. **the straits** the Straits of Dover
2. **the cliffs of England** 指英国多佛岸边高耸的白色峭壁
3. **the moon-blanched land** 月光照白的陆地
4. **At their return** at the waves' return (to the beach)
5. **Sophocles** 索福克勒斯（约公元前496–公元前406），希腊悲剧作家
6. **it** 指上两行的The eternal note of sadness
7. **the Aegean** the Aegean Sea
8. **it** Here it refers to thought.
9. **distant** far away (from the Aegean)

10. **The Sea of Faith** 主要指宗教信仰
11. **Lay like the folds of a bright girdle furled** lay furled like the folds of a bright girdle
12. **the vast edges drear** 广阔而阴郁的边沿
13. **Ah, love, let us be true / To one another** 在荒原般的世界上，人们只能依靠相互的忠诚了。

参考译诗

多佛海滩

今夜大海平和安静：
月色朗朗潮水满，
月照海峡——法国海岸的灯光
忽明忽灭；英格兰的峭壁矗立，
在宁静的海湾里巨大的形象闪烁。
来，到窗边，晚风香甜！
可是，你听！从那条长长的浪花线，
在海与月光漂白了的陆地连接的地方，
你听到刺耳的涛声，
那是卵石被海浪卷走
又抛回到高高海滩上的声音，
抛起，停止，然后又抛起，
以缓慢而颤动的节奏
传来永远的悲哀的声音。

索福克勒斯很久以前
在爱琴海听过这声音，于是心中想起
滚滚不停的
人类苦难的潮汐；我们还在
在遥远的北海
在这声音里听到一种思想。

信仰之海
也曾如此满潮，把全球的海岸环绕

像一根腰带，曲折、闪光、静卧。
但如今我只听见
它忧伤、长久的退潮，
伴着夜风的呼吸退去，
沿着广阔而阴郁的边沿退去，
只留下光秃秃的满世界卵石。

啊，亲爱的，愿我们彼此忠诚！
因为这世界
展现在我们面前的似乎是梦幻之光，
如此多彩，如此美丽，如此新鲜，
却实际上没有欢乐，没有爱，没有光明，
没有肯定，没有和平，没有对苦难的帮助；
并且我们待在一个黑暗的旷野
争斗和逃逸混乱地扫掠一切，
无知的军队在黑夜中冲突流血。

（李正栓　译）

思考题

1. What is the basic tone of the whole poem?
2. Why does Arnold mention Sophocles in his poem?

Christina Georgina Rossetti
克里斯蒂娜·乔治娜·罗塞蒂
（1830–1894）

Christina Rossetti, different from her brother Dante Gabriel, was a devout High Church Anglican. She was educated at home and led a quiet life with her parents, having twice declined marriage on account of her Anglican religious scruples. She started to write poetry early in life but did not publish her first collection of poetry *Goblin Market and Other Poems* till 1862. She wrote with intensity as much as her brother though in a simpler style. The long narrative poem *Goblin Market*, primarily meant for children and written in sing-song short-lined couplets, is about two sisters Lizzie and Laure who were tempted by goblins to taste of the forbidden fruit in their childhood and about the lesson they thereby learned. Actually it is nothing more than a charming nursery rhyme, though the poet herself probably tried to insert much religious significance into the tale.

As an important woman poet in England in late 19th century, Christina Rossetti is chiefly celebrated for her short lyrics, several of which are truly gems as elegies and love lyrics in the English language.

All these lyrics were outpourings, as it were, from the poet's innermost recesses of mind and served as priceless expressions of her genuine emotions on the occasions of their composition. And these poems, no less than those of Emily Dickinson, have had their influence upon a number of English and American women poets in the 20th century, especially upon Sarah Teasdale, Elinor Wylie and Edna St. Vincent Millay.

Remember

Remember me when I am gone away,
    Gone far away into the silent land;[1]
    When you can no more hold me by the hand,

Nor I half turn to go yet turning stay.[2]
Remember me when no more day by day
　You tell me of our future that you planned:
　Only remember me; you understand
It will be late to counsel[3] then or pray,
Yet if you should forget me for a while
　And afterwards remember, do not grieve:
　For if the darkness and corruption leave
　　A vestige of the thoughts that once I had,
Better by far you should forget and smile
　Than that you should remember and be sad.

注释

1. **Gone far away into the silent land** 指死去
2. **Nor I half turn to go yet turning stay** 我也不再半转身要走，却又留下来。
3. **counsel** 给予忠告

参考译诗

记 住 我

记住我，当我离开这世界后，
　远离这世界，去那寂静的国度；
　那时你再也不能把我的手握住，
我也不能再转身犹疑，欲走还留。
记住我，当你不能再夜以继昼
　把我们未来的生活给我描述。
　只祈求记住我；你心里清楚
到那时已来不及忠告或祈求。
不过如果你一时把我忘掉，
　之后又把我记起，你别悲哀，
　因为黑暗和腐败

还留一些我曾有过的思念痕迹，
我宁愿你能忘记我并露出微笑，
也不愿你把我记住而惨惨凄凄。

（李正栓　译）

思考题

1. In what way does the speaker ask to be remembered?
2. What's the figurative meaning of "the silent land"?
3. Do you like this poem? Why?

Thomas Hardy
托马斯·哈代
(1840–1928)

Thomas Hardy was born at Upper Bockhampton, Dorset in 1840. His father was a violinist, mason and builder. His mother was a well-read woman who was interested in singing folk songs and telling legends to her son. From his parents, he gained interest that would influence both his life and career: architecture and music, the ways of rural life and literature. His mother taught him at home until he was eight. Then he went to Jilia Martin's school. Being a boy with academic potential, he taught himself French, German and Latin. However, his family's lack of financial support could not enable him for further university education. At the age of sixteen, he was sent to become apprenticed to James Jicks, a local architect, from whom Hardy learned architectural drawing and the restoration of the old buildings. Later he moved to London and worked with Arthur Blomfield for five years during which he was involved in visiting museums, theatres and churches, learning classic literature, and writing poetry. Because of poor health, he returned to Dorset and opted for a career in writing.

In 1870, while restoring a church at St. Juliot in Cornwall, Hardy fell in love with Emma Gifford. They got married in 1874. Although their marriage was not so harmonious, Emma's death in 1912 exerted a traumatic influence upon Hardy. He was stricken a terrible sense of blame which led to some of his best poems in memory of his late wife. In 1914, he remarried. He died of pleurisy on January 11, 1928 at Max Gate and his ashes were buried at Westminster Abbey.

Hardy is better known as a novelist than as a poet. His best works include *Desperate Remedies* (1871), *Under the Greenwood Tree* (1872), *Far From the Madding Crowd* (1874), *The Return of the Native* (1878), *The Mayor of Casterbridge* (1886), *Tess of the D'Urbervilles* (1891), *Jude the Obscure* (1894). The publication of the last two novels attracted severe criticism for the sympathetic description of a "fallen woman" and obvious attack on the institution of marriage. Then he made a decision to give up writing novels and began to write poetry. His notable collections of poetry are: *Wessex Poems* (1898), *The Dynasts* (1908), *Time's Laughingstocks* (1909), *Satire of Circumstance* (1914), *Moments of Being* (1917), *Winter Words in Various Moods and Meters* (1928), and *Collected Poems* (1932).

The main concerns of Hardy's poetry focus on the forces and circumstances beyond human control with a somber tone, people's struggle against indifference to suffering, tender feeling for the ancient landscape and cultural roots of rural England. His poetry is characterized with colloquial directness and plainness of language, frequent use of archaic words, all of which can be seen as a deliberate reaction against the ornate, elaborate language of late-Victorian verse. Hardy is now recognized as one of the greatest poets of the 20th century. He was once awarded the Order of Merit in 1910. He influenced the later generation such as David Herbert Lawrence, Virginia Woolf, Robert Graves, John Cowper Powys, Dylan Thomas and Philip Larkin.

The Man He Killed[1]

Had he and I but met
 By some old ancient inn,
We should have sat us down to wet
 Right many a nipperkin[2]!

 But ranged as infantry,
 And staring face to face,
I shot at him as he at me,
 And killed him in his place.

 I shot him dead because—
 Because he was my foe,
Just so: my foe of course he was;
 That's clear enough; although

 He thought he'd list, perhaps,
 Off-hand-like—just as I—

Was out of work—had sold his traps—
No other reason why.

Yes; quaint and curious war is!
You shoot a fellow down
You'd treat if met where any bar is,
Or help to half-a-crown[3].

注释

1. 这首诗写于1902年，即波尔战争结束之时。诗人在此表达了对战争的厌恶之情。
2. **nipperkin** a small container of liquor
3. **half-a-crown** a small amount of money like 60 cents

参考译诗

他杀死的那个人

假若我与他偶遇
在一家古老的酒馆，
我们会相坐畅饮，
喝下一杯又一杯！

但被列队进步兵，
只能面对面地瞪视，
彼此向对方射击，
我将他当场击毙。

我将他击毙因为——
因为他是我的敌人，
仅此而已：他肯定是我的敌人；
那再清楚不过；虽然

他应募参军，或许
未加思索——和我一样——

或因失业——卖掉了随身物品——
再无别的什么缘由。

是的；战争多么离奇！
你将一个家伙击毙，
若相遇在酒吧你会宴请
或接济他半个克朗硬币。

（白凤欣 译）

思考题

1. Why does the speaker pause and then repeat the word "because"?
2. What kind of attitude does the poem show toward the war?

Hap[1]

If but some vengeful god would call to me
From up the sky, and laugh: "Thou suffering thing,
Know that thy sorrow is my ecstasy,
That thy love's loss is my hate's profiting!"[2]

Then would I bear, and clench myself, and die,
Steeled by the sense of ire unmerited;
Half-eased, too, that a Powerfuller than I
Had willed and meted me the tears I shed.

But not so. How arrives it joy lies slain,
And why unblooms the best hope ever sown?—
Crass Casualty[3] obstructs the sun and rain,
And dicing Time for gladness casts a moan...
These purblind[4] Doomsters had as readily strown
Blisses about my pilgrimage[5] as pain.

注释

1. **Hap** (古用法) 偶然
2. **That thy love's loss is my hate's profiting** 你爱的亏损正是我仇恨的盈利。profiting: reward
3. **Crass Casualty** 纯粹的偶然。crass: crude and unrefined; causalty: a situation being governed by chance, or hap
4. **purblind** half-blind
5. **my pilgrimage** my life journey

参考译诗

偶　然

倘若有一位复仇之神
从天上召唤我，并笑道：
“受苦之人，你的痛苦即我的狂喜，
你爱的亏损正是我仇恨的盈利！”

那么我只有忍受，咬紧牙关而死，
因他不当的忿怒而变得坚强；
我将稍感轻松，由于他比我更有力，
让我遭罪流泪正是他的意向。

但事实并不然。为何欢乐遭杀戮？
为何播撒的美好却总不能实现？——
是纯粹的偶然遮挡了阳光雨露，
掷骰子消磨时间取乐不成反铸悲叹……
这些半瞎的预言者欣然地撒布
我人生路途上的福佑与痛苦。

（白凤欣 译）

思考题

1. Identify the form of this sonnet.
2. How does Hardy express his fatalism in this poem?

Gerard Manley Hopkins
吉拉德·曼莱·霍普金斯
（1844－1889）

Gerard Manley Hopkins was born at Stratford, Essex on July 28, 1844 in a religious family. His father was once the British consul general in Hawaii, the church warden at St. John-at-Hampstead, and a poet. His mother was talented in music and reading. At an early age, Hopkins was taught to draw by his aunt and uncle. Thus he had his first ambition to become a painter throughout his life. He was inspired and influenced by the work of John Rustin and the pre-Raphaelites. From 1854 to 1863 he studied at Highgate School, where he began to read John Keats and modelled on him. His intelligence, sensitivity and sensuous response to natural beauty excelled all of his fellow classmates, yet he was physically fragile. In 1863 he entered Balliol College, Oxford, to study classics and established friendly relationship with Robert Bridges, the later poet laureate, and Walter Pater, a critic and writer. There he became a keen socialite and prolific poet. He was also influenced by the Oxford Movement, which sought to revive the ritualistic and dogmatic traditions of the Church of England, and its original leader John Henry Newman. Under Newman's sponsorship, Hopkins joined the Roman Catholic Church on October 21, 1866. By January 1868 he was determined to become a priest and entered the Society of Jesus. In 1877 he became an ordained priest and served in parishes in London, Oxford, Liverpool and Glasgow. In 1884 he taught Greek and Latin at University College, Dublin. On June 8, 1889 he died of typhoid fever at the age of forty-four and was buried in Glasnevin Cemetery.

Before being a Jesuit, Hopkins burnt all the poems he had written up to that time, because he thought them inappropriate to his profession. He began writing in 1875 or 1876, but he decided never to publish his poetry. He realized that any true poet should accept criticism and encouragement from his reader. The tension between his religious responsibility and his poetic endowment made him feel that he failed both. His poems were finally published from 1918 by Robert Bridges, Charles Williams and William Henry Gardner.

Being one of the most individual of Victorian poets, he is best remembered for his impressive language, compressed sentence structure, innovations in rhythm and meter. He invented sprung rhythm, which is composed of a set number of stressed syllables per line of poem, but the number of unstressed syllables may vary considerably in each line. Generally the number of syllables varies between one to four per foot, and the stress always falls on the first syllable in a foot. Hopkins deemed it a way to rid the restrictions of the conventional rhythm and meter. His famous poems include *The Wreck of the Deutschland*, *God's Grandeur*, *Pied Beauty*, *Spring* and *The Windhover*. He is regarded as a precursor to modernist poetry. He influenced many poets of the 20th century.

Pied[1] Beauty

Glory be to God for dappled[2] things—
For skies of couple-colour as a brinded[3] cow;
For rose-moles all in stipple upon trout that swim;
Fresh-firecoal chestnut-falls[4]; finches' wings;
Landscape plotted and pieced—fold, fallow, and plough;
And áll trádes,[5] their gear and tackle and trim.[6]

All things counter, original, spare, strange;
Whatever is fickle, freckled[7] (who knows how?)
With swift, slow; sweet, sour; adazzle, dim;
He fathers-forth whose beauty is past change:[8]
Praise him.

注释

1. **Pied** multicolored
2. **dappled** mottled
3. **brinded** (古用法) streaked with dark hairs
4. **Fresh-firecoal chestnut-falls** 霍普金斯曾在日记中写道："栗子像煤炭或朱色斑点

一样鲜亮。”（Chestnuts are bight as coals or spots or vermilion.）。因此，此语在此处有两种解释：一指经炭火烤后外壳剥落的栗子；二指从树上掉下来的栗子有着炭火的颜色。

5. **And áll trádes** 这里是诗人自己加的重音。
6. **their gear and tackle and trim** 这三个词意思相近，指各行各业及其使用的工具和设备。gear: 齿轮；tackle: 滑车；trim: 设备
7. **Whatever is fickle, freckled** anything that is fickled is freckled.
8. **He fathers-forth whose beauty is past change** He fathers forth anything whose beauty is past change.

参考译诗

斑斓之美

为万物的斑斓，光荣归于上帝——
　为炫彩的天空犹如牛身的花斑；
　　为游动鳟鱼身上的玫瑰花痣，
为熟落的栗子似炭火；为燕雀的双翼；
　为条块状的农田——圈舍，休耕和耕翻；
　　为各行各业，还有齿轮、滑车和设施。

万物相对，新颖，简朴，奇异，
　一切变化无常，都带有（谁知会怎样？）
　　快慢，酸甜，明暗的斑点；
是他创造这一切，其美永驻不易：
　　　　　　　　让我们将他颂赞。

（白凤欣 译）

思考题

1. Hov [illegible] beauty of nature?
2. Wh [illegible] things counter”?
3. Who [illegible]
4. Whi [illegible] ?

Alfred Edward Housman
阿尔弗莱德·爱德华·霍斯曼
（1859—1936）

Alfred Edward Housman was born in Fockbury, Worcestershire, a county in western England, near the Shripshire border. His father was a country solicitor. His mother died when he was only twelve. This was one of the personal events that affected him enormously and erode his religious faith. Later he claimed that he "became a deist at thirteen and an atheist at twenty-one." He was educated at Bromsgrove School, where he acquired a strong grounding for Greek and Latin studies, where he won prizes for his poetry. In 1877 he won a scholarship to St. John's College, Oxford to study classical literature and philosophy, but in 1881 he mysteriously failed to obtain a pass degree in spite of being a natural academic.

At Oxford he established a friendship with Moses Jackson, a handsome undergraduate with whom Housman fell hopelessly and enduringly in love. In 1882 he took a post in a London Patent office for ten years. He shared a West End flat with Moses and Adalbert, who was Moses' younger brother until 1885 when Housman moved into lodgings of his own. Moses emigrated to India in 1888 and got married in 1889. But he did not [illegible] Housman
was heart [illegible] rt's death
of typhoi [illegible] about the
appearanc [illegible] ns. When
the collect [illegible] the critics
and the pu [illegible] He died in
Cambridge [illegible]

While [illegible] interest
in classical [illegible] eputation
through his [illegible] holarship
was charact [illegible] lmost no
trace of the [illegible] offered the

professorship of Latin at University College, London, and in 1911 he took the similar professorship of Latin at Trinity College, Cambridge until his death.

Most of Housman's poems have a rural or pastoral setting, and many of them focus on the experiences of the "Shropshire Lad", whom he himself described as "an imaginary figure, with something of my own temper and view of life." He is aware of the grimness and pain of life, but his awareness takes the form of a more subdued irony and a more poignant melancholy. His writing has a smooth, carefully wrought cadence.

Loveliest of Trees

Loveliest of trees, the cherry now
Is hung with bloom along the bough,
And stands about the woodland ride[1],
Wearing white for Eastertide[2].

Now, of my threescore years and ten[3],
Twenty will not come again,
And take from seventy springs a score,
It only leaves me fifty more.

And since to look at things in bloom
Fifty springs are little room,
About the woodlands I will go
To see the cherry hung with snow.

注释

1. **woodland ride** 为骑马穿过树林而开辟的小道
2. **Eastertide** 复活节期，5月前后40–50天之间
3. **my threescore years and ten** 70岁。《旧约・诗篇》中写道："我们的生命期限是70年（threescore years and ten）。"

参考译诗

最可爱的树

樱桃树，最可爱，
朵朵樱花枝头开，
亭亭立，林道旁，
迎接“复活”着银装。

人生六十又十年，
其中二十不复还，
若从七十减二十，
我仅只享余五十。

世间繁花不胜数，
五十春光短不足，
我赴密林去观赏，
樱花如雪挂枝上。

（白凤欣　译）

思考题

1. Identify the rhyme scheme.
2. Learn the first stanza by heart.

With Rue[1] My Heart Is Laden[2]

With rue my heart is laden
  For golden friends I had,
For many a rose-lipt maiden
  And many a lightfoot[3] lad.

By brooks too broad[4] for leaping
The lightfoot boys are laid[5];
The rose-lipt girls are sleeping
In fields where roses fade.

注释

1. **Rue** 悲伤
2. **Laden** 充满，满载
3. **lightfoot** 脚步轻松的，步态轻盈的
4. **broad** wide
5. **laid** 指死后长眠

参考译诗

我的内心充满悲伤

我的内心充满悲伤
因拥有的金玉良朋，
因玫瑰红唇的姑娘
和步履轻快的小伙。

宽阔难跃的溪涧边
矫健的少年已安葬；
红颜的少女也安眠
玫瑰凋零的田野上。

（白凤欣 译）

思考题

1. What gives the poet so much pain?
2. Learn this poem by heart.

William Butler Yeats
威廉·巴特勒·叶芝
(1865—1939)

One of the great names in English poetry in the first four decades of the 20th century is that of an Irishman, William Butler Yeats. Yeats was born in Dublin in a Protestant painter's family. He went to school in London and in Dublin and then he entered the Dublin School of Art but soon left it to devote himself to poetry. His first poems were published in the *Dublin University Review* in 1885, and in 1887 he went to London where he got acquainted with William Morris and Oscar Wilde and began to work on an edition of William Blake. In 1889 appeared his book *The Wanderings of Oisin* and in 1891 he became one of the founders of the Rhymers' Club and fell under the influence of the Pre-Raphaelites and of Spenser and Shelley. He had fallen in love with Maud Gonne for whom he wrote a verse play *The Countess Cathleen* which appeared in 1892. In 1894 he visited Paris and was introduced to modern French poetry, especially the Symbolists, by his friend the poet-critic Arthur Symons. In 1896, he met Lady Augusta Gregory and John Millington Synge, and he got to know not only the great stories of the heroic age of Irish history but also Gaelic poetry through translations. In 1899, he published another volume of lyrics *The Wind Among the Reeds*.

In 1904, Yeats became President of the Irish National Dramatic Society and, together with Lady Gregory and with the financial help of Miss A. E. F. Horniman, he founded the Abbey Theatre in Dublin. After that, for a number of years Yeats was busily involved in the management of the theatre, and from 1904 to the end of his life in 1939 he wrote more than twenty plays, mostly in verse, and had many of them staged in the Abbey Theatre. In the meantime he kept on writing poetry until his eight-volume *Collected Works* was published in 1908. In 1911, Yeats went on an American tour with the Abbey troupe and began his friendship with Ezra Pound who introduced to him the Japanese Noh plays and started him on to the writing of plays for dancers.

The Easter Rising of 1916 in Dublin, which a number of his friends including

Maud Gonne participated, had its strong effect upon him. He not only wrote a poem on the event but also referred to the revolutionary activities in Ireland in a number of his later writings. However, he never had much enthusiasm for revolutionary work himself but stood aloof with his aristocratic pose.

In 1917, Yeats bought an old Norman tower at Ballylee in Galway, on the west coast of Ireland, and had it repaired and then moved in to live there following his marriage in the same year. In 1922, he was appointed a senator of the new Irish Free State and in 1923, he was awarded the Nobel Prize for literature. He kept on publishing his poems: *The Green Helmet and Other Poems* in 1910, *Responsibilities* in 1914, *The Wild Swan at Coole* in 1917, *Later Poems* in 1922, *The Tower* in 1928 and *The Winding Stair* in 1929; while his autobiographical work in prose, *The Trembling of the Veil* appeared in 1922 and *A Vision* in 1925 and 1937, this last being an attempt to work out his symbolic "system" of personality and history for "a fuller realization" of himself as an artist. At this last stage he was more and more under the influence of occultism and much of his poetry was very complicated and obscure.

Yeats had a very long poetic career, stretching from his early works in the 1880s and 1890s to the 1930s. He also distinguished himself as a playwright, particularly of verse drama, and devoted much of his energy to the founding and the management of the Dublin Abbey Theatre as the core of the Irish Literary Renaissance. But his fame rested chiefly on his poetry, and T. S. Eliot considered him to be the greatest English-speaking poet of his age.

The Old Men Admiring Themselves in the Water

I heard the old, old men say,
"Everything alters,
And one by one we drop away."
They had hands like claws, and their knees
Were twisted like the old thorn trees
By the waters.

I heard the old, old men say,
"All that's beautiful drifts away
Like the waters."

参考译诗

老人们自赏水中影

我听到年迈苍老的人们说，
"一切都在变，
我们都要消失，一个接一个。"
他们的手像爪子，他们的膝
歪歪扭扭，弯而不直，
像水边枯老的荆棘。
我听到年迈苍老的人们说，
"一切美好的事和物都在消逝，
像河水流去。"

（李正栓　译）

思考题

1. What's the central idea of this poem?
2. Find some other poems or songs about aging.

When You Are Old

When you are old and gray and full of sleep,
And nodding by the fire, take down this book,
And slowly read, and dream of the soft look
Your eyes had once, and of their shadows deep;

How many loved your moments of glad grace,

And loved your beauty with love false or true,
But one man loved the pilgrim soul in you,
And loved the sorrows of your changing face[1];

And bending[2] down beside the glowing bars,
Murmur, a little sadly, how Love[3] fled
And paced upon the mountains overhead
And hid his face amid a crowd of stars.

注释

1. **changing face** 变化着的脸，日渐苍老的面孔
2. **bending** 可指弯下身躯，也可指人变老后形成的驼背
3. **Love** 指一个男性，与以往诗歌中 love 多指女性的情况不同

参考译诗

当你老了

当你老了，满头白发，充满睡意，
在火炉旁打盹时，你取下这本书，
慢慢地读，慢慢回忆你昔日眉目的
柔和还有你眼中深深的忧郁；

多少人爱过你美好温雅的时光，
多少人或真或假爱过你的美貌，
只有一个人爱你那圣洁的灵魂，
还爱你日渐衰老的容颜的哀伤；

在散发柔光的炉火旁，你弯着身躯，
有些凄然，低声诉说，爱如何消散，
如何爬上头顶上的山巅，
把自己的脸藏在繁星紧簇的天宇。

（李正栓　译）

思考题

1. What's the difference between the speaker's love for her and other people's?
2. What book do you think the speaker is asking the woman to read?
3. Learn the first stanza by heart.
4. Find other Chinese versions of this poem.

Lake Isle of Innisfree[1]

I will arise and go now, and go to Innisfree,
And a small cabin build there, of clay and wattles made:
Nine bean-rows will I have there, a hive for the honeybee,
And live alone in the bee-loud glade.

And I shall have some peace there, for peace comes dropping slow,
Dropping from the veils of the morning to where the cricket sings;
There midnight's all a glimmer, and noon a purple glow,
And evening full of the linnet's wings.

I will arise and go now, for always night and day
I hear lake water lapping with low sounds by the shore;
While I stand on the roadway, or on the pavements gray,
I hear it in the deep heart's core.

注释

1. Innisfree 是爱尔兰北部的一个小岛。诗人表达了对大自然的热爱，也表达了远离尘嚣的愿望。

参考译诗

茵尼斯弗利岛

我要起身，现在就走，去茵尼斯弗利岛，
用泥土和枝条建造一个小屋，
种上九架芸豆，为蜜蜂建一蜂巢，
在蜜蜂高唱的林间幽居独处。

在那儿我会有安宁，安宁慢慢来到，
从晨曦的面纱降落到蟋蟀歌唱的地方；
那里午夜一片闪光，中午有紫霞高照，
暮色中也到处飞舞着红雀鸟的翅膀。

我要起身，现在就走，因为我日夜都听到
湖水轻声地拍打着湖滨；
不管站在路上，还是在灰色的人行道，
在心灵深处我总听到水拍湖滨的声音。

（李正栓　译）

思考题

1. What idea is expressed in this poem?
2. Why does the speaker idealize life on the Lake Isle of Innsfree?
3. Make a comparative study of this poem with Tao Yuanming's *Gui Yuan Tian Ju*.
4. What is the significance of Nature in this poem?
5. Learn the first stanza by heart.

David Herbert Lawrence
戴维·赫伯特·劳伦斯
(1885–1930)

David Herbert Lawrence was born in a small village of Eastwood, Nottinghamshire, England on September 11, 1885. His father, Arthur Lawrence, was a coal miner and a heavy drinker. His mother, Lydia Beardsall, came from a middle-class family. Before marriage, she was a former schoolteacher and a lover of literature. Due to the differences in background and financial predicament, the couple fell into frequent conflicts. Thus Lawrence's childhood was shadowed by his parents' continuous quarrelling and poverty. Lawrence was very close to his mother, from whom, he acquired an interest in reading and art. He was sent to Beauvale Board School from 1891 to 1898. Being a fragile boy, he was not good at sports; being an intelligent boy, he excelled his classmates in reading and writing. He became the first local pupil to win a scholarship to Nottingham High School. After leaving school in 1901, he worked for three months as a junior clerk at a Nottingham surgical appliances manufacture. In 1902, he was employed as a teacher at the British school in Eastwood. In 1906, he attended the University College of Nottingham, where he obtained his teacher's certificate in 1908. From 1908 to 1911, he began his teaching career at Davidson Road School in Croydon, a southern suburb of London.

Lawrence's life changed suddenly and irrevocably in 1912 after he met and fell in love with Frieda von Richthofen, a German woman, wife of Ernest Weekley, a professor of French at Nottingham. Frieda left her husband and three children. They eloped and travelled to Bavaria, Austria, Germany and Italy. In 1914, they went back to England and got married. The outbreak of World War I stopped their plan to go to Italy. They had to retreat to Tregerthen in Cornwall near the south coast where they stayed from 1914 to 1919. They were officially expelled from Cornwall in 1917 because the local government believed that they were German spies for the Germans. Only after the war ended in 1919 did they leave England once more, embarking on his "savage pilgrimage" from European continent to Ceylon, Australia, Mexico, and the

United States. Finally they settled in a villa in Northern Italy.

From his childhood on, Lawrence suffered from a poor health. He died of tuberculosis on March 2, 1930 at the age of 44 at Vence in the south of France. He was buried in the old Vence cemetery.

Lawrence is regarded as one of the most important modernist writers of the 20th century. As a novelist, he is a controversial figure because of his frank treatment of sex and his outspoken insistence upon a need for readjustment in the relationship between the sexes. His notable novels include *Sons and Lovers* (1913), *The Rainbow* (1915), *Women in Love* (1920) and *Lady Chatterley's Lovers* (1928). As a literary critic, his ideas are startling, even revolutionary. His representative criticisms are: *Study of Thomas Hardy and other Essays* (1914), *Movements in European History* (1921), *Psychoanalysis and the Unconscious* (1921), *Studies in Classic American Literature* (1923). As a poet, his poetry is a systematic declaration to represent the real life and genuine emotion. His major collections of poetry are: *Love Poems and Athers* (1913), *Look! We Have Come Through!* (1917), *New Poems* (1918), *Bay: a Book of Poems* (1919), *Tortoises* (1921), *Birds, Beasts and Flowers* (1923), *The Collected Poems of D. H. Lawrence* (1928), *Pansies* (1929), *Nettles* (1930).

Cherry Robbers

Under the long, dark boughs, like jewels red
In the hair of an Eastern girl
Shine strings of crimson[1] cherries, as if had bled
Blood-drops beneath each curl.

Under the glistening cherries[2], with folded wings
Three dead birds lie:
Pale-breasted throstles[3] and a blackbird, robberlings
Stained with red dye.

Under the haystack a girl stands laughing at me,
With cherries hung round her ears—
Offering me her scarlet fruit: I will see
If she has any tears.

注释

1. **crimson** deep red in color，此处形容樱桃的嫣红
2. **glistening cherries** 亮晶晶的樱桃
3. **throstles** 画眉鸟

参考译诗

樱 桃 盗 贼

在长长的黑树枝下，像红宝石
嵌于一位东方少女的秀发
闪亮着串串妍红的樱桃，好似
血滴落在每个发卷下。

在晶莹的樱桃下，躺着三只死鸟，
羽翼收拢着
白脯画眉与一只黑鹂，小强盗
被染成了红色。

在草垛下，一个姑娘站着冲我笑，
棵棵樱桃悬挂在耳际边——
送我鲜红的果子：我想知道
她的双眼是否泪水噙满。

（白凤欣　译）

思考题

1. Discuss the theme of the poem.
2. What does the image of cherry symbolize?

Piano

Softly, in the dusk, a woman is singing to me;
Taking me back down the vista of years[1], till I see
A child sitting under the piano, in the boom of the tingling strings[2]
And pressing the small, poised feet of a mother who smiles as she sings.

In spite of myself, the insidious[3] mastery of song
Betrays me back, till the heart of me weeps to belong
To the old Sunday evenings at home, with winter outside
And hymns in the cosy parlour, the tinkling piano our guide.

So now it is vain for the singer to burst into clamour
With the great black piano appassionato[4]. The glamour
Of childish days is upon me, my manhood is cast
Down in the flood of remembrance, I weep like a child for the past.

注释

1. **the vista of years** 对往事的连绵回忆
2. **in the boom of the tingling strings** 在钢琴琴弦颤动的隆隆声响中。boom：（拟声词）隆隆声，嗡嗡声; string: 弦
3. **insidious** 潜在的，不知不觉间加剧的
4. **appassionato** 热情的

参考译诗

钢　琴

黄昏时分，一位女子轻柔地对我吟唱；
勾起我对往事的连绵回想，直到我看见
一个孩童坐在钢琴下面，在琴弦震颤的隆鸣中
按弄边唱边笑的母亲那平放的小脚。

不由自主地，那歌声对我悄然的掌控
背叛我追忆起往昔，直到我的内心流着泪
回到那家中星期天的夜晚，屋外是严冬，
而温暖的客厅却赞歌回荡，琅琅琴声是我们的向导。

此刻随着黑色的大钢琴热情的演奏，
那演唱者爆发出的高歌也是徒劳。魔力的
青涩童年浮现眼前，我的成年被抛进
记忆的洪流，孩子般地为失去的过去哭泣。

（白凤欣 译）

思考题

1. What is the symbolic meaning of "piano"?
2. Do you think that this poem expresses the poet's Oedipus Complex?

Rupert Brooke
鲁波特·布鲁克
(1887–1915)

Rupert Brooke was born in Rugby, Warwickshire, on August 3, 1887. His father was a housemaster at Rugby School. At an early age, he showed his interest and talent in poetry, academics and athletics. He received his education from 1897 to 1901 in Hillbrow School and then until 1905 in Rugby School, where he twice won the school prize. In 1906, he entered King's College, Cambridge, where he joined the Fabian Society. He thus talked of the Fabians: "They're really sincere, energetic, useful people, and they do a lot of good work." In 1911 he wrote a thesis on John Webster and Elizabethan drama, and travelled in Germany and Italy. He was known as a leader of "Neo-pagans", a group of young writers who shared an enthusiasm for some outdoor activities such as long walks, camping and nude bathing. At the same time, he made friends with members of the Bloomsbury Group. But he himself belonged to the Georigan Poets.

Although Brooke was a popular figure on his contemporary literary scene, he underwent a severe emotional crisis in his life. After the failures of his troubled love, he successively travelled in France, Germany, America, Canade New Zealand and South Seas. When World War Ⅰ broke out, he returned to England. He was assigned to Winston Churchill's Royal Navy Division. In October 1914, he took part in the Antwerp expedition. On February 28, 1915 he sailed with the British Mediterranean Expeditionary Force on the Grantully Castle for the Dardanelles. Unhappily he developed acute blood poisoning from a mosquito bite. He died at the age of 28 on April 23, 1915 and was buried on the Greek island of Skyros.

During his life, Brooke travelled extensively. This resulted in his travel letters for *Westminster Gazette*, which was collected in *Letters from America* (1916). He published two collections of poetry: *Poems* (1911) and *Georgian Poetry* (1913). He wrote five *War Sonnets*, including *Peace*, *Safety*, *The Dead*, *The Dead*, and *The Soldier*. He is seen as a major representative of the poets during World War Ⅰ. Traditional not only in form, his poems were the last of that period to express idealistic patriotism in the face of war. Thus his war poetry was laden with cheerful friendship and idealism with sacrifice and death as an honor for England.

The Soldier

If I should die, think only this of me:
That there's some corner of a foreign field
That is for ever England. There shall be
In that rich earth a richer dust[1] concealed;
A dust whom England bore, shaped, made aware,
Gave, once, her flowers to love, her ways to roam,
A body of England's, breathing English air,
Washed by the rivers, blest by suns of home.
And think, this heart, all evil shed away,
A pulse in the eternal mind[2], no less
Gives somewhere back the thoughts by England given;
Her sights and sounds; dreams happy as her day;
And laughter, learnt of friends; and gentleness,
In hearts at peace, under an English heaven.

注释

1. **dust** 这是一个圣经典故，取自《创世纪》3：17上帝的诅咒："你本是尘土，仍要归于尘土。"
2. **the eternal mind** the immortal mind of God

士　兵

假若我战死沙场，请这样想起我：
在异国他乡田野上的某个角落

那将永属英国。将有
一粒更富饶的尘埃在肥沃的土壤里埋藏；
一粒尘埃，在英国出生，成长，变得有思想，
曾给鲜花让他恋爱，给他道路随其漫游，
属于英国的身躯啊，呼吸着它的空气，
被河流洗涤，被故乡的太阳赐福。
还要想起，这颗心，抛弃一切邪念，
在不朽精神中跳动的脉搏，依然
将英国赋予他的思想送还；
她的音容笑貌；她生日的甜美梦想；
朋友的欢歌笑声；在英国的天空下，
在安宁的心底，还有那高贵的温和。

（白凤欣 译）

思考题

1. What is the poet's feeling toward England?
2. Characterize the major features of Georgian poetry.

Wystan Hugh Auden
温斯坦·休·奥登
(1907–1973)

Wystan Hugh Auden was born into a middle-class family in York, England, on February 21, 1907. His father, George Augustus Auden, was a physician and a psychologist. His mother, Constance Rosalie Bicknell Auden, was a devout Anglican. He was brought up under strict Anglo-Catholic atmosphere. In 1908, he and his family moved to Solihull, near Birmingham. He attended St. Edmund's School and Gresham's School to receive his earlier education. In 1925, he went to Christ Church College at the University of Oxford, where he won a scholarship in biology. At the same time he made friends with a group of left-wing young poets including Cecil Day Lewis, Louis MacNeice and Stephen Spender, who were influenced by literary Modernism represented by T. S. Eliot. They preferred to use concrete imagery and free verse in their poetic creation. This group was later known as the "Thirties Poets" or the "Auden Group".

After graduation in 1928, he travelled abroad in Germany, Iceland and China. From 1930 to 1935 he became a schoolmaster in several boys' schools for five years. He once served in the Spanish Civil War in 1937. From 1935 to 1939 he worked as a freelance reviewer, lecturer, essayist and documentary filmmaker. In 1939, he took up residence in the United States, teaching at different universities. In 1940, he returned to the formal practice of Christianity he had abandoned at his young age. In 1946, he became an American citizen. His poetic works were widely recognized by American public. He received the Pulitzer Prize and the Bollingen Award. In 1973, he died in his sleep in Vienna and was buried in Kirchstetten.

Auden was a prolific writer. His major collections of poetry are *Poems* (1928), *Poems* (1930), *The Orators Prose and Verse* (1932), *For the Time Being* (1944), *The Age of Anxiety: A Baroque Eclogue* (1947), *The Old Man's Road* (1956), *City Without Walls* (1969), *Thank You, Fog: Last Poems* (1974). He, a man with remarkable wit and talent, began his poetry writing at the age of thirteen. His poems displayed the influence of William Wordsworth, Thomas Hardy and T. S. Eliot. He often combined deliberate irreverence with verbal craftsmanship to awaken what he saw as the complacent middle class to the hollowness of their society and the need for reform. His later poetry, though often as satirical as the early poems had been, became increasingly concerned with religious and ethical themes. But his poetry never lost its moral quality, nor did it abandon its concern with the troubles of the modern world.

Auden's poetry is characterized by its vitality, variety and originality. He imposes new and unexpected patterns on a wide range of forms—from archaic ballads to street-corner blues. One of his most important contributions to the 20th century poetry is his experimentation in versification, combining an off-hand informality with remarkable technical skill. Therefore, he is generally regarded as one of the greatest modern poets in the 20th century.

Funeral Blues[1]

Stop all the clocks, cut off the telephone.
Prevent the dog from barking with a juicy bone,
Silence the pianos and with muffled drum[2]
Bring out the coffin, let the mourners come.

Let aeroplanes circle moaning overhead
Scribbling in the sky the message He is Dead[3],
Put crêpe bows round the white necks of the public doves,
Let the traffic policemen wear black cotton gloves.

He was my North, my South, my East and West,
My working week and my Sunday rest,
My noon, my midnight, my talk, my song;
I thought that love would last forever, I was wrong.

The stars are not wanted now; put out every one,

Pack up the moon and dismantle the sun.
Pour away the ocean and sweep up the wood;
For nothing now can ever come to any good.

注释

1. **Blues** 产生于美国19世纪末的一种黑人流行音乐形式，意为悲伤、忧郁。Funeral Blues指在葬礼上颂唱的挽歌
2. **muffled drum** 沉闷的鼓声
3. **Dead** 指死亡的不可改变

参考译诗

葬礼布鲁斯

把所有时钟停止，把电话切断。
给狗一块多汁的骨头，别让它叫唤，
把钢琴静音，随着沉闷的鼓声敲响
抬出灵柩，让吊唁的人群前来瞻仰。

让飞机在头顶上盘旋悲戚
在空中急速写下“他逝去”的讯息，
把黑纱围系在鸽子那雪白的脖项，
让交警将黑色的棉手套戴上。

他曾是我的北、我的南、我的东、我的西，
我的工作周还有那休息日，
我的午、我的夜、我的话、我的歌；
我以为爱将长久永存，但我错了。

再也不需要繁星；把颗颗星都熄灭，
将明月包住，将骄阳拆卸。
将海洋倾尽，将树木清掉；
因为至此再也不会有美好。

（白凤欣　译）

思考题

1. What's the tone of this poem?
2. What's the difference between a dirge and an elegy?

Musée des Beaux Arts[1]

About suffering they were never wrong,
The Old Masters[2]: how well they understood
Its human position; how it takes place
While someone else is eating or opening a window or just walking along;
How, when the aged are reverently, passionately waiting
For the miraculous birth[3], there always must be
Children who did not specially want it to happen, skating
On a pond at the edge of the wood:
They never forgot
That even the dreadful martyrdom must run its course[4]
Anyhow in a corner, some untidy spot
Where the dogs go on with their doggy life and the torturer's horse
Scratches its innocent behind on a tree.[5]

In Brughel's *Icarus*[6], for instance: how everything turns away
Quite leisurely from the disaster; the ploughman may
Have heard the splash, the forsaken cry,
But for him it was not an important failure; the sun shone
As it had to on the white legs disappearing into the green water;
And the expensive delicate ship that must have seen
Something amazing, a boy falling out of the sky,
Had somewhere to get to and sailed calmly on.

注释

1. **Musée des Beaux Arts** （法语）指位于布鲁塞尔的美术陈列馆
2. **The Old Masters** referring to the classic painters in general
3. **the miraculous birth** referring to the birth of Jesus
4. **run its course** progress to its usual end
5. **Scratches its innocent behind on a tree** 马靠在树上擦屁股搔痒的画面。behind: buttock
6. **Icarus** 古希腊神话中的人物伊卡洛斯

参考译诗

美　术　馆

关于苦难，他们从未搞错，
古典大师们：他们多么悉知苦难
在人间的位置；它如何发生
当某个人正吃东西，或打开一扇窗户，
或只是无精打采地走路；
当上年纪的人虔诚地、热切地等待
那奇迹的发生，总会有些
孩子并不特别希望它发生，却在
林边的池塘上溜冰：
他们从未忘记
即使可怕的殉难也必将前行至终点。
在某个角落，某个凌乱不堪的地方，
狗仍过着狗的生活，施刑者的马
在树上不停地蹭挠它那无辜的屁股。

比如说，在勃鲁盖尔的《伊卡洛斯》里，
一切是如何悠闲地掉转脸而无视灾难；农夫或许
听到了落水声，还有那无助的呼救，
可对他来说这并非大不了的事故；太阳
像往日一样照在淹没白净双腿的

碧水上；那豪华精美的轮船一定目睹了
惊人的事件，一个男孩从空中坠落，
但它有自己的目的地，继续平静地航行。

（白凤欣　译）

思考题

1. Explain the function of the poem's title.
2. How do you evaluate Icarus and the ploughman?

Philip Larkin
菲利浦·拉金
(1922–1985)

Philip Larkin was born on August 9, 1922 in Coventry. His father Sydney Larkin, once being Coventry City Treasurer, was a lover of literature and a fanatic of Nazism. The father guided the son into the world of literature, where Philip voraciously read Ezra Pound, T. S. Eliot, James Joyce and D. H. Lawrence. His mother Eva Emily Day was a nervous and passive woman whose life was completely arranged by her husband. Philip received his earliest education at home from his mother and sister. At eight he was sent to Coventry's King Henry Ⅲ Junior School and later proceeded to King Henry Ⅲ Senior School. In 1940, he entered St. John's College, Oxford to study English. After World War Ⅱ broke out, he volunteered to go to the front. But he was turned down because of his poor eyesight. So he was able to complete his study without interruption within the three years. At Oxford he met Kingsley Amis, Bruce Montgomery and others, with whom he formed a group named "The Seven". The members met regularly to discuss and communicate their own poetic creation, listen to jazz, and drink heavily. After graduation in 1943, he worked as a librarian in several universities. In 1955 he became a librarian in the University of Hull, an office that he held until his death. It was during his work as a librarian for more than thirty years that he produced the most important works in his life. He died of cancer in 1985 at the age of 63 and was buried at the Cottingham municipal cemetery.

World War Ⅱ produced a series of poets like Dylan Thomas whose response to the catastrophe was emotionally intense and often highly rhetorical. This group of poets is sometimes referred to as the "New Apocalypse". In contrast to this group is "The Movement"—a group of British poets that were loosely associated during the 1950s. They were educated at Oxford and strongly influenced by W. H. Auden and Thomas Hardy. They were concerned with creating a less intense and colloquial experience and the changes in everyday English life and in traditional forms. They consciously and strictly avoided sentimentality and self-pity. Larkin has proved to be one of the best poets of the group, represented by Kingsley Amis, Donald Davie and Tom Gunn.

Larkin claimed that his earliest poetry was influenced by W. B. Yeats, T. S. Eliot and W. H. Auden; but his more mature works at later time were mainly under the influence of Thomas Hardy. His poetic publications include *The North Ship* (1945), *XX Poems* (1951), *Poems* (1954), *The Less Deceived* (1955), *The Whitsun Weddings* (1964), *Gorgi Modern Poets in Focus 5* (1971), *High Windows* (1974), *Femmes Damnées* (1978), *Aubade* (1980) and *Collected Poems* (1989). In their quiet, reflective tone and ironic understatement, his best poems continue the traditional forms. He has the rare gift of clarity and of casually suggesting the importance of the ordinary.

Water

If I were called in
To construct[1] a religion
I should make use of water.

Going to church
Would entail[2] a fording
To dry, different clothes;

My litany would employ
Images of sousing[3],
A furious devout drench[4],

And I should raise in the east
A glass of water
Where any-angled light
Would congregate endlessly.

注释

1. **construct** 用具体的材料制造某物；构筑思想体系等，诗中两种含义兼而有之。
2. **entail** 需要
3. **sousing** 浸泡，浸透
4. **drench** 湿透

参考译诗

水

倘若我被召见
去建构一种宗教
我会用水。

去教堂
需涉水过河，
晾干，不同的衣服；

我的连祷会用
浸泡的意象，
一个既热烈又虔诚的浸透，

我在东方会举起
一杯水
在那里调整了角度的光线
将不断地聚集。

（白凤欣 译）

思考题

1. What's the symbolic meaning of "water" in this poem?
2. Identify allusions in this poem and explain them.

Ted Hughes
塔特·休斯
（1930—1998）

Edward James Hughes, known as Ted Hughes, is routinely regarded as one of the best poets of his generation.

Ted Hughes was born on August 17, 1930 in Mytholmroyed, West Riding of Yorkshire. The family origin of his mother, Edith Hughes, could trace back to William the Conqueror. His father, William Henry Hughes, had once enlisted during World War I and fought in the battle of Gallipoli. Being one of the 17 survivors from his regiment, he often told his son stories of Flanders field. This made young Ted full of imagination in his mind. Ted was educated firstly at the Burnley Road School. At seven, his family moved to Mexborough, a coal mining town of South Yorkshire. He then went to Schofield Street junior school. His upbringing of his hometown proved to shape his future poetic creation. It was at Mexborough Grammar School that he met with some teachers who encouraged him to write and cultivated his interest in poetry. It was also at Mexborough Grammar School that he won a scholarship to Pembroke College, Cambridge. But he chose to serve two years in the Royal Air Force on an isolated three-man station in east Yorkshire. During this period of National Service, he read and memorized a large number of Shakespeare's plays and Yeats' poetry.

In 1951, Ted Hughes began to study at Pembroke College, Cambridge, where he studied English in his first two years, but in his third year he transferred to anthropology and archaeology. This helped him to develop an interest in mythological systems that later intrigued him deeply into astrology, shamanism and hermeticism. After graduation he did many odd jobs such as a rose gardener, a night watchman, a worker at a local zoo, and a reader for a British film company. On February 26, 1956, he found *St. Botolph's Review*, a literary magazine, together with his friends. At the party he met his future wife Sylvia Plath, an American poet. The two quickly fell in love and got married on June 16, 1956. Unfortunately their marriage was a tragic one: Plath committed suicide on February11, 1963. After Plath's death, Hughes stopped his poetry writing for three years. He was busily involved in broadcasting, writing critical essays and running international poetry festivals. In 1970 he settled on a farm in Devon. In the same year he set up the Rainbow Press with his sister Olwyn. In 1984 he was appointed Poet Laureate. On October 28, 1998, he died of myocardial infarction and was cremated in Exeter.

Ted Hughes's major collection of poetry include *The Hawk in the Rain* (1957), *Crow: From the Life and the Songs of the Crow* (1970), *Cave Birds* (1975), *Gaudete* (1977), *Remains of Elmet* (1979), *Moortown* (1979), *Flowers and Insects* (1986), *Wolfwatching* (1989), *Rain-charm for the Duchy* (1992). He admitted his main influence from John Donne, William Blake, Gerard Hopkins and T. S. Eliot. His poetry is characterized with restrained diction, controlled style and loose structure. This creates a sense of order and meaning in the natural world, especially in the world of wild animals such as hawks, wolves, and crows, for which he is frequently labelled as the poet of animals. Animals are used as an implication to reflect his own view on life and nature. His poems represent the combination of beauty, savage and violence in the natural world.

Hawk Roosting

I sit in the top of the wood, my eyes closed.
Inaction, no falsifying dream[1]
Between my hooked head and hooked feet:
Or in sleep rehearse perfect kills and eat.

The convenience[2] of the high trees!
The air's buoyancy[3] and the sun's ray
Are of advantage to me;
And the earth's face upward for my inspection.

My feet are locked upon[4] the rough bark.
It took the whole of Creation[5]
To produce my foot, my each feather:

Now I hold Creation in my foot

Or fly up, and revolve it all slowly—
I kill where I please because it is all mine.
There is no sophistry in my body[6]:
My manners are tearing off heads —

The allotment of death.
For the one path of my flight is direct
Through the bones of the living.
No arguments assert my right:

The sun is behind me.
Nothing has changed since I began.
My eye has permitted no change.
I am going to keep things like this.

注释

1. **no falsifying dream** 没有虚幻的梦
2. **convenience** 方便
3. **buoyancy** the ability to float on a liquid or in the air
4. **locked upon** 紧紧抓住
5. **Creation** the universe and all the things in it
6. **no sophistry in my body** 在我身上用不着诡辩术。sophistry: the practice of using clever arguments that sound convincing but are in fact false

栖 息 的 鹰

我坐在树梢，双眼紧闭，
一动不动，没有虚幻的梦
在我钩状的头和钩状的爪间：
或在酣睡中排练精湛的捕杀和吞食本领。

高高的树木真是方便！
空气的托力和太阳的光线
都对我非常有利；
大地的面庞朝上任我视察。

我的双爪牢牢抠住粗粝的树皮。
还需造物主
来创造我的脚爪，我的根根羽毛：
而今我把造物攫在爪中

或高高飞起，把它缓缓旋转——
我可随意捕杀，因为它的一切都归我所有。
我的身上没有什么诡辩术：
我的方式是把脑袋撕断——

就这样分配死亡。
因为我的飞翔之路是直接
穿透活物的骨骼。
我的权利无须论证：

太阳就在我身后。
自我开始从未有任何改变。
我的眼睛不许有丝毫变化。
我打算像这样保持一切。

（白凤欣　译）

思考题

1. What is the image of the hawk?
2. What view of nature emerges in this poem?
3. By imparting human motives to the hawk, what might the poet be implying about human tyranny?
4. Which stanza do you like best? Learn it by heart.

Seamus Heaney
西默斯·希尼
(1939–2013)

Seamus Heaney is an Irish poet, playwright, translator, lecturer and winner of Nobel Prize in Literature.

Heaney was born on April 13, 1939 and was brought up on a farm in County Londonderry, Northern Ireland. In 1953, his family moved to Bellaghy. Although his father Patrick Heaney was a farmer, his real commitment was to cattle-dealing. His mother Margaret McCann came from a more industrialized McCann family. He was educated at Anahorish Primary School. In 1951, he won a scholarship to St. Columb's College where he studied Latin and Irish. In 1957 he went to Queen's University, Belfast, to study English and Literature. After graduation with a First Class Honours degree in 1961, he was trained as a teacher in St. Joseph's Teacher Training College in Belfast. It was during this period of time that he began to publish poetry in 1962. After publishing some articles in local magazines, he was attracted by an English lecturer Philip Hobsbaum, who established a Belfast Group of local young poets. This provided Heaney with the opportunity to get in touch with other poets such as Derek Mahon and Michael Longley. In 1966, he became a lecturer in Modern English Literature at Queen's University. In 1972, he moved to Carysfort College as a teacher. In 1981, he became a visiting professor at Harvard University, where he was appointed Boylston Professor of Rhetoric and Oratory from 1985 to 2006. In 1995, he was awarded the Nobel Prize for Literature. From 1989 to 1994, he was the Oxford Professor for Poetry. He died on August 2013 at the age of 74 in Dublin and was buried in Bellaghy.

During his life, Heaney received a number of awards for his remarkable contribution to the literature. His major works include: *Death of a Naturalist* (1966), *Door into the Dark* (1969), *Wintering Out* (1972), *North* (1975), *Field Work* (1979), *Poems* (1980), *The Haw Lantern* (1987), *The Spirit Level* (1996) and *District and Circle* (2006). His subject matter is about Northern Ireland, its farms, its cities, its natural landscape, its culture and language overrun by English rule. His poetry focuses on characters in his own family and family history, on the evocation of Irish rural life and events, on the local surroundings of the Northern Ireland, on his extraordinary connection with nature. His Nobel Prize nomination ran "for works of lyrical beauty and ethical depth, which exalt everyday miracles and the living past."

Digging

Between my finger and my thumb
The squat pen[1] rests; as snug[2] as a gun.

Under my window a clean rasping sound[3]
When the spade sinks into gravelly ground[4]:
My father, digging. I look down

Till his straining rump[5] among the flowerbeds
Bends low, comes up twenty years away[6]
Stooping in rhythm through potato drills[7]
Where he was digging.

The coarse boot nestled on the lug,[8] the shaft
Against the inside knee was levered firmly.[9]
He rooted out tall tops, buried the bright edge[10] deep
To scatter new potatoes that we picked
Loving their cool hardness[11] in our hands.

By God, the old man could handle a spade,
Just like his old man.

My grandfather could cut more turf[12] in a day
Than any other man on Toner's[13] bog.

Once I carried him milk in a bottle
Corked sloppily with paper.[14] He straightened up
To drink it, then fell to[15] right away
Nicking[16] and slicing neatly, heaving sods
Over his shoulder,[17] digging down and down
For the good turf. Digging.

The cold smell of potato mold, the squelch and slap[18]
Of soggy peat[19], the curt cuts of an edge
Through living roots awaken in my head.
But I've no spade to follow men like them.

Between my finger and my thumb
The squat pen rests.
I'll dig with it.

注释

1. **The squat pen** 矮胖的笔
2. **snug** warm and comfortable
3. **rasping sound** 刺耳声
4. **gravelly ground** 多砂砾的地
5. **straining rump** 使劲的臀部
6. **twenty years away** 20年来
7. **drills** a long line in the earth in which seeds are sown
8. **The coarse boot nestled on the lug** 粗劣的靴子踩在铁铲上。nestle: 放置；lug:（用作把手或柄等的）耳状物，手柄
9. **the shaft / Against the inside knee was levered firmly** 长柄顶着膝盖内侧使劲地翻撬
10. **the bright edge** the edge of the spade
11. **cool hardness** 又凉又硬的感觉
12. **turf** 泥煤
13. **Toner** 地名或人名
14. **Corked sloppily with paper** 草草地用纸把瓶口塞住
15. **fell to** began to (work)
16. **Nicking** cutting
17. **heaving sods / Over his shoulder** 把泥煤甩过肩膀
18. **the squelch and slap** 吧唧声（咯吱声）和啪啪声
19. **soggy peat** 潮湿的泥煤

参考译诗

挖　地

在我的手指和拇指间
放着一支短粗的笔；舒服地像支枪。

窗下一阵清晰刺耳的声音响起
当铁铲铲进满是砾石的地里：
我爹，正在挖地。我低头

看见他那用力的臀部在花圃中
弯下，直起，已有二十余年
有节奏地弯着腰穿行在土豆垄沟里
挖呀挖。

粗劣的靴子踩在铁铲上，长柄
顶着膝盖内侧使劲地翻撬。
他翻平高高的地面，将锃亮的铲边插入地里
把刚挖出的土豆撩撒在地上，我们捡起
手中那又凉又硬的感觉真好。

天啊，这个老头的确是一位铲子高手，
就像他的老头那样。

我爷一天挖的泥煤
比土纳沼泽地的任何人都多。
我曾给他送去一瓶牛奶
草草地用纸把瓶口塞住。他直起腰
喝完，又马上干起来
熟练地剪断切块，把泥煤
甩过肩膀，往深处挖

为了挖到好泥煤。挖呀挖。

土豆冷冰冰的泥霉味，嘎吱吱啪哒哒
湿透的泥煤，短促的铲断
仍生长的根部声唤醒我的头脑。
可我却没有铁铲在手像他们那样干。

在我的手指和拇指间
放着一支短粗的笔。
我将用它来挖地。

（白凤欣　译）

思考题

1. What is the image of the speaker's father?
2. Why does the speaker focus on digging?
3. What kind of relationship can you find between the speaker and his father?
4. What is the tone of the poem?

The Play Way

Sunlight pillars through glass, probes each desk
For milk-tops, drinking straws and the old dry crusts.
The music strides[1] to challenge it
Mixing memory and desire with chalk dust.

My lesson notes read: Teacher will play
Beethoven's Concerto Number Five[2]
And class will express themselves freely
In writing. One said: "Can we jive[3]?"

When I produced the record, but now
The big sounds has silenced them. Higher
And firmer, each authoritative note[4]
Pumps the classroom up as tight as a tyre

Working its private spell[5] behind eyes
That stare wide. They have forgotten me
For once. The pens are busy, the tongues mime[6]
Their blundering embrace of the free

Word. A silence charged with sweetness
Breaks short on lost faces where I see
New looks. Then notes stretch taut as snares[7]. They trip
To fall into themselves unknowingly.

注释

1. **strides** to walk quickly with long steps
2. **Beethoven's Concerto Number Five** 贝多芬第五协奏曲
3. **jive** a very fast dance, popular especially in the 1930s and 1940s, performed to swing music
4. **authoritative note** 强有力的音符
5. **spell** incantation
6. **mime** to act with actions or movements without any words
7. **notes stretch taut as snares** 音符绷得像罗网那样紧

参考译诗

播放的方式

光柱穿过玻璃，探寻每张书桌上的
奶瓶盖，吸管和久放的干面包屑。
音乐大步走来向它挑战
将记忆与愿望和粉笔灰混在一起。

我的教案上写着：老师要播放
贝多芬第五协奏曲
同时班上的学生可自由地表达
他们的感受。一个学生问："能跳摇摆舞吗？"

当我播放唱片时，随即
响亮的声音使他们安静。不断升高
不断坚定，每一个强有力的音符
把教室胀满的像打足气的轮胎

施展它独有的魔力在双双
瞪大的眼睛背后。此刻他们忘记了
我的存在。钢笔急促着，舌头模仿着
他们误读的对"自由"

一词的信奉。一种充满甜蜜的安静
骤然消失在迷失的面庞。在那里我看见
全新的神情。这时音符紧绷如罗网。他们绊倒
而不知不觉地陷入他们自己之中。

（白凤欣　译）

思考题

1. Analyze the influence of music on the students in this poem.
2. Read the poem and pay special attention to the vivid images. Try to explain them.

PART TWO

American Poetry

William Cullen Bryant
威廉·柯伦·布莱恩特
(1794–1878)

In 1817, the stately poem called *Thanatopsis* (Greek, meaning "view of death") introduced the best poet to appear in America up to that time. This remarkable poem was written in 1810 when William Cullen Bryant was at the age of sixteen. (The author later added lines at both the beginning and the end of the poem.)

Coming to New York City from his native Massachusetts, Bryant began working on the *New York Review*, and a few years later became an editor with the *New York Evening Post*. He was to remain with the latter newspaper for fifty years, during most of that time as editor-in-chief and partner. Apart from his fame as a poet, Bryant merits a reputation as one of the great editors of American journalism. He supported such causes as free speech, free trade and the abolition of slavery. When Abraham Lincoln came to New York in 1860 to make his famous Cooper Union speech, which greatly increased his chances for the Presidential nomination, Byrant presided at the meeting and introduced the Illinois politician, who was then little known to the New York public.

Greater poets than Bryant were to follow, but none possessed more of the quality of serene and noble imaginative power. *To a Waterfowl* is perhaps the peak of his work. Mathew Arnold, the eminent English critic and poet, called it the "most perfect brief poem in the language."

The finest of Bryant's poems were written in his youth, before Bryant felt the pressures of his career in journalism. Nevertheless, he continued to write poetry throughout much of his life, publishing a number of volumes. Among his most important later works are his translations of the *Iliad* and the *Odyssey* into English blank verse. As Irving had shown that American prose had come of age, Bryant demonstrated to European readers that American poetry was ready to demand serious attention. He was the first American to gain the stature of a major poet.

To a Waterfowl[1]

Whither, 'midst falling dew,
While glow the heavens with the last steps of day,
Far, through their rosy depths, dost thou pursue
Thy solitary way?

Vainly the fowler's[2] eye
Might mark thy distant flight to do thee wrong,
As, darkly painted the crimson sky,
Thy figure floats along.

Seek'st thou the plashy[3] brink
Of weedy lake, or marge of river wide,
Or where the rocking billows rise and sink
On the chafed ocean-side?

There is a Power whose care
Teaches thy way along that pathless coast, —
The desert and illimitable air, —
Lone wandering, but not lost.

All day thy wings have fann'd
At that far height, the cold thin atmosphere;
Yet stoop not, weary, to the welcome land,
Though the dark night is near.

And soon that toil shall end,
Soon shalt thou find a summer home, and rest,
And scream among thy fellows; reeds shall bend

Soon o'er thy sheltered nest.

Thou'rt gone, the abyss of heaven
Hath swallowed up thy form; yet, on my heart
Deeply hath sunk the lesson thou hast given,
And shall not soon depart.

He, who, from zone to zone,
Guides through the boundless sky thy certain flight,
In the long way that I must tread alone,
Will lead my steps aright.

注释

1. This poem, called by Mattew Arnold "The most perfect brief poem in the language", was composed by Bryant after a walk from Cummington to Plainfield, Massachusetts, in December 1815. Arranged in alternating rhymed quatrains, it expressed both the poet's grateful view, at the close of a day of self-doubt and despair, of a solitary bird on the horizon, and his sense of a divine power guiding and protecting everything in nature. The clarity of the central image and the aptness and simplicity of the moral analogy have always been admired, even by those who dislike "preaching" in poetry. The effect of the stanza form has been described as "gliding", appropriate to the visual image of the second stanza. The poem was first published in the *North American Review* for March 1818 and collected in the *Poems* of 1821.
2. **fowler's** hunter's
3. **plashy** marshy, swampy

致水鸟

露珠正在滴落，
白昼将退，天际遍洒柔辉，
天上玫瑰红一抹，
你要往何处孤独远飞？

猎鸟者也许已注意到
你振翅远飞却无法伤害你，
红霞满天，神秘轻罩，
看着你飘一般飞去。

你要寻觅杂草丛生
泥泞的湖滨、宽广河流的岸沿？
还是要寻觅波涛汹涌
海浪冲击的洋边？

有一种神力关心着你，
教你如何沿无路的海滨飞翔，
在沙漠和无可比拟的长空里，——
你虽然独往却不迷失方向。

一整天，你拍翅飞翔，
忍受那高处寒冷稀薄的空气，
你已疲惫不堪，黑夜已临降，
可你却不肯屈栖欢迎你的大地。

这辛苦即将告一段落，
你很快会找到爱巢去歇息，
在同伴间欢鸣不已；你筑的巢窝
很快会让芦苇弯腰俯视。

你走啦。深邃的无际
已吞没了你的形象；但在我心里
已留下一个深深的教益，
它将永存我心底。

他教你跨区飞翔，
指引你飞越无垠长空，
也会在我必须独自跋涉的征途上
指引我正确的航程。

（李正栓　译）

思考题

1. This poem is praised by Matthew Arnold as "The most perfect brief poem in the language." Discuss why Arnold said so.
2. What's the central idea of this poem?
3. William Cullen Bryant is entitled "American Wordsworth". Discuss the similarities and differences between Wordsworth and Bryant's poems.
4. Learn the first and the last stanzas by heart.

Edgar Allan Poe
爱德加·爱伦·坡
(1809–1849)

Edgar Allan Poe, the child of traveling actors, was born in Boston. Before he was three, his father deserted the family, and his mother died. He was taken into the home of John Allan, a rich merchant of Richmond, Virginia. In 1815, Poe followed the Allans to England. In 1820, the Allans returned to Virginia.

When he was seventeen, Poe entered the University of Virginia. He distinguished himself in Latin and French and soon gained a reputation as a self-proclaimed "aristocrat", a poet, a wit, a gambler and a heavy drinker. The next year, after bitter quarrels with Allan, who refused to pay Poe's gambling debts of $ 2,000 at cards, Poe left the university and ran off to Boston where he enlisted in the United States Army.

In Boston, he got his first book of poetry *Tamerlane and Other Poems* (1827) published. In April 1829, he left the army, and eight months later, his second volume of poems *Al Aaraaf, Tamerlane, and Minor Poems* came out in Baltimore.

In 1832, five of his stories were published. In 1833, he won first prize of $ 100 in a short story contest run by a Baltimore newspaper. Then he became an editor in Richmond where more stories, poems were published. When he was twenty-seven, he married his thirteen-year-old cousin, Virginia Clemm, and late in 1836 he left Richmond.

The remaining years of his life were filled with intense creativity punctuated by fits of acute mental depression and drinking bouts. In 1838, he published a novel. Other works followed, *The Fall of the House of Usher* (1839), *Tales of the Grotesque and Arabesque* (1839), his sonnet *Silence* (1840), *The Murders in the Rue Morgue* (1841) because of which he was regarded as the ancestor of American detective stories.

While in New York in 1844, he wrote *The Raven* which was a success and was reprinted many times.

In 1847, his wife died. Assaulted by her death, his extreme poverty and his own instability, Poe nonetheless continued to write. In 1849, he returned briefly to Richmond, where he became engaged to a childhood sweetheart, and he set out for Philadelphia for yet another editing job, stopping on the way in Baltimore. There on

October 2, 1849, he was found unconscious on the street. Four days later he died.

Poe found his works in a romanticism divorced from the actualities of American life, a world of disorder, perversity and romantic emotion. He helped establish one of the world's most popular literary genres, detective story. His writing influenced later writers such as A. Conan Doyle, Robert Louis Stevenson, William Faulkner and T. S. Eliot. He was among the first modern literary theorists of America. His arguments against the didactic motive for literature and for the creation of beauty and intensity of emotion, although they ran counter to the prevailing literary ideals of his time, have had profound effect on the writers and critics who followed him. To the modern age he stands as one of the foremost writers of America, and he is now, long after his death, one of the most popular authors in the world.

To Helen[1]

Helen, thy beauty is to me
  Like those Nicéan[2] barks of yore,
That gently, o'er a perfumed sea,
  The weary, way-worn wanderer bore
  To his own native shore.

On desperate seas long wont to roam,
  Thy hyacinth[3] hair, thy classic face,
Thy Naiad[4] airs have brought me home
  To the glory that was Greece,
And the grandeur that was Rome.

Lo! in yon brilliant window-niche
  How statue-like I see thee stand,
  The agate lamp within thy hand!

Ah, Psyche[5], from the regions which
Are Holy-Land!

注释

1. One of Poe's most famous lyrics, this poem was inspired by Mrs. Jane Stith Stanard, the mother of a schoolmate of Poe, in Richmond, Virginia. Poe described the poem as "lines written, in my passionate boyhood, to the first, purely ideal love of my soul." The Helen of Greek myth was the beautiful daughter of Zeus. Her abduction by Paris was the cause of the Trojan War and the source of the *Iliad* of Homer. 海伦是希腊神话中的宙斯的女儿，她以美貌而闻名。此处爱伦·坡灵感来自于同学之母海伦·史坦纳太太。但全诗仍是指古典美人海伦。是同学之母让诗人想起神话中的海伦。也只有神话中美丽的海伦才能与同学的母亲相提并论。
2. Nicéan victorious. Poe's meaning is unclear. He may have intended reference to the ancient city of Nicea (or Nicaea) in Turkey, which was associated with the god Dionysus, a wanderer. Although many different interpretations have been put forward, all agree on the musical quality of the term and its implications of classical antiquity. 奈西亚（Nicaea）是小亚细亚北海岸之古城。"芬芳的海"应该是指爱琴海。
3. **hyacinth** curly
4. **Naiad** Nymphs of more placid fresh water, contrasted to the "desperate seas" above.
5. **Psyche** soul in Greek. In classical mythology, Psyche, the lover of Cupid, was a woman so beautiful that the goddess Venus was jealous of her.

致 海 伦

海伦，对于我，你的美
　正像古时奈西亚帆船，
载着疲惫的旅人
　悠悠飘过芳香的海域，
　驶向他故乡的海岸。

在长久习于汹涌的海面，
　你那卷发及典雅的脸，
你海仙女的风姿使我熟记

古希腊的荣耀、
古罗马的庄严。

瞧！我见你玉立婷婷，
在光彩的壁龛里，
如玉雕神女，
手里还握着玛瑙油灯！
呵，你是赛琪，来自天国的圣地。

（李正栓　译）

思考题

1. Poe makes use of allusions to illustrate the supernatural beauty of "Helen". Identity the allusions.
2. What's the rhyme scheme of the poem?
3. The rhyme scheme of the Chinese version is different from that of the English version. Try to improve it to make the poem sound better.
4. Learn this poem by heart.

Annabel Lee[1]

It was many and many a year ago,
In a kingdom by the sea,
That a maiden there lived whom you may know
By the name of ANNABEL LEE;
And this maiden she lived with no other thought
Than to love and be loved by me.

I was a child and she was a child,
In this kingdom by the sea;
But we loved with a love that was more than love—

I and my ANNEBEL LEE;
With a love that the winged seraphs[2] of heaven
Coveted her and me.

And this was the reason that, long ago,
In this kingdom by the sea,
A wind blew out of a cloud, chilling
My beautiful ANNEBEL LEE;
So that her highborn kinsmen came
And bore her away from me,
To shut her up in a sepulchre[3]
In this kingdom by the sea.

The angels, not half so happy in heaven,
Went envying her and me—
Yes! —that was the reason (as all men know,
In this kingdom by the sea)
That the wind came out of the cloud by night,
Chilling and killing my ANNABEL LEE.

But our love it was stronger by far than the love
Of those who were older than we—
Of many far wiser than we—
And neither the angels in heaven above,
Nor the demons down under the sea,
Can ever dissever[4] my soul from the soul
Of the beautiful ANNABEL LEE:

For the moon never beams without bringing me dreams
Of the beautiful ANNABEL LEE;
And the stars never rise but I see the bright eyes

Of the beautiful ANNABEL LEE;
And so, all the night-tide, I lie down by the side
Of my darling, my darling, my life and my bride,
In her sepulcher there by the sea—
In her tomb by the sounding sea.

注释

1. This is the last poetic work of Edgar Allan Poe. It is believed to be dedicated to the memory of Poe's wife, Virginia Clemm. In 1836, Poe married his cousin, Virginia Clemm. She died in 1847 at the age of 26. The poem was first published on October 9, 1849 in *New York Tribune* with the author's name as *Ludwig*.
2. **seraph** (in the *Bible*) a member of the highest order of angels
3. **sepulchre** = Sepulcher：grand grave, tomb
4. **dissever** separate. 爱伦·坡在这首诗中用词极简，使整首诗听起来像童话故事一样。同时又点缀了像seraph，sepulchre，dissever这样相对正式的词汇，增加了整首诗庄严肃穆的气氛。

参考译诗

安娜贝尔·李

很多很多年以前，
海边一个王国里，
君知住着一少女，
名叫安娜贝尔·李；
她在世上无杂念，
唯知与我相爱怜。

我们两人皆孩童，
住在海边王国里；
相爱程度比爱浓，
我和安娜贝尔·李；
天上六翼众天使，
垂涎我和我的李。

因为我们长相爱，
就在海边王国里，
云中吹出寒风来，
冻死我的漂亮李；
于是高贵亲属来，
从我手中掠她去，
墓穴把她关起来，
就在海边王国里。

天上天使并不悦，
开始妒忌她和我——
的确此因人人解，
（就在海边这王国。）
寒风乘夜云端起，
冻杀我的安娜·李。

但是我们爱更浓，
胜比我们年长者——
胜比几许智多星——
天上众多神天使，
海里无数怪妖精，
妄想拆散灵与魂！
我们生死不分离！

因为月辉带我梦，
梦见漂亮安娜·李；
除非见她明亮眸，
否则星辰难升起；
所以长夜邀我睡，
伴我新娘我的命，

就在海边墓穴内，
滔滔海边她墓内。

（李正栓　译）

思考题

1. *Annabel Lee* is often regarded as Poe's most beautiful poem and a perfect piece of "word music". Discusss why it is thus regarded.
2. The poem reads like a beautiful fairy tale. How does it achieve such an effect?
3. Libai, a Chinese poet in the Tang Dynasty, wrote *The River-Merchant's Wife: A Letter* (《长干行》), which also talks about the innocent childhood sweetheart. Make a comparative study of them.
4. Learn the first stanza by heart.

Henry Wadsworth Longfellow
亨利·瓦兹华斯·朗费罗
(1807–1882)

Henry Wadsworth Longfellow was the only American to be honored with a commemorative bust in the Poet's Corner of Westminster Abbey in London. He expressed pleasantly for many readers, the world over, the sincerity of pure morality, good tales well versified, and the everyday joys and sorrows of human life lovingly ornamented. His great virtue is his humility, and some of his best poems are *Paul Revere's Ride*, *The Village Black Smith*, *Evangeline*, *The Song of Hiawatha*, and *The Courtship of Miles Standish*.

Longfellow came from an old New England family, and lived comfortably in Portland, Maine. He attended Portland Academy and entered Bowdoin College, where he was a fellow classmate of Hawthorne. He published his first poem at 13, impelling him to make a career of writing. In college, he modeled his early literary ambition on Irving, who received him in Spain during a journey there. His linguistic abilities gained him a professorship at Bowdoin and, in 1834, at Harvard, after a trip to Europe to encounter Scandanavian and German romantic poetry. On the trip, his wife accompanied him, but died in childbirth. Returning, alone, to teach at Harvard, he mused about the charm of the galleries and cafes of Europe—its cathedrals, its romanticism and its history. He combined this sense of appreciation with a renewed sense of the colonial past of the New World. He seemed to have given the young civilization a cultural past by blending the unrealities of both worlds. He revered Europe and idealized the American past, and therefore provided for many readers a sense of pride in their heritage and culture. He published a semi-autobiographical romance in 1839. He remarried in 1843.

Always torn between being a teacher or a poet, Longfellow eventually resigned his post to James Russell Lowell in 1854. He settled at his home in Cambridge and completed *The Song of Hiawatha* (1855), and *The Courtship of Miles Standish* (1858), which popularized the legend of Plymouth Colony. These poems became extremely popular, increasing his appeal in Europe as well.

Longfellow's life was rooted in Cambridge and Boston. His great fame began with the publication of his first volume of poems, *Voices of the Night* (1839), which contained *A Psalm of Life*, one of the nineteenth century's best-loved poems. His reputation continued to grow with the appearance of *Ballads* (1841) which included *The Village Blacksmith*. Then came *Evangeline* (1847); *Hiawatha* (1855); *The Courtship of Miles Standish* (1858); and *Tales of a Wayside Inn* (1863).

Hawthorne placed him at "the head of our list of native poets," voicing the opinion of the vast number of readers who made Longfellow the most popular poet of his age. *Hiawatha* sold 30,000 copies in six months. When *The Courtship of Miles Standish* was published, more than 15,000 copies were sold the first day. Longfellow became a national institution. His seventy-fifth birthday was celebrated by school-children throughout the nation; people rose when he entered a room; gentlemen took off their hats in his presence. His poetry was translated throughout Europe; he was revered in England, where his popularity exceeded even that of Tennyson and Browning; and after his death his home became a literary shrine.

Longfellow transmitted European culture to his countrymen, popularized native American themes, and helped establish a national literature. His work was musical, mildly romantic, high-minded, and flavored with sentimental preachment. Yet the very qualities that brought excessive praise in his lifetime have since brought excessive reaction against him. His melodious measures are now condescendingly discounted as sing-song versification. He has been judged unduly didactic, passionless, and sweetly untouched by the social controversies of his time. As one of America's "schoolroom poets," Longfellow represented the ideals and aspirations of a young nation and a genteel tradition. He remains an index to a nineteenth-century culture whose ideals still survive, although its once-favorite poet has now been largely relegated to the elementary schoolroom. Here his masterful storytelling verses are still cherished as guides to genteel morality and as rhymed introductions to the legends of American history.

A Psalm of Life

WHAT THE HEART OF THE YOUNG MAN SAID TO THE PSALMIST

1

Tell me not, in mournful numbers[1],
Life is but an empty dream!
For the soul is dead that slumbers,
And things are not what they seem.

2

Life is real—Life is earnest—
And the grave is not its goal:
Dust thou art, to dust returnest,[2]
Was not spoken of the soul.

3

Not enjoyment, and not sorrow,
Is our destin'd end or way;
But to act, that each to-morrow
Find us farther than to-day.

4

Art is long, and time is fleeting,[3]
And our hearts, though stout and brave,
Still, like muffled drums, are beating
Funeral marches to the grave.

5

In the world's broad field of battle,
In the bivouac of Life,
Be not like dumb, driven cattle!
Be a hero in the strife!

6

Trust no Future, howe'er pleasant!
  Let the dead Past bury its dead!
Act—act in the glorious Present!
  Heart within, and God o'er head!

7

Lives of great men all remind us
  We can make our lives sublime,
And, departing, leave behind us
  Footsteps on the sands of time.

8

Footsteps, that, perhaps another,
  Sailing o'er life's solemn main,
A forlorn and shipwreck'd brother,
  Seeing, shall take heart again.

9

Let us then be up and doing,
  With a heart for any fate;
Still achieving, still pursuing,
  Learn to labor and to wait.

注释

1. **numbers** poetic meters, rhythms
2. **Dust thou art, to dust returnest** Dust thou art, and unto dust shalt thou. 你来自泥土，得重归泥土。
3. **Art is long, and time is fleeting** Adapted from *Aphorisms* of Hippocrates（希波拉底）, Greek physician. 希波拉底是希腊的名医（约公元前460–约公元前370），被称为“医药之父”，又是和苏格拉底和柏拉图齐名的著名哲学家。希波拉底的原句是：Ars longa, vita brevis. 翻译成英语是：Art is long, life is short.

参考译诗

生命礼赞

——青年人的心灵对赞歌作者所言

1

不要用哀婉的诗句对我说：
　人生只是梦幻一场!——
因为昏睡的灵魂不再有生活，
　而事物也不是表面的模样。

2

人生即真，不能虚度!
　坟墓并非人生追求的目标；
你来自尘土，归于尘土，
　这并非对灵魂的写照。

3

我们命运的道路或终点，
　不是享乐，也不是忧伤；
只是行动，并且每一个今天
　发现我们比前一个今天更加辉煌。

4

学艺须日久，时光飞如箭。
　我们的心尽管勇敢又坚强，
总像蒙住的鼓敲着
　葬礼的鼓点向死亡挺进并走向墓场。

5

在世界辽阔的战场，
　在人生临时的营站，
不要像无言无语任人驱使的牛羊!
　要在奋斗中做个英雄好汉！

6

别指望未来，不管它多么光明!
　让死的过去把死的事物埋葬!
行动吧，在活生生的现实中行动!
　赤心胸中存，上帝在天堂!

7

伟人的生平把我们提醒：
　我们能使生命崇高无限，
即使辞世去也留下身后美名，
　在时间的沙滩上留下脚印一串串。

8

或许另有人会看到这脚印，
　他在人生肃穆的航行中
偶遭不幸：船沉后只剩孤独一人，
　见这脚印便又有希望重生。

9

那么就让我们起来行动，
　准备一个应对一切命运的胸怀，
成就总是有但永处追求中，
　学会苦干还要学会等待。

（李正栓　译）

思考题

1. Tell the meaning of the poem in your own words.
2. What kind of advice does the poet give to people?
3. Choose three stanzas that you like and tell the reasons why you like them.
4. Learn the first two stanzas by heart.

Snow-Flakes

Out of the bosom of the Air,
Out of the cloud—folds of her garments shaken,
Over the woodlands brown and bare,
Over the harvest—fields forsaken,
    Silent, and soft, and slow
    Descends the snow.

Even as our cloudy fancies take
Suddenly shape in some divine expression,
Even as the troubled heart doth make
In the white countenance confession,
    The troubled sky reveals
    The grief it feels.

This is the poem of the air,
Slowly in silent syllables recorded;
This is the secret of despair,
Long in its cloudy bosom hoarded,
    Now whispered and revealed
    To wood and field.

雪　　花

从太空的胸怀，
从抖动的云衣褶缝，
飘过深褐色光秃的森林地带，
飘过收获后的田垄，

乘柔风，慢悠悠，无声响，
雪花在纷纷下降。

就像我们云一样的模糊虚幻
突然呈现出神圣的身影，
还像是我们内心焦虑不安，
脸色苍白中暴露出隐情，
这不安的天空
透露了自己的哀痛。

这是一首太空的诗，
用无声的音节来写成；
这诗隐藏了绝望的秘密，
这绝望已久藏在云的心中，
此刻他对森林和田野
正透露原委、正低声诉说。

（李正栓　译）

思考题

1. Identify the use of alliteration in the poem.
2. What does the poet try to convey in the poem?
3. Learn this poem by heart.

The Tide Rises, the Tide Falls

The tide rises, the tide falls,
The twilight darkens, the curlew calls;
Along the sea-sands damp and brown
The traveller hastens toward the town,
And the tide rises, the tide falls.

Darkness settles on roofs and walls,
But the sea, the sea in the darkness calls;
The little waves, with their soft, white hands,
Efface the footprints in the sands,
And the tide rises, the tide falls.

The morning breaks; the steeds in their stalls
Stamp and neigh, as the hostler calls;
The day returns, but nevermore
Returns the traveller to the shore,
And the tide rises, the tide falls.

参考译诗

潮起潮又落

潮起潮又落，
黄昏渐黑，鹬鸟哀歌；
沿着潮湿褐色的海滩
那旅人急匆匆往城镇赶，
潮起潮又落。

夜色栖落在墙壁和房顶，
大海仍在黑暗中轰鸣；
微波的手洁白柔软，
抹去沙滩上的脚印串串。
潮起潮又落。

东方已破晓，
厩里马儿踢踏嘶鸣，马夫喊叫；
白昼复旧，那旅人却永远

不能回到海岸。
　　潮起潮又落。

（李正栓　译）

思考题

1. What's the rhyme scheme of this poem?
2. What's the main idea of the poem?
3. What's the implication of "The tide rises, the tide falls"? What effect does the repetition produce?
4. Learn the poem by heart.

Walt Whitman
沃尔特·惠特曼
(1819–1892)

Both in theme and technique, Walt Whitman was an American poet. He extolled an emergent America, its expansion, its individualism and its Americanness. In technical terms, he added to the literary independence of the new nation by breaking free of the convention of the iambic pentameter and exhibiting a freedom in form.

In 1855, after first reading *Leaves of Grass*, Ralph Waldo Emerson wrote to Walt Whitman, "I am not blind to the worth of the wonderful gift of *Leaves of Grass*. I find it the most extraordinary piece of wit and wisdom that America has yet contributed... I greet you at the beginning of a great career, which yet must have had a long foreground somewhere, for such a start."

When *Leaves of Grass* was published in 1850, Whitman was thirty-six years old, and nothing in his "long foreground" suggested that he would write the greatest single book of poetry in American literary history. He was born in 1819 in a rural village on Long Island, New York. His parents were semiliterate and could give him little more than sympathy for political liberalism and a deistic faith shaped by the teachings of Quakerism. He had only five or six years of formal schooling, but he was a voracious reader of the nineteenth century novelists, the English romantic poets, the "classics" of European literature, and *The New Testament*. His teachers characterized him as a "dreamy and impractical youth", and he drifted through a series of jobs as an office boy, a printer, and a country schoolteacher. He had a natural talent for journalism. For a short time he edited a *Long Island* weekly newspaper and when he was twenty-two and attracted by the Bohemian life of Manhattan he went to New York City.

In New York, Whitman worked as a printer, an editor and a freelance journalist contributing essays, short stories, and poems to the popular newspapers and magazines of the 1840s. When he was twenty-seven he became editor of *The Brooklyn Daily Eagle*, but after only two years he was dismissed because of his radically liberal political views. He next made a brief visit to New Orleans, but he soon returned to

New York City, where he opened a printing office and stationery store and began to write his greatest poetry.

The first edition of *Leaves of Grass* contained twelve poems which Whitman himself reportedly had set in type and printed at his own expense. Few copies of his slim book of poetry were sold, yet those who read it were rarely indifferent. His apparently formless free-verse departures from poetic convention, his incantations and boasts, his sexuality, and his exotic and vulgar language caused critics to steep in the gentilities of the nineteenth century to label his work "poetry of barbarism" and warn that it was "not to be read aloud to a mixed audience."

From 1857 to 1859 Whitman edited the *Brooklyn Times*, and undaunted by the critical response to the first edition, he reworked *Leaves of Grass*, publishing expanded second and third editions in 1856 and 1860. When the Civil War began, he traveled south to Washington D.C., where he obtained an appointment as a government clerk and worked as a volunteer nurse, a "wound-dresser", in nearby military hospitals. While living in Washington he published *Drum-Taps* (1865), Civil War poems that he gathered into the fourth edition of *Leaves of Grass* (1867).

By the appearance of the fifth edition (1871), Whitman's poetry had begun to receive increasing critical recognition in England and America. He had come to see his work as a single "poem" to be revised and improved through a lifetime, but in 1873, when he was fifty-four, he suffered a paralytic stroke. He moved from Washington D.C. to his brother's home in Camden, New Jersey, and there, declining in his poetic abilities and cared for by a small group of devoted friends, Whitman spent most of the remaining nineteen years of his life, revising successive editions of *Leaves of Grass* until the final version was published shortly before his death in 1892.

The more than four hundred poems that had appeared in the nine editions of *Leaves of Grass* printed in Whitman's lifetime were unprecedented in American literature. They were a compound of commonplaces, of disorganized and raw experience, of sentimentalism, and of true poetic inspiration. They were filled with "barbaric yawps". They had ecstatic perceptions of man and nature, united and divine. Whitman had an expansive oceanic vision, an urgent desire to incorporate the entire American experience into his life and into poetry. He aspired to be a cosmic consciousness, to experience and glorify all humanity and all human qualities, including "sex, womanhood, maternity, lusty animations, organs, acts."

He had yearned to be the "bard of democracy," a public poet celebrated by democratic men "en-masse", but while he lived, the bulk of his poetry was read only by the literary enthusiasts and intellectuals. In his final years, Whitman's devoted followers solemnized him as "The Good Gray Poet". He became a national figure, America's whiskery sage, but the wide popularity he had yearned to have nonetheless escaped him. He was defeated in his greatest literary ambitions, yet his poems came to exert more influence on modern American poetry than the work of any other writer. Whitman had been a radically new poet, had made his own rhythms, created his own mythic world, and in writing his sprawling epic of American democracy he helped make possible the free-verse unorthodoxies and the private literary intensities of a twentieth century world that would one day come to honor him as one of the great poets of all time.

O Captain! My Captain![1]

O captain! My Captain! our fearful trip is done,
The ship has weather'd every rack, the prize we sought is won,
The port is near, the bells I hear, the people all exulting,
While follow eyes the steady keel, the vessel grim and daring;
  But O heart! heart! heart!
    O the bleeding drops of red!
      Where on the deck my Captain lies,
        Fallen cold and dead.

O Captain! my Captain! rise up and hear the bells;
Rise up—for you the flag is flung—for you the bugle trills,
For you bouquets and ribbon'd wreaths—for you the shores
  crowding,

For you they call, the swaying mass, their eager faces turning;
  Here, Captain! dear father!
    This arm beneath your head;
      It is some dream that on the deck
        You've fallen cold and dead.

My Captain does not answer, his lips are pale and still,
My father does not feel my arm, he has no pulse nor will,
The ship is anchor'd safe and sound, its voyage closed and done;
From fearful trip the victor ship comes in with object won;
  Exult, O shores! And ring, O bells!
    But I, with mournful tread,
      Walk the deck my Captain lies,
        Fallen cold and dead.

注释

1. 这首诗是为纪念林肯而作的，以一个掌舵的船长来比喻林肯再贴切不过。本诗非常出名，引起很多人模仿它的形式和字句。

参考译诗

啊，船长！我的船长！

啊，船长！我的船长！可怕的航程已完成；
这船历尽风险，企求的目标已达成。
港口在望，钟声响，人们在欢欣。
千万双眼睛注视着船——平稳，勇敢，坚定。
  但是痛心啊！痛心！痛心！
    瞧一滴滴鲜红的血！
      甲板上躺着我的船长，
        他倒下去，冰冷，永别。

啊！船长！我的船长！起来吧，倾听钟声；
起来吧，号角为您长鸣，旌旗为您高悬；
迎着您，多少花束花圈——候着您，千万人蜂拥岸边；
他们向您高呼，拥来挤去，仰起殷切的脸；
　啊，船长！亲爱的父亲！
　　我的手臂托着您的头！
　　　莫非是一场梦：在甲板上
　　　　您倒下去，冰冷，永别。

我的船长不作声，嘴唇惨白，毫不动弹；
我的父亲没感到我的手臂，没有脉搏，没有遗言；
船舶抛锚停下，平安抵达；航程终了；
历尽艰险返航，夺得胜利目标。
　啊！岸上钟声齐鸣，啊！人们一片欢腾！
　　但是，我在甲板上，在船长身旁，
　　　心悲切，步履沉重：
　　　　因为他倒下去，冰冷，永别。

（杨霖　译）

思考题

1. Explain the four metaphors in the poem: captain, ship, trip and prize.
2. Why does Whitman use the traditional metrical pattern in this poem instead of the free verse he loves?
3. What is the tone of the poem?

I Hear America Singing

I hear America singing, the varied carols I hear,
Those of mechanics, each one singing his as
　　it should be blithe and strong,

The carpenter singing his as he measures his
plank or beam,
The mason singing his as he makes ready for
work, or leaves off work,
The boatman singing what belongs to him in
his boat, the deckhand singing on the
steamboat deck,
The shoemaker singing as he sits on his
bench, the hatter singing as he stands,
The wood-cutter's song, the ploughboy's on
his way in the morning, or at noon
intermission or at sundown,
The delicious singing of the mother, or of
the young wife at work, or of the girl
sewing or washing,
Each singing what belongs to him or her and
to none else,
The day what belongs to the day—at night
the party of young fellows, robust, friendly,
Singing with open mouths their strong
melodious songs.

参考译诗

我听见美利坚国在歌唱

我听见美利坚在歌唱，听见各种颂歌在回响：
机械工在唱，每个人都心情愉快、歌声嘹亮；
木匠在唱，边唱歌边把木板和大梁来丈量；
泥瓦匠在唱，上工前后都在唱；
船夫在唱船上事，水手歌唱在汽艇甲板上；
鞋匠坐着凳子把歌唱，帽匠站在店铺里唱；

伐木工、农村青年清晨走路、中午时分、黄昏回家都在唱；
母亲在甜唱，少妇在边工作边唱，少女在边缝洗边唱；
每个人都在唱自己关心而不属于别人的事；
白天唱着白天的事，夜里身强力壮互相友好的青年人
张口大唱，歌声悦耳、雄壮嘹亮。

（李正栓　译）

思考题

1. What kind of people does Whitman describe?
2. Why is almost everyone singing?
3. What does the title of the poem mean?
4. In terms of rhythm and rhyme scheme, what is new in this poem?
5. Do you like such free verse?
6. Is free verse really free?

I Sit and Look Out

I sit and look out upon all the sorrows of the world, and upon
all oppression and shame,
I hear secret convulsive sobs[1] from young men at anguish with
themselves, remorseful after deeds done,
I see in low life the mother misused by her children, dying,
neglected, gaunt, desperate,
I see the wife misused by her husband, I see the treacherous[2]
seducer of young women,
I mark the ranklings[3] of jealousy and unrequited love[4]
attempted to be hid, I see these sights on the earth,
I see the workings of battle, pestilence[5], tyranny, I see martyrs[6]
and prisoners,
I observe a famine at sea, I observe the sailors casting lots who

shall be kill'd to preserve the lives of the rest,
I observe the slights and degradations cast by arrogant persons
upon laborers, the poor, and upon negroes, and the like;
All these—all the meanness and agony without end I sitting
look out upon,
See, hear, and am silent.

注释

1. **convulsive sobs** very sad, uncontrollable crying
2. **treacherous** disloyal, deceitful
3. **ranklings** 极度的怨恨。rankle: make resentful or angry
4. **unrequited love** love of one person which was not reciprocated by the other sex.
5. **pestilence** a disease that causes death and spreads swiftly
6. **martyrs** a person who by his death or sufferings proves the strength of his belief

参考译诗

我坐着眺望

我坐着眺望世间的一切悲苦、
一切压迫和羞辱，
我听见年轻人因悔恨往事而痛苦时
暗中发出抽搐的呜咽，
我看见卑微的母亲为子女所折磨而奄奄待毙，
无人照应、消瘦如柴、濒临绝境，
我看见受丈夫虐待的妻子，我看见
诱骗青年妇女的奸诈之徒，
我注视着企图掩盖的嫉妒和单恋的痛苦，
我看见芸芸众生，
我看见战争、瘟疫、暴政，我看见
殉教者和囚徒，
我望见海上发生饥荒，水手们在拈阄决定
谁作牺牲来保全他人的性命，

我看见傲慢自大的人们加于劳动者、穷人、黑人
等人身上的轻蔑和侮辱，
我坐着眺望这一切——
一切无尽无休的丑行和痛苦，
我看着、听着，我默然。

（李正栓　译）

思考题

1. What are the main techniques used in the poem?
2. What is the basic tone in this poem?

Emily Dickinson
艾米莉·狄金森
(1830–1886)

Like Whitman, Emily Dickinson was American in theme and technique. But unlike Whitman, Dickinson explored the inner life of the individual.

Only eight of Emily Dickinson's poems were published while she lived, and it was not until the appearance of *Poems by Emily Dickinson* (1890), four years after her death, that her work became available to the general reading public for the first time. Some reviewers found the poetry "balderdash" suffering from lack of rhyme, faulty grammar, and incomprehensible metaphors, a "farrago of illiterate and uneducated sentiment." But other readers found them remarkably pointed and evocative. As the years passed and as more poems were published, critical estimates grew more favorable until, with the publication of all her known poetry, in *The Poems of Emily Dickinson* (1955), the shy, reclusive poet had come to be regarded, with Whitman and Poe, as one of America's greatest lyric poets.

The range of Emily Dickinson's worldly experience was small by any standard. Her entire life, except for brief visits to nearby Boston and to Washington D.C., was spent in and around her birthplace, Amherst.

As she grew older, she increasingly withdrew from society, seldom leaving her garden and her large family house. There she wrote poems and letters to her friends and watched the life of the town from her upstairs bedroom window. Her friends, she said, were her "estate", and among them were men, other than Higginson, her father, and her brother, who profoundly affected her creative and emotional life. One of them was her second "preceptor", the Reverend Charles Wadsworth, whom she met in Philadelphia in the mid-1850s, (the first being Higginson who remained her friend and adviser). The facts of their relationship are obscure, but there is little doubt about her love for him and for his "kindly spiritual counsel", although they seldom met, and he was a married man with a family. His departure to California perhaps caused the emotional crisis she experienced in 1862, provoking a great creative outburst, for in that single year she wrote the astonishing total of 366 poems.

Dickinson lived a more intense and passionate life than was thought by neighbors and acquaintances who saw her only as an eccentric maiden lady, the "moth" of Amherst, dressed only in white, who flitted almost ghostlike through her house and garden. Not even those closest to her knew fully the depth and extent of her emotions or that the nearly 1,800 poems, tied neatly in packets found after her death, would reveal an immensely complex and passionate sensibility.

Her subjects were love, death, nature, immortality and beauty. Written largely in meters common to Protestant hymn books, her poems employed irregular rhythms, off-or-slant-rhymes, paradox, and a careful balancing of abstract Latinate and concrete Anglo-Saxon words. Her lines were gnomic and her images kinesthetic, highly concentrated, and intensely charged with feeling. Her greatest lyrics were on the theme of death, which she typically personified as a monarch, a lord, or a kindly but irresistible lover, yet her moods varied widely, from melancholy to exuberance, grief to joy, and leaden despair to spiritual intoxication.

Dickinson's poetry at times descended to coyness and sentimentality. She had no first-hand contact with contemporary writers or critics of the highest order. Her favorite authors included Shakespeare, Keats, the Brownings, Ruskin and Sir Thomas Browne, whose uneasy balance of faith and skepticism she shared. Early in life she rebelled against the Calvinism of the Amherst Congregational Church, yet she retained the Calvinist tendency to look inwardly, and she had a Calvinist sense of both the inherent beauty and the frightening coldness of the world. With her fellow New Englanders Jonathan Edwards and Emerson, she perceived beauty in the wholeness and harmonious relationships of nature, and like Edwards and Emerson she has come to stand as a dominant figure in her nation's literary history, a poet whose work reflects a spiritual unrest and a sense of the human predicament that defy all easy categories.

A Bird Came Down the Walk

A Bird came down the Walk—
He did not know I saw—
He bit an Angleworm in halves
And ate the fellow, raw,

And then he drank a Dew
From a convenient Grass—
And then hopped sidewise to the Wall
To let a Beetle pass—

He glanced with rapid eyes
That hurried all around—
They looked like frightened Beads, I thought—
He stirred his Velvet Head

Like one in danger, Cautious,
I offered him a Crumb
And he unrolled his feathers
And rowed him softer home—

Than Oars divide the Ocean,
Too silver for a seam—
Or Butterflies, off Banks of Noon
Leap, plashless as they swim.

参考译诗

鸟儿沿着小径过来

一只鸟儿沿着小径走过来——
他不知道我已看见他——
他把一条蚯蚓撕成两段,
活生生地把这家伙吞下。

之后他从就近的草上
吸喝了一滴露珠——
之后跳到一旁的墙下,
为了给一只甲虫让路。

他用眼快速扫视
看了看四周——
双眼像受了惊的珠子——
之后他晃了晃毛茸茸的头

我像在险境时小心翼翼地
给他投了点面包渣子,
他却张开翅膀
像划着船桨轻轻地回到家里。

但比起划桨破海水
更为轻柔,不留痕迹——
或像正午岸边的蝴蝶
不激起一点浪花就能腾翼飞起。

(李正栓　译)

思考题

1. What is the image of the bird? Why is it so vigilant?

2. What do "I" think of the bird?
3. How does the poet describe the bird's home-going?
4. Which stanza do you like best? Why? Learn the first stanza by heart.
5. Emily Dickinson is often entitled "American Li Qingzhao". Why?

I Died for Beauty

I died for Beauty—but was scarce
Adjusted in the Tomb
When One who died for Truth, was lain
In an adjoining Room—

He questioned softly "Why I failed"?
"For Beauty", I replied—
"And I—for Truth—Themself are One—
We Bretheren, are", He said—

And so, as Kinsmen, met a Night—
We talked between the Rooms—
Until the Moss had reached our lips—
And covered up—our names—

我为美而死

我为美而死——但还不怎么
适应坟墓里的生活，
这时一个为真理而死的人
被安放在隔壁墓室里。

他柔声问我我为什么失败而亡；

"为了美"，我回答说——
"我——为了真理——美和真一样——
我们俩是兄弟"，他说。

就这样，像近亲在夜里相遇——
我们隔墙而谈——
直到青苔把我们的嘴封闭——
将我们的名字埋掩——

（李正栓　译）

思考题

1. For what did the speaker die?
2. How did the speaker feel when she found a neighbor?
3. What is the relationship between Beauty and Truth?
4. What does the poet want to express here?
5. Learn the whole poem by heart.

"Hope" Is the Thing with Feathers[1]

"Hope" is the thing with feathers—
That perches[2] in the soul—
And sings the tune without the words—
And never stops—at all—

And sweetest—in the Gale[3]—is heard—
And sore must be the storm—
That could abash[4] the little Bird
That kept so many warm—

I've heard it in the chillest land[5]—

And on the strangest sea[6]—
Yet, never, in extremity,
It asked a crumb[7]—of Me.

注释

1. Emily Dickinson is good at describing abstract thing by making them concrete. In this poem, she compares the abstract "hope" to a concrete appearance—a bird, which can fly far and high.
2. **perch** (a bird) to come to rest from flying, to go into the stated position. 狄金森用了很多用来描述小鸟动作的词生动地刻画了"希望有如小鸟"这一核心比喻。
3. **Gale** strong and violent wind.
4. **abash** to cause to feel uncomfortable or ashamed in the presence of others
5. **the chillest land** the severest state, the most difficult situation
6. **the strangest sea** the most unexpected places
7. **crumb** very small amount of reward

参考译诗

"希望"是个长着羽毛的东西

"希望"是个长着羽毛的东西——
它栖息在灵魂之中——
唱着没有歌词的旋律——
永远唱个不停——

大风中——能听到——最美的歌声——
暴风雨肯定最让人心痛——
令那只小鸟惊惧
它却曾使多人感到暖意——

在最寒冷的陆地，我听到它——
在最陌生的海上，我听到它——
在即便是绝境中，
连面包碎屑它也不向我索取。

（李正栓　译）

思考题

1. What is the central metaphor in the poem?
2. What are the functions of the dashes in Dickinson's poems?
3. Why is Dickinson regarded as one of the precursors of modern imagism?

Nature, the Gentlest Mother[1]

Nature, the gentlest mother,
Impatient of no child,
The feeblest or the waywardest[2],—
Her admonition[3] mild

In forest and the hill
By traveller is heard,
Restraining rampant[4] squirrel
Or too impetuous[5] bird.

How fair her conversation,
A summer afternoon,—
Her household, her assembly;
And when the sun goes down,

Her voice among the aisles
Incites the timid prayer
Of the minutest[6] cricket,
The most unworthy flower.

When all the children sleep
She turns as long away
As will suffice to light her lamps;

Then, bending from the sky

With infinite affection
And infinite care,
Her golden finger on her lip,
Wills silence everywhere.

注释

1. Emily here gives nature a concrete image—a mother with all virtues.
2. **waywardest** self-willed, not easily controlled or guided
3. **admonition** warning, scolding
4. **rampant** beyond control, unchecked
5. **impetuous** moving quickly or violently, said or done hastily
6. **minutest** very small, tiny and humble

参考译诗

自然，最温柔的母亲

自然，最温柔的母亲，
对所有孩子都那么耐心，
即使孩子最柔弱或最任性，
她的训诫均似细雨柔风。

在树林里，在小山中，
每位旅者都可以倾听，
她在驯服猖獗的松鼠，
或者鲁莽冒失的飞禽。

她的话语总是那么公平，
在夏日的午后，
在家里或是在聚会中，
抑或是夕阳西下的光景。

她的声音回荡在过道中，
激发最小型的蟋蟀，
和最卑微的花朵
开始祈祷，羞怯但是虔诚。

当所有的孩子进入梦境，
母亲转身离去，
边点亮夜空中的繁星，
然后俯下身躯。

满怀无限的关爱，
和无限的柔情，
把金色的手指放在唇边，
让一切回归寂静。

（张青梅　译）

思考题

1. What is nature compared to? Do you think this comparison proper?
2. In what way is nature fair and gentle?
3. Learn the last stanza by heart.

Edwin Arlington Robinson
埃德温·阿灵顿·罗宾逊
（1869–1935）

When Robinson was born, American literature was flourishing with fictional works. Francis Harte, Mark Twain and Henry James were all at the summit of their creation. It was the time when the novel had developed into full scale and poetry had entered an era confronted with crises: poets were no longer being honored as the King's respected guests. Because of the rapid development of industry, poets were forced to try any new themes or styles possible for their survival, to have a revolution of language so as to reconstruct poetry in a new literary form. This is why Robinson, as the transitional poet of the time, was not recognized as a poet of the first class until he won the Pulitzer Prize in 1922 for his *Collected Poems*.

Robinson, whose initials spell E. A. R. (ear), was ironically born deaf in one ear. He was born on December 22 in Head Tide, but grew up in Gardiner, Maine. He was a descendant of Anne Bradstreet. After a lonely childhood, Robinson managed to enter Harvard University where he stayed for two years, which, though not enough for creating a prominent poet, widened his eyesight and brought him some new friends and new ideas.

Robinson's only ambition was to become a poet. However, being introspective by nature and poor in health, he was always lonely. While fond of his family, he felt himself an outsider among the other members. Friendship seemed a great favor, and he always felt alienated from the society of his own. As a result, his life was often isolated and miserable.

Fortunately, Robinson, even in the darkest part of his time, did not give up his belief in man's highest duty that each one is to develop his best attributes as fully as possible. Being by nature introspective and conscious of psychological depth, Robinson, the one who was often at a loss as a social creature, was actually rather quick and accurate in catching and interpreting the spiritual world of human beings. With his wide reading of classic works and the influence of Thomas Hardy, Robinson succeeded in bringing his attributes to the summit by winning the Pulitzer Prize in 1922, in spite of the pessimistic mood in most of his works.

For Robinson, the year 1921 was a dividing line. Before 1921, several volumes of poems were published but attracted little public attention, though President Roosevelt helped him to get a better job after reading his poems. In 1921, his *Collected Poems,* poems about wasted, or impoverished life in American society, was published and brought him his first Pulitzer Prize.

From 1921, his career as a poet was smooth. *The Man Who Dies Twice* came out in 1924 and gained him a second Pulitzer Prize.

Three years later, a long narrative poem, *Tristram* (1927) won him the Pulitzer Prize for the third time.

Richard Cory[1]

Whenever Richard Cory went down town,
We people on the pavement looked at him:
He was a gentleman from sole to crown[2],
Clean favored[3], and imperially slim.

And he was always quietly arrayed[4],
And he was always human when he talked;
But still he fluttered pulses when he said
"Good-morning," and he glittered when he walked.

And he was rich—yes, richer than a king—
And admirably schooled in every grace[5]:
In fine[6], we thought that he was everything
To make us wish that we were in his place.

So on we worked, and waited for the light,

And went without the meat, and cursed the bread;
And Richard Cory, one calm summer night,
Went home and put a bullet through his head.

注释

1. The poem was published in 1897. The turn of the century was a period full of crises, including the snapping of the American Dream. The futility of human life is the very frequent theme of Robinson. He created out of the model of his hometown, a naturalistic world, Tilbury town, where life seemed futile and meaningless. Richard Cory is one of the Tilbury town characters that Robinson created "to hold up some fragment of humanity for a moment's contemplation."
2. **a gentleman from sole to crown** (he was) gentlemanlike from top to feet; (he was) a standard gentleman. 罗宾逊用了"crown, imperially, king"等字眼暗示理查德·科里出身高贵，为衬托他的和蔼随和制造了悬念。
3. **Clean favored** clean and tidy; neat and elegant in appearance
4. **quietly arrayed** properly dressed. 用quietly 形容科里的穿着打扮，运用了通感，突出他的穿着很有品味，不奢华，低调但很优雅。
5. **admirably schooled in every grace** well educated and strictly trained in all manners and in every aspects
6. **In fine** to make a long story short; in short

参考译诗

理查·科里

理查·科里走在大街上，
我们驻足路旁把他看：
他绅士气派、仪表堂堂，
他从脚到头，苗条若仙。

他穿着朴素不彰显，
谈吐文雅又达理；
他向人们问"早安"，
声音令人悦，步态光四溢。

家缠万贯胜国王——

学问美德令人羡：
人间一切唯他强
令人欲把其位换。

我们苦苦劳作盼荣光，
无肉可吃，诅咒面包坏；
一个宁静夏天的晚上，
他回家，枪推子弹穿脑袋。

（李正栓　译）

思考题

1. What kind of person is Richard Cory?
2. What is the theme of the poem?
3. Why did Richard Cory kill himself?
4. Could you find some other Chinese versions of this poem?
5. Learn the second stanza by heart.

Miniver Cheevy[1]

Miniver Cheevy, child of scorn,
Grew lean while he assailed the seasons[2];
He wept that he was ever born;
And he had reasons.

Miniver loved the days of old
When swords were bright and steeds were prancing;
The vision of a warrior bold
Would set him dancing

Miniver sighed for what was not,
And dreamed, and rested from his labors;

He dreamed of Thebes[3] and Camelot[4],
And Priam's neighbors[5].

Miniver mourned the ripe renown
That made so many a name so fragrant;
He mourned Romance, now on the town,
And Art, a vagrant.

Miniver loved the Medici[6],
Albeit he had never seen one;
He would have sinned incessantly
Could he have been one.

Miniver cursed the commonplace
And eye a khaki suit[7] with loathing;
He missed the medieval grace
Of iron clothing[8].

Miniver scorned the gold he sought,
But sore annoyed was he without it;
Miniver thought, and thought, and thought,
And thought about it.

Miniver Cheevy, born too late,
Scratched his head and kept on thinking;
Miniver coughed, and called it fate,
And kept on drinking.

1. **Miniver Cheevy** sound rather similar to "mini achiever", is the lively sketch of an ambitious and cynical young man who believed he would be successful in any other

age but the present one. 这首诗生动刻画了一个用世俗的眼光看一事无成的弥尼沃·切维。他雄心勃勃地认为在任何其他时代他都会功成名就，唯独他所在的时代不能给他的成功提供条件。

2. **assailed the seasons** kill the time. 作为一个愤世嫉俗的青年，弥尼沃·切维步履艰辛，度日如年。
3. **Thebes** capital city in Boeotia, rival of ancient Athens and Sparta
4. **Camelot** the legendary court of king Arthur and the knights of the Round Table located close to the present Winchester.
5. **Priam's neighbors** Priam: the last king of Troy; Priam's neighbors refer to the neighboring countries of Troy. In this poem, together with Priam, they all indicate the embodiments of ancient heroes.
6. **Medici** Family of wealthy merchants, statesmen and art patrons in Renaissance Florence. Many businessmen, politicians and literary men came from the family and some of them were notorious for ruthlessness and sinfulness.
7. **khaki suit** military uniform of a yellowish brown color; the military uniform of modern time
8. **iron clothing** ancient military uniform made of iron; armor and helmet

弥尼沃·切维

弥尼沃·切维怨天又怨地，
　　他终日虚度，身材削瘦，
他常恨自己生不逢时，
　　他却哭得有理由。

弥尼沃喜欢遥远古日子：
　　那时候，宝剑锋利，战马奔腾，
想象着勇敢的战士
　　便会点燃他狂热的激情。

他慨叹不是其中一员，
　　心神恍惚，荒废手中的活计，
梦见古城底比斯，又梦见亚瑟王的宫殿，
　　还梦见普里阿摩斯的古邻居。

弥尼沃悲痛那远扬的名声，
　　它使无数美名如此传世流芳；

他悲叹传奇文学遗废城，
　　他哀叹艺术沦落于丐帮。

弥尼沃热爱梅第奇这家族，
　　尽管家族风貌从未看见。
倘若真能属于这家族，
　　他也会罪孽累累不间断。

弥尼沃诅咒这平凡界，
　　看见黄色军装就生恨，
他盼望中世纪优雅永不灭，
　　他思念铁甲铠衣威风凛凛。

弥尼沃鄙视自己聚巨财，
　　无财富，他又忧恨心中生；
他思来想去又思来，
　　试图把这事想明白。

生不逢时的弥尼沃
　　骚首皱眉又思索；
他咳嗽完后认了命
　　杯复一杯酒不停。

（李正栓，韩志华　译）

思考题

1. This poem is often regarded as the poet's self-portraiture. Why?
2. Robinson's poems are characterized by a striking ironic tone. Illustrate the tone in the poem.
3. Why are well-known places and people mentioned in the poem?
4. Comment on the character of Miniver Cheevy.
5. Find some other translations of this poem and compare them.
6. Learn the last two stanzas by heart.

Stephen Crane
斯蒂芬·克兰
(1871–1900)

In spite of the limitation of a short life, Stephen Crane was well-known as the first American Naturalist novelist. However, another surprise is that, besides novels, Crane also contributed some valuable poems to the literary history of the States.

Crane was born in Newark, New Jersey, the 14th and the youngest child of a Methodist clergyman's family. Though sickly and frail in appearance from the very beginning, Crane was a rebel in the religious, conventional family. He attended the university but devoted more time to sports than to his studying of any curriculum and thus, he left the school and started his writing career as a roving reporter. His first novel *Maggie, a Girl in the Street* was published in 1893 at his own expense. The book, though later regarded as the first naturalist work in American literary history, was rejected by both the editors and the critics due to its stark description of the seamy side of the society. Crane's fame as a writer came to him in 1895 with the publication of his second novel *The Red Badge of Courage*. The revealing, alarming honesty of the effects of war on a raw recruit won the appreciation of such prominent writers as Howells and Henry James, and what's more, it won the admiration of some veterans of the Civil War.

As a poet, Crane was recognized also in the same year with the publication of his first collection of poems *The Black Riders and Other Lines*, which was, as a matter of fact, composed in very experimental form and with many startling images and appeared too unconventional to be widely accepted. His second volume of poetry came out in 1899 under the title of *War Is Kind*. Crane died of tuberculosis in Germany on June 5, 1900 at the age of 29. It is a pity he died too early; however, as a very diligent writer, Crane contributed to the world novels, short stories, and poetry of about 12 volumes.

Probably due to his poor health, Crane was by nature a pessimist. Influenced by Charles Darwin's Evolution Theory, Crane believed that when God died and people are left alone in an indifferent or even hostile world, and when a human's fate is completely decided by heredity and environment, where might is power, human beings are rather helpless and nothing like dignity or honor is able to exist before the crushing forces of nature. Consequently, as a person with social responsibility, Crane took up his pen to expose the cruelty of modern society by interpreting the naturalist ideas in various written forms and thus became a pioneer in the American naturalist tradition.

Whether as a novelist, short story teller, or a poet, Crane dwelt on the depiction of the truth of the harsher realities of American life.

Insisting in telling the truth at all costs, Crane made every effort to report reality, truthfully and objectively, to expose the darkness of the world. As a result, the tone of his works is often pessimistic and gloomy.

With the influence of the impressionistic painters, Crane was good at taking advantage from private symbols, namely picking an object from an experience and giving it a symbolic meaning. This exerted a significant influence on later imagist poetry and his poetic works were hence recognized as the earliest imagist poetry.

In his novels as well as in poetry, Crane tells everything directly but vividly. His syntax is usually simple; however, he is very careful in choosing a narrative point of view. Most frequently, Crane would start from a scientific observer's view to present nature's indifference to man, or to record the physical, emotional, and intellectual response of man under extreme pressure.

Black Riders Came from the Sea[1]

Black riders came from the sea.
There was clang and clang of spear and shield,
And clash and clash of hoof and heel,
Wild shouts and the wave of hair
In the rush upon the wind:
Thus the ride of Sin.

注释

1. This is the first poem in *Black Riders Came from the Sea* (1895).

参考译诗

黑色骑手来自海上

黑色骑手来自海上。
盾矛叮当响，
蹄根闪闪亮，
匆忙赶来落狂风，
呼喊狂，发飞扬：
罪恶骑来也这样。

（李正栓　译）

思考题

1. What do “black riders” symbolize?
2. What figures of speech are used in the poem to make it rhythmical though without rhyme?
3. Why is Stephen Crane regarded as one of the precursors of imagism in America? Can you find some clues from this poem?
4. Learn this poem by heart.

I Walked in a Desert[1]

I walked in a desert.
And I cried,
“Ah, God, take me from this place!”
A voice said, “It is no desert.”
I cried, “Well, But—
The sand, the heat, the vacant horizon.”
A voice said, “It is no desert.”

注释

1. This poem was published in 1905 in the volume *The Black Rider & Other Lines*.

参考译诗

我走在沙漠里

我走在沙漠里
大声呼唤
“主啊，带我离开！”
有个声音传来，“这不是沙漠。”
我呼唤：“可是，那——
沙粒、炙热和空旷的地平线。”
有个声音传来，“这不是沙漠。”

（张青梅　译）

思考题

1. What kind of world is revealed in the poem?
2. This following line is repeated in the poem: A voice said, “It is no desert.” What does it intensify?
3. Learn this poem by heart.

William Carlos Williams
威廉·卡洛斯·威廉姆斯
(1883–1963)

William Carlos Williams, whose fame as a poet paralleled that of Ezra Pound and T. S. Eliot, was a physician factually all his adult life.

Dr. Williams was born in Rutherford, New Jersey, and studied medicine at the University of Pennsylvania, where he came into contact with two masters of imagism: Ezra Pound and Hilda Doolittle, whose imagist ideals had a tremendous impact on Williams' early poetic works. Nevertheless, as a professional physician, he derived from his practice of medicine the knowledge of people that inspired the best of his poems. With a special knowledge of humanity and a diagnostic reserve towards the frailty or strength of mankind, Williams soon distinguished himself as a poet who was able to illustrate a probing and clinical realism by seeking beauty and truth in plain reality.

As a poet, though overshadowed by Pound and T.S. Eliot all his life, he had been experimenting to give up the conventional and metaphysical interest, and seek signs of permanence in the local and concrete by applying the natural American idiom and the variable rhythms and vocabulary, by concerning himself with the ordinary, the commonplace, and the specific American atmosphere.

While busily occupied with his engrossing medical practice, Williams managed to compose more than 25 volumes of fictional and poetic works. His first published work is *Poems,* a collection of his early works, coming out in 1909. It was very poorly accepted by the public. However, it started the composition of poems of a long list: the collection was followed up by a lot of others, among them, the most popular are *The Tempers* (1909), *Kora in Hell* (1920), *Sour Grapes* (1921), *Spring and All* (1922), *Complete Collected Poems* (1938), *The Desert Music* (1954), *Journey to Love* (1955) and *Pictures from Brueghel* (1963), which brought him the Pulitzer Prize of the year. Above all else, he accomplished *Paterson*, a tremendous epic of 5 volumes (1946, 1948, 1949, 1951, 1958). The poetic fragments he left were compiled into the 6th volume posthumously in 1963.

This Is Just To Say

I have eaten
the plums
that were in
the icebox

and which
you were probably
saving
for breakfast

Forgive me
they were delicious
so sweet
and so cold

参考译诗

也就是说

我吃掉了
那些李子
他们原本放在
冰箱里

这些
可能是你准备
早餐要吃的美食

原谅我

真好吃
真甜
真凉

（李正栓　译）

思考题

1. This is one of the many "found poems" by Williams. Make comments on this "found poem".
2. In what way is this poem different from other poems?
3. Learn this poem by heart.

Spring and All

By the road to the contagious hospital[1]
under the surge of the blue
mottled[2] clouds driven from the
northeast—a cold wind. Beyond, the
waste of broad, muddy fields.
brown with dried weeds, standing fallen
patches of standing water
the scattering of tall trees

All along the road the reddish
purplish, forked, upstanding, twiggy
stuff of bushes and small trees
with dead, brown leaves under them
leafless vines—

Lifeless in appearance, sluggish[3]
dazed spring approaches—

They enter the new world naked,
cold, uncertain of all
save that they enter. All about them
the cold, familiar wind—

Now the grass, tomorrow[4]
the stiff curl of windcarrot leaf
one by one objects are defined[5]—
It[6] quickens: clarity, outline of leaf

But now the stark dignity of
Entrance—still, the profound change
has come upon them: rooted, they
grip down[7] and begin to awaken.

注释

1. **contagious hospital** contagious: disease that can be spread by contact. 象征疾病和死亡。
2. **mottled** marked with spots or areas with different colors
3. **sluggish** slow, having little motion; inert. 生动表现了春天的步伐在开始时候的状态。
4. **Now the grass, tomorrow** 春天的步伐加快了，每天都有新气象。
5. **one by one objects are defined** the leaves, the grass, etc. take shape one by one with the coming of spring.
6. **It** refers to the pace of spring
7. **grip down** takes a firm hold of soil and root in it. 表现了春天勃勃的生命力。

参考译诗

春天和全部

在去传染病院途中，
抬望蓝天：
云彩斑驳飘自

东北方——冷风吹来。眺望远处：
广阔泥泞的荒田，
枯叶棕黄，像宁静倒落的
一片一片的死水潭，
树木参天处处现。

一路上，那红色的、
紫色的、劈了叉的、挺直而上的、多枝的
灌木丛和小树，
树下枯叶棕红，
藤蔓裸枝——

春天来了：
面无生机、慵懒疲惫，行动迟缓。

这一切景物也进入春天，赤裸裸，
冷冰冰，对一切无把握，
只知他们进来了。周围尽是
野风凄寒，司空见惯——

现在，是草，明天，
僵僵的卷叶，就象萝卜叶，
一件一件，清晰可辨——
春天催发：叶有轮廓，形状可见。

现在，这样进入春天，
十足的尊严——还有，深刻的变化
已发生在它们身上：根深扎，它们
紧抓着大地，生机勃发。

（李正栓，韩志华 译）

思考题

1. Why does the poem give mixed images of the winter and the spring at the beginning?
2. What does the title imply?
3. Learn the last two stanzas by heart.

Ezra Pound
埃兹拉·庞德
（1885–1972）

Ezra Loomis Pound was born in Hailey, Idaho, on October 30, 1885. He attended the University of Pennsylvania and then Hamilton College, from which he graduated in 1905. He returned to the University of Pennsylvania for graduate study in romance languages and took an M.A. in 1906. He spent the summer abroad, and returned to Pennsylvania on a fellowship for another year of study in Renaissance literature. In 1908 he again went abroad, and by 1920 he regarded himself as a permanent expatriate.

By 1912, he was the author of seven volumes which identified him as a distinct poetic personality, who combined a command of the older tradition with impressive and often daring originality. When Harriet Monroe in 1912 issued from Chicago the prospectus for her new magazine *Poetry*: *A Magazine of Verse*, Pound characteristically proposed himself as its foreign correspondent.

He was a prolific essayist for the little magazines of New York, London, and Paris, which then constituted a large and exciting literary world. He unselfishly and persistently championed the experimental and often unpopular artists whom he approved—Antheil, the musician; Gaudier-Brzeska, pioneer abstractionist sculptor, killed in World War Ⅰ; and James Joyce, among others. Most important of all, perhaps, was the advice and encouragement which he gave to T. S. Eliot, who has candidly acknowledged the value of Pound's assistance in the final revision of *The Waste Land* and in connection with other poems of that period. Both poets of independent power and interest, they became the early leaders in restoring to poetry the use of literary reference as an imaginative instrument. Such referential figures of speech assume that the poet and his readers share a common cultural inheritance. In the present age increasing complexity, diffuseness, and specialization of knowledge, both Pound and Eliot required of their readers a familiarity with the classics, the productions of the Italian and English Renaissance, and specialized areas of Continental literature, including the works of the French symbolists. After *The Waste Land* (1922), Eliot's poetry became somewhat less difficult in this respect, while Pound continued to draw fundamentally upon his formidably recondite culture. A large part of his work consists of "reconst-ructions" in modern English of poems from earlier literatures, chiefly Greek, Latin, Italian, Provencal, and Chinese. Among his reconstructions, his *Homage to Sextus Propertius* is a masterpiece. He called the often-expanded volume of his poems his Personae, or "masks", referring to the conventionalized masks of the Greek drama.

A final obstacle for the reader is the violence of Pound's distrust of capitalism and his allegiance to the Utopian concept of "social credit". Nevertheless, *Hugh Selwyn Mauberley* (1920), considered as a satire of the materialistic forces involved in World War I is a masterpiece. In *The Cantos*, begun in 1917, the satire became intensified. The progressive series, exceeding the proposed limit of one hundred poems, are loosely connected cantos, like Dante's *Divina Commedia* in three sections, but representing a comedy human, not divine, dealing with the wreck of civilizations by reason of the infidelity of mankind in the three epoch—the ancient world, the Renaissance, and the modern period. A considerable number of them contain lyrical passages of genuine power; they are in Maces supremely witty, and many of their topical references are shrewd and valuable. But their complexity renders them controversial. Somewhat resembling *Finnegans Wake* in structure, Pound's vast poem now has a position similar to that of Joyce's novel before critical scholarship provided its explication. Pound's critics have developed a voluminous commentary concerning *The Cantos*, which, like Joyce's work, employs the complex association of scholarly lore, anthropology, modern history and personages, private history and witticisms, and obscure literary interpolations in various languages, including Chinese ideograms.

In 1924 Pound 1eft Paris for Rapallo, Italy, attracted by Mussolini's faithless promises of democratic state socialism. During World War II, Pound, on behalf of the Italian government, conducted radio broadcasts beamed at the American troops. He was returned to the United States as a citizen accused of treason, but on examination he was declared insane. After the treason charges were dismissed in 1958, Pound returned to Italy, where he died in 1972.

Pound was an influential poet in the history of American literature. He even translated many Chinese poems into English. His translation is poor, but he learned a lot from Chinese poetry. In some way, he introduced imagery system of Chinese poetry into American literature.

A Pact

I make a pact with you, Walt Whitman—
I have detested you long enough.
I come to you as a grown child
Who has had a pig-headed father;
I am old enough now to make friends.
It was you that broke the new wood,
Now is a time for carving.
We have one sap and one root—
Let there be commerce between us.

参考译诗

合　约

沃尔特·惠特曼，我与你有约在先——
我以前一直把你讨厌。
我现在向你走近，
因为长大的孩子已离开愚蠢的父亲；
我已长大成人，能交友择朋。
是你砍下了新木，
现在已适合雕刻。
我们合一种树汁，合一条根——
愿你我之间存有流通和交易。

（李正栓　译）

思考题

1. Pound says in the poem that "It was you that broke the new wood." What does it refer to?
2. Pound's attitude to Whitman is ambivalent. Can you see it from the poem?
3. Learn the poem by heart.

In a Station of the Metro[1]

The apparition of these faces in the crowd;
Petals on a wet, black bough.

注释

1. 这首诗指的是巴黎的地铁站。

参考译诗

在地铁车站

人群中幽灵般的一张张面孔；
黑色潮湿枝头上的一片片花瓣。

（李正栓　译）

思考题

1. Do you think the faces can be beautiful in the subway?
2. What does the word "apparition" suggest?
3. Are the petals beautiful on a wet, black bough?
4. Learn the poem by heart.
5. Write two poems by modeling on this one.

Robert Frost
罗伯特·弗洛斯特
(1874–1963)

Robert Frost was born in San Francisco and spent his early childhood in the Far West. At the death of his father when Frost was eleven, the family moved to Salem, New Hampshire. After graduating from high school as valedictorian and class poet in 1892, Frost entered Dartmouth College but soon left to work at odd jobs and to write poetry. In 1897 he tried college again—Harvard—but he left at the end of two years, having acquired an enduring dislike for academic convention.

For the next twelve years, Frost eked out a minimal living by teaching and farming while continuing to write poems. In 1912 he decided to venture everything on a literary career. Leaving New Hampshire, he sailed for England, where he hoped "to write poetry without further scandal to friends or family."

In London, he soon found a publisher, and his first book, *A Boy's Will* (1913), brought him to the attention of influential critics, among them the American expatriate Ezra Pound, who praised Frost as an authentic poet.

Following the publication of a second volume of poems, *North of Boston* (1914), Frost returned home, determined to win recognition in his native land. To support himself he taught in colleges and gave poetry readings in the United States. His fame grew with the appearance of a succession of books: *Mountain Interval* (1916), *New Hampshire* (1923), W*est-Running Brook* (1928), *A Further Range* (1936), *A Witness Tree* (1942), *Steeple Bush* (1947), *In the Clearing* (1962). By the end of his life he had become a national bard; he received honorary degrees from forty-four colleges and universities and won four Pulitzer Prizes; the United States Senate passed resolutions honoring his birthdays, and when he was eighty-seven he read his poetry at the inauguration of President John F. Kennedy.

Frost had rejected the revolutionary poetic principles of his contemporaries, choosing instead "the old-fashioned way to be new." He employed the plain speech of rural New Englanders and preferred the short, traditional forms of lyric and narrative. As a poet of nature he had obvious affinities with romantic writers, notably Wordsworth and Emerson. He saw nature as a storehouse of analogy and symbol, announcing, "I'm always saying something that's just the edge of something more," but he had little faith in religious dogma or speculative thought. His concern with nature reflected deep moral uncertainties, and his poetry, for all its apparent simplicity, often probes mysteries of darkness and irrationality in the bleak and chaotic landscapes of an indifferent universe where men stand alone, unaided and perplexed.

The Road Not Taken

Two roads diverged in a yellow wood,
And sorry I could not travel both
And be one traveler, long I stood
And looked down one as far as I could
To where it bent in the undergrowth;

Then took the other, as just as fair,[1]
And having perhaps the better claim,
Because it was grassy and wanted wear[2];
Though as for that the passing there
Had worn them really about the same,

And both that morning equally lay
In leaves no step had trodden black.
Oh, I kept the first for another day!
Yet knowing how way leads on to way,
I doubted if I should ever come back.

I shall be telling this with a sigh
Somewhere ages and ages hence:

Two roads diverged in a wood, and I—
I took the one less traveled by,
And that has made all the difference.

注释

1. **Then took the other, as just as fair** Then I took the other road, which is as proper as it is fair.
2. **wanted wear** was not quite worn

参考译诗

一条未走的路

两条路岔开在黄叶秋林，
遗憾我不可能同时都走，
遗憾我只是孤身一人，
我伫立远眺想看到路遥终尽，
只见那路拐进矮树林里头。

于是我选了另一条，同样不错，
或许我更有理由选择它，
因为这路上长满了野草未经踩磨；
尽管这条路经人走过
与第一条路同样足迹乱杂。

那天早晨，两条路同时摆在我面前，
树叶埋住台阶，还没被踩黑；
第一条留待日后再去选！
但又知道，路尽路始紧接连，
我怀疑我是否还能再回归。

很久很久以后在某处，

我会叹息着把这事情讲：
两条路岔开在一林，我未踟躇——
选择了一条人们较少走的路，
而这选择竟决定了人间与天上。

（李正栓　译）

思考题

1. Does the speaker think that he has made a wrong choice in taking the road "less traveled by"?
2. What does this choice imply in the poet's life?
3. What lessons about life can you learn from this poem?
4. Learn the first stanza by heart.

Stopping by Woods on a Snowy Evening

Whose woods these are I think I know.
His house is in the village though;
He will not see me stopping here
To watch his woods fill up with snow.

My little horse must think it queer
To stop without a farmhouse near
Between the woods and frozen lake
The darkest evening of the year.

He gives his harness bells a shake
To ask if there is some mistake.
The only other sound's the sweep
Of easy wind and downy flake.

The woods are lovely, dark and deep,
But I have promises to keep,
And miles to go before I sleep,
And miles to go before I sleep.

参考译诗

雪夜停林边

这是谁家的树林我想我知道，
尽管他家住在村子里；
他看不见我在这儿停住并观瞧
他的林中雪栖树枝落满地。

我那匹小马肯定认为很古怪，
在这一年中最灰暗的黄昏，
湖面冰封，近无人家，林木雪盖，
停在这儿是什么原因？

它摇动缰铃，似乎在问：
你停在这里，有没有搞错？
此外别无任何的声音，
只有清风徐来，雪花飘落。

树林幽深，景色迷人，
不过，我有约要赴，
须走路程遥远才能投宿，
须走路程遥远才能投宿。

（李正栓　译）

思考题

1. What does "sleep" imply?
2. "The woods are lovely, dark and deep." What implications can you find?
3. What is your view on the didactic function of poetry? Take this poem as an example.
4. The poem exemplifies Frost's ability to join the pastoral and philosophical modes in lyrics of unforgettable beauty. Elaborate on this opinion.
5. What is the relationship between the poet and the owner of the woods? Are they friends or foes? Why?
6. The translator of this poem in this textbook changed the rhyme scheme of aaba in the original poem to abab in the Chinese version in the first three stanzas. Is this change acceptable? Read the translation and tell your feeling.

Carl Sandburg
卡尔·桑德堡
(1878–1967)

Like his contemporary Robert Frost, Carl Sandburg lived to enjoy enormous popular acclaim. By the end of his life he had become a familiar figure to national television audiences who listened to him read his poems, sing folk ballads, and relate anecdotes about Lincoln.

Sandburg was the son of Swedish immigrant who settled in Galesburg, Illinois. His father was a machinist's blacksmith. Sandburg had irregular schooling and worked as an itinerant laborer and jack-of-all-trades in the Midwest before enlisting in the army during the Spanish-American War and serving as correspondent for the Galesburg *Evening Mail*. After the war he attended Lombard College, working for the fire department to support himself at the same time, but withdrew without a degree in 1902. He worked as advertising writer, roving reporter and organizer for the Social Democratic party in Wisconsin, and he married the sister of famed photographer Edward Steichen in 1908. He served as secretary to the Socialist mayor of Milwaukee (1910–1912) and wrote editorials for the Milwaukee *Leader* before moving to Chicago in 1913. He had published a pamphlet of poems privately in Galesburg in 1904, and *Poetry* magazine published his poem *Chicago* in 1914.

The poems that made Sandburg famous appeared in four volumes: *Chicago Poems* (1914), *Cornhuskers* (1918), *Smoke and Steel* (1920), and *Stabs of the Sunburn West* (1922). With the precedent of Whitman behind them, they present a sweeping panorama of American life, encompassing prairie, eastern, and western landscapes as well as vignettes of the modern city. They celebrate, from the standpoint of a Populist radical, the lives of outcasts, the contributions of immigrants and common people to urban culture, and the occupations of those who have survived or been sacrificed in the rise of industrial civilization. Sandburg's language draws on the colorful diction of immigrants and the lingo of urban dwellers, but unvarnished directness of statement takes precedence over subtleties of imagery or rhythm in his verse, even in such poems as *Cool Combs*, where the consistency of tone is impressive, or in *Flash Crimson*, where the techniques of symbolism are used. Sandburg avoided regular stanza patterns and traditional blank verse and wrote an utterly free verse, developing Whitman's long line but moderating its rhetorical impact and intensity, and composing what are often in effect prose paragraphs. As one who undertook as a spokesman for the common people to inscribe "public speech", he was proud late in his career to "favor simple poems for simple people."

His most ambitious attempt to accomplish that aim was *The People, Yes* (1936), consisting of prose vignettes, anecdotes and verse, which drew on his studies of American folksongs that preoccupied his attention after the publication of *The American Songbag* in 1927. Indeed, from 1918 on, other professional activities took precedence over his verse. He was a columnist, editorial writer, and feature writer on the *Chicago Daily News* from 1918 to 1933, and he published an account of *The Chicago Race Riots* in 1919. He published *The Rootabaga Stories* (for children) and two sequels between 1922 and 1930, and his biographies include *Steichen the Photographer* (1929) and *Mary Lincoln* (1932). His major work in prose was a monumental and celebratory biography of Abraham Lincoln, beginning with the two-volume *Prairie Years* in 1926 and culminating in *The War Years* (1939), a four-volume work which won the Pulitzer Prize in 1940.

The Harbor

Passing through huddles and ugly walls
By doorways where women
Looked from their hunger-deep eyes,
Haunted with shadows of hunger-hands,
Out from the huddled and ugly walls,
I came sudden, at the city's edge,
On a blue burst of lake,
Long lake waves breaking under the sun

On a spray-flung curve of shore;
And a fluttering storm of gulls,
Masses of great gray wings
And flying white bellies
Veering and wheeling free in the open.

参考译诗

港　口

穿过拥挤的人群和丑陋的街墙，
门廊里妇女们饥饿深陷的眼睛
带着饥饿魔掌的阴影
向行人张望。
离开拥挤的人群和丑陋的街墙，
突然间发现我已到了城市的边沿。
在蓝色的湖里
湖水波涌在阳光下闪现，
沿着那浪花飞溅的湖弯。
一群飞起的海鸥，
一片硕大的灰色翅膀，
飞翔中的白色肚皮
在空中一会儿变向一会儿滑翔。

（李正栓　译）

思考题

1. What is the main idea of this poem?
2. How does the poet use the comparison to convey his idea in this poem?

Fog[1]

The fog comes
on little cat feet.

It sits looking
over harbor and city
on silent haunches
and then moves on.

注释

1. 这首诗被认为是典型的意象派作品。由于经常被选入各种诗集，人们称此诗是“按字数计算稿费拿得最多的美国诗”。

参考译诗

雾

雾来了
迈着碎小猫步。

它坐下来张望
港口与城市
悄悄地蹲息
之后又继续前行。

（李正栓　译）

思考题

1. Discuss the image in the poem. In what way is fog like a cat?
2. What impresses you most in the poem?
3. Learn the poem by heart.

Grass

Pile the bodies high at Austerlitz and Waterloo[1].
Shovel them under and let me work—
I am the grass; I cover all.

And pile them high at Gettysburg[2]
And pile them high at Ypres[3]and Verdun[4].
Shovel them under and let me work.
Two years, ten years, and passengers ask the conductor:
What place is this?
Where are we now?

I am the grass.
Let me work.

注释

1. **Austerlitz and Waterloo** 奥斯特里兹，捷克地名；滑铁卢，比利时地名
2. **Gettysburg** 葛底斯堡，美国宾夕法尼亚州地名，1863年美国南北战争时在此发生大战，南军被击败。
3. **Ypres** 伊普勒斯，比利时地名
4. **Verdun** 凡尔登，法国地名

参考译诗

草

让尸首在奥斯特里兹和滑铁卢堆积成山，
把它们铲下去，然后交给我来处理——
我是草，我能把一切覆盖掉。

让尸首在葛底斯堡堆高成山，

让尸首在伊普勒斯和凡尔登高高堆起，
把它们铲下去，然后交给我来处理。
两年后，十年后，游客们便会问导游：
　　　　　这是什么地方？
　　　　　我们现在何处？

　　　　　我是草。
　　　　　交给我来处理。

（李正栓　译）

思考题

1. What's the central idea of this poem?
2. What does "grass" represent? Does it remind you of the "grass" in Whitman's *Leaves of Grass*?

Wallace Stevens
华莱士·史蒂文斯
(1879—1955)

As a poet, Stevens had a stronger passion for perfecting what he wrote than for his literary fame; for all his life, he was well-known as a lawyer, and later, a successful businessman.

Stevens was born in Reading, Pennsylvania, into a prosperous attorney's family of Dutch stock. With the encouragement of his father, Stevens studied at Harvard and New York University Law School, preparing for a career to the bar. In 1916, after practicing law for many years, he was engaged by the Hartford Accident and Indemnity Company and secured the position of vice-president of this insurance company until 1955, the year of his retirement and his death.

Stevens began to write poems during his time at Harvard. Even when he was busily associated with business, he never gave up his interest in poetry. As a matter of fact, Stevens made great efforts to bridge the world of reality with the world of imagination. Consequently, he was recognized as a successful businessman, and an outstanding poet as well.

Most of Stevens' important poems were composed during the time of the Great Depression and the two World Wars. Yet he showed little concern with the sufferings and frustrations of the time, for he believed that, as a poet, what he should and could do was not to heal or reform society, but to help his people to become more happily aware of the beauty and pleasure and excitement and meaning in the sordidness of reality.

However, Stevens was not blindly optimistic, nor was he the one who escaped from reality. Instead, he was interested in the "ideas of order", that is, true ideas correspond with an innate order in the universe. He was interested in the relationship of chaos and order, the reconciliation of reality and imagination, by insisting that an artist should observe reality and create reality out of his imagination, and that the order and faith we have lost in modern society can be recreated in artistic work through imagination.

Having been regarded as a poet of the imagist group, Stevens was good at applying metaphors and symbols. As with all the other imagists, he experimented a lot with styles, sound, and rules of rhymes.

The earliest poetic work of Stevens came out in 1914, but he did not have his poems collected into a book *Harmonium* until 1923. After it, more and more poems poured out over the next 20 years, including *Ideas of Order* (1935), *Owl's Clover* (1936), *The Man with the Blue Guitar* (1937), *Parts of a World* (1942), *The Auroras of Autumn* (1950), *The Necessary Angel: Essays on Reality and the Imagination* (1951), and *The Collected Poems of Wallace Stevens* (1954).

The Snow Man[1]

One must have a mind of winter[2]
To regard the frost and the boughs
Of the pine-trees crusted with snow.

And have been cold a long time
To behold the junipers shagged with ice[3],
The spruces[4] rough in the distant glitter

Of the January sun; and not to think
Of any misery in the sound of the wind,
In the sound of a few leaves,

Which is the sound of the land,
Full of the same wind
That is blowing in the same bare place

For the listener, who listens in the snow,
And, nothing himself, beholds,
Nothing that is not there[5] and the nothing that is[6].

注释

1. *The Snow Man* is a poem from Wallace Stevens's first book of poetry, *Harmonium*. *The Snow Man* was first published in 1921 in the journal *Poetry*. It was written in the Modern era, but reflects more of a transcendentalist style, which appeared during the Romantic era.
2. **mind of winter** the state of mind harmonious with the atmosphere of winter
3. **junipers shagged with ice** trees roughly covered with ice
4. **The spruces** a type of evergreen tree with dense foliage
5. **Nothing that is not there** nothing substantial
6. **the nothing that is** the nothingness exists there; the state of emptiness there

雪　　人

人若喜看冬严霜，
心怡冬雪披青松。
他心必与冬相通。

严寒时节已久长，
刺柏树上冰狼卧，
云杉挂冰熠熠光。

那是一月寒太阳；
莫忌风声多凄厉，
莫忌疏叶好凄凉。

此乃大地恒声音，
相同寒风总充盈，
那是空地神智音。

听者站在雪中听，
忘掉自我独自看
原本无物万事空。

（李正栓，韩志华 译）

思考题

1. What do "the snow" and "the man" represent respectively?
2. What is the main idea of the poem?

Edward Estlin Cummings
爱德华·艾斯特林·肯明斯
(1894—1962)

In the first half of the 20th century, Edward Estlin Cummings remained a controversial figure for all the dexterous novelty of his versification and for his daring experimentation.

Edward Estlin Cummings was born in Cambridge, Massachusetts, the town in which Harvard University is located. Cummings' father was a professor at Harvard, and in 1915 Cummings himself graduated from Harvard with a master's degree. The next year, Cummings was recruited by the Red Cross for World War Ⅰ and was sent to France. But he was soon, very unfortunately, charged with treason because of a censor's mistake, and stayed in a French detention camp for three months. This experience, fortunately, provided the raw material for his first literary work, *The Enormous Room* published in 1922. After the war, Cummings went to Paris to study painting, with all the fascination for suchpost-Impressionist and Cubist painters as Cézanne and Picasso. His genius in art, harmoniously combined with his talent in language, freed him from the bondage of conventional style and distinguished him as one of the most outstanding poets of the 20th century.

All his life, Cummings was absorbed in the pursuit of perfection in art and literature. He was not like most writers in history, who toiled to add something of novelty to enlarge the content of the treasure house of art; nor was he like those who arrogantly spurned convention and started anew. Cummings was a poet who defined independently his own universe by expressing conventional ideas through employing modern techniques.

As a poet, Cummings was famous for the experiments he executed. His experimental techniques are evident first in the defying or complete rejection of the capitalization. He deliberately ignored the conventional capitalization of the proper names "god" and "america" and even refused to capitalize the word "i".

Then there is the violation of regular grammar by freely splitting or combining words, purposeful underpunctuation, and breaking phrases by cadence to the advantage of the melody. Sometimes Cummings would arrange the letters of a word or lengthen the space between letters or words, all for the same aim to convey the vividness of life and present the power of rhythm.

Besides, Cummings, a master of the stream-of-consciousness technique, often employed words and phrases symbolically or simply as an image to display something meaningful in mind but probably illogical in appearance. Whereas, compared with the works of other poets in this group, Cummings' works are shorter and more flexible.

The experimental poet in Cummings was very traditional in mind. Science, industry and machines are often the object of condemnation in his works. Instead, love for nature, children, normal family life and artistic work are the frequent themes of his poems. What's more, as a professional painter, he was much more concerned than other poets with the typographical order of words: the arrangement of them into a picture. Some of his poems are virtually unreadable because of his experimental skills—Cummings deliberately presented them as "picture-poems" to please the reader's eye with all the beauty contained in a pattern.

Immediately after the publication of his first book in 1922, Cummings' first collection of poems *Tulips and Chimneys* came out the next year. His other works include & (1923), *is 5* (1926), *Viva* (1931), *No Thanks* (1935), and *50 poems* (1940).

in Just—[1]

in Just—
spring   when the world is mud—
luscious[2] the little
lame balloonman

whistles   far   and wee[3]

and eddieandbill[4] come

running from marbles and
piracies and it's
spring

when the world is puddle-wonderful

the queer
old balloonman whistles
far   and   wee
and bettyandisbel[5] come dancing

from hop-scotch[6] and jump-rope and
it's
spring
and
  the
        goat-footed[7]

balloonman   whistles
far
and
wee

注释

1. This poem presents a vivid picture of childhood in spring.
2. **luscious** rich and sweet in taste and smell; attractive
3. **wee** little; very small; to stay a little longer and in vibrating sound. 此行的词语之间的距离表示口哨声从很远的地方传来，声音断断续续。
4. **eddieandbill** the combination of two boys' name, Eddie and Bill. 生动刻画了孩子们因为卖气球的人的到来推来搡去，挤作一团的兴奋热闹的情景。
5. **bettyandisbel** the combination of two girls' names, Betty and Isbel
6. **hop-scotch** children's game of throwing a stone into numbered squares a etc. marked on the ground and hopping from square to square to collect it

7. **goat-footed** lame. The character of the "goat-footed" balloonman with his whistle strongly suggests the god of shepherds, Pan, who is half-man, half-animal and carries the sense of spring to the world with a pipe.

参考译诗

正　好

正好在——
春天，当大地散发泥香——
味道甘美，那个跛脚的
卖气球的小老头
从远处吹着口哨哨音微弱，
艾迪和比尔跑过来
本来丢石子和
抓海盗，原来
春天到了。

当大地冰雪消融，一展魅力，

那个卖气球的
古怪的老头吹着哨子
从远处走来哨音微弱，
贝蒂和伊莎贝尔跳着过来

她们正在跳房子，跳绳子，
原来是
春天到了，
还有，
那
山羊脚的
卖气球的人吹找哨子
来自远处

还有
啸音微弱。

（李正栓，韩志华　译）

思考题

1. Edward Estlin Cummings is a juggler with syntax, grammar and diction. Is this poem an illustration?
2. “Whistles far and wee” appears three times in the poem while each time it appears differently. Why?
3. What does “the goat-footed balloonman” suggest?

Thomas Stearns Eliot
托马斯·斯特恩斯·艾略特
(1888–1965)

Thomas Stearns Eliot (T. S. Eliot) was born in St. Louis, Missouri, on September 26, 1888, of New England stock. At that time, his grandfather had gone west as a Unitarian minister. T. S. Eliot studied at private academies, entered Harvard at eighteen, and there attained the M.A. degree in 1910. A student of languages and belles-lettres, especially the writings of the Elizabethans and the metaphysical poets and the literature of the Italian Renaissance, he was attracted to the study of philosophy, taught by such men as Irving Babbitt and George Santayana. In the winter of 1910 he went to the University of Paris, where he was influenced by the lectures of the philosopher Henri Bergson. Again at Harvard (1911–1914), he studied Sanskrit and Oriental philosophy in the graduate school, and acted as an assistant in the philosophy department. In 1914, he was awarded a traveling fellowship for study in Germany.

At Merton College, Oxford, in 1915, he again studied philosophy. That year he married the daughter of a British artist. For two years he taught in English academies while bringing to fruition his first book of poems. In 1917, he published *Prufrock and Other Observations.* Few poets in their first book have so prophetically suggested the direction and power of what was to follow. *The Love Song of J. Alfred Prufrock*, still holds its place in the development of Eliot's poetry as a whole; like much of his later work it concerns various aspects of the frustration and enfeeblement of individual character as seen in perspective with the decay of states, peoples, and religious faith.

From 1918 to 1924, he was in the service of Lloyd's Bank in London. In 1920, his fourth volume, *Poems*, with *Gerontion* as its leading poem, again developed the same general pattern of ideas. It is remarkable that he excluded almost no poem of his early volumes from his later collected works. In 1920 also appeared *The Sacred Wood*, containing, among other essays, *Tradition and the Individual Talent*, the earliest statement of his aesthetics.

Also in 1920, Eliot began *The Waste Land*, one of the major works of modern literature.

Eliot's next major accomplishment, the *Four Quartets* originated during his visit to the United States (1932, 1934), his first return to his native country in seventeen years. During this period he wrote the small *Landscapes*, some of them drawn from American scenes, which are spiritually connected with the theme of the *Quartets*. His lectures at Harvard University in 1932 resulted in the influential volume *The Uses of Poetry* and *the Uses of Criticism* (1933). In 1934, he lectured at the University of Virginia and produced the study of orthodoxy and faith entitled *After Strange Gods, A Primer of Modern Heresy*. Presumably it was during this year that he conceived the subject of *Burnt Norton*, the first of the *Quartets*.

Few men of letters have been more fully honored in their own day than T. S. Eliot, and even those who strongly disagreed with him seemed content with his being selected for the Nobel Prize in 1948. *The Complete Poems and Plays* (1952) is a relatively small volume, but it represents an artist whose ideas are large, whose craftsmanship is the expression of artistic responsibility, and whose poems represent the progressive refinement and illustration of his aesthetics.

T. S. Eliot, though difficult to understand and profound in ideas, has been highly acclaimed by poets and critics.

Preludes

1

The winter evening settles down
With smell of steaks in passageways.
Six o'clock.
The burnt-out ends of smoky days.
And now a gusty shower wraps
The grimy scraps
Of withered leaves about your feet
And newspapers from vacant lots;

The showers beat
On broken blinds and chimney-pots.
And at the corner of the street
A lonely cab-horse steams and stamps.
And then the lighting of the lamps.

2

The morning comes to consciousness
Of faint stale smells of beer
From the sawdust-trampled street
With all its muddy feet that press
To early coffee-stands.
With the other masquerades
That time resumes,
One thinks of all the hands
That are raising dingy shades
In a thousand furnished rooms.

3

You tossed a blanket from the bed,
You lay upon your back, and waited;
You dozed, and watched the night revealing
The thousand sordid images
Of which your soul was constituted;
They flickered against the ceiling.
And when all the world came back
And the light crept up between the shutters
And you heard the sparrows in the gutters,
You had such a vision of the street
As the street hardly understands;
Sitting along the bed's edge, where

You curled the papers from your hair,
Or clasped the yellow soles of feet
In the palms of both soiled hands.

4

His soul stretched tight across the skies
That fade behind a city block.
Or trampled by insistent feet
At four and five and six o'clock;
and short square fingers stuffing pipes,
And evening newspapers, and eyes
Assured of certain certainties,
The conscience of a blackened street
Impatient to assume the world.

I am moved by fancies that are curled
Around these images, and cling:
The notion of some infinitely gentle,
Infinitely suffering thing.

Wipe your hand across your mouth, and laugh;
The worlds revolve like ancient women
Gathering fuel in vacant lots.

序　曲

1

冬天的傍晚降临，
走廊里还有牛排味儿。
六点钟。
烟蒙蒙白天烧尽的烟蒂。

此刻，一阵斜风急雨
卷起一堆堆
枯叶，卷到你脚旁，
还刮来些报纸，从空荡荡的地方；
阵雨拍打
破旧的叶窗和烟囱的顶上。
在街角处
一匹孤零零的拉车的马冒着汗，蹬着地。
之后油灯的灯光亮起。

2

清晨复苏，
微闻啤酒的淡味儿
这味道来自踩满锯屑的大街。
街上沾满泥的脚
都在急急地奔向早市的咖啡货架。
随时光恢复
另一种装束，
人们想起所有的手
在数千个有陈设的房间里
拉起暗淡的窗帘。

3

你把毯子掀下床去，
你仰面躺着，等着；
你昏昏欲睡，凝望黑夜展示
千百个肮脏的形象，
这些形象充满你头脑；
它们在天花板上忽隐忽现。
当人们都回来
当灯光从百叶窗缝爬进来

当你听到麻雀在路边槽沟鸣叫，
你便看到街上这样一景
这一景那街上人难以弄懂；
你这时坐在床边
解开卷发的纸，
或把你发黄的脚底
紧紧抱在你的脏手里。

4

街上人灵魂紧紧向天空延伸
在街区后天空渐暗。
或在不停不绝的脚踩踏着，
从四点、五点到六点；
短胖的手指往烟斗里装烟丝，
还有一份份晚报，还有
对某些事情充满自信的眼睛，
昏黑街道的良心
已迫不及待地要征服世界。

这些形象周围的幻想
令我感动，我紧紧地抓住这幻想：
对某种事无限温柔
也无限伤痛。

用手抹一把你的嘴，之后笑吧；
大千世界在转，就像古代妇女
在空地上捡柴一样。

（李正栓　译）

思考题

1. What's the implication of "smoky days" and "a gusty shower"?
2. What features of modernism are shown in this poem?
3. What is the rhyme scheme of this poem?
4. Learn the first stanza by heart.

Hilda Doolittle
希尔达·杜立特尔
(1886−1961)

Hilda Doolittle, a woman poet, novelist and translator, was born in a professor's family in Pennsylvania. In 1904, she attended Bryn Mawr College, but she didn't finish her study. She once had a close touch with Pound. In 1911, she went to London and indulged in the poetic creation of Imagism. In 1913, she married an imagist poet, Richard Aldington. In 1916, she became a literature editor of *The Egoist*. In the same year, she published her first collection of poems *Sea Garden*. From 1920 to 1923, she traveled in America, Greece and Egypt. She settled down in Switzerland. In 1925, she published *Collected Poems*, which includes *Oread*, *Pear Tree* and *Orchard*. After World War Ⅱ, she got divorced with Aldington. From 1944 to 1946, she published *The Walls Do Not Fall* (1944), *Tribute to the Angels* (1945) and *The Flowering of the Rod* (1946). When she was old, she was deeply influenced by Freud, and published *Tribute to Freud* (1956). In 1961, she published her last work, A lyric *Helen in Egypt*.

Oread

Whirl up, sea—
whirl your pointed pines,
splash your great pines
on our rocks,
hurl your green over us,
cover us with your pools of fir.

参考译诗

山林女神

大海，旋翻吧，——
旋起你针松般细浪，
溅起你松树般巨浪
拍打我们的岩石，
把你的碧波绿浪向我们投来，
用你冷杉般漩涡把我们覆盖。

（李正栓　译）

思考题

1. What are the effects of the imperative sentences and the violent verbs at the beginning of almost each line?
2. Discuss the juxtaposition or mingling of images in the poem.
3. Learn the poem by heart.

Never More Will the Wind

Never more will the wind
cherish you again,
never more will the rain.

Never more
shall we find you bright
in the snow and wind.

The snow is melted,
the snow is gone,
and you are flown:

Like a bird out of our hand,
like a light out of our heart,
you are gone.

参考译诗

风再也不会

风再也不会，
对你惺惺相惜，
雨也不会。

我们再也不会
发现你在雪里和风中
那样明亮。

雪化了
雪消了
你也飞逝而去。

像小鸟飞出我们的掌心，
像光束离开我们的心房，
你无影无踪。

（张青梅　译）

思考题

1. What is the basic tone in the poem?
2. What images are used to express the sense of loss?
3. Learn this poem by heart.

Hart Crane
哈特·克兰
(1899–1932)

Hart Crane was born in a merchant family in Ohio. His parents got divorced, which brought him great misery. He began to write poems at the age of 13 and published his first poem *My Grandmother's Love Letters* at 21. In 1922, he published *Praise for an Urn* on *The Dial*. In 1923, he finished his first noticeable poem *For the Marriage of Faustus and Helen*. In the same year, he went to New York. In the following years he published his love poem *Voyage*. In 1926, he had his first collection of poetry *White Buildings*. His poems are full of symbolism and hints, which are difficult to understand. In 1930, he finished his masterpiece *The Bridge*. In 1932, he committed suicide on the way from Mexico to New York.

The Bridge

From going to and fro in the earth
and from walking up and down in it.
—The Book of Job

To Brooklyn Bridge[1]

How many dawns, chill from his rippling rest
The seagull's wings shall dip and pivot him,
Shedding white rings of tumult, building high
Over the chained bay waters Liberty—

Then, with inviolate curve, forsake our eyes
As apparitional as sails that cross

Some page of figures to be filed away;—
Till elevators drop us from our day...

I think of cinemas, panoramic sleights
With multitudes bent toward some flashing scene
Never disclosed, but hastened to again,
Foretold to other eyes on the same screen;

And Thee, across the harbor, silver-paced
As though the sun took step of thee, yet left
Some motion ever unspent in thy stride,—
Implicitly thy freedom staying thee!

Out of some subway scuttle, cell or loft
A bedlamite speeds to thy parapets,
Tilting there momently, shrill shirt ballooning,
A jest falls from the speechless caravan.

Down Wall, from girder into street noon leaks,
A rip-tooth of the sky's acetylene;
All afternoon the cloud-flown derricks turn...
Thy cables breathe the North Atlantic still.

And obscure as that heaven of the Jews,
Thy guerdon...Accolade thou dost bestow
Of anonymity time cannot raise:
Vibrant reprieve and pardon thou dost show.

O harp and altar, of the fury fused,
(How could mere toil align thy choiring strings!)
Terrific threshold of the prophet's pledge,[2]

Prayer of pariah, and the lover's cry, —

Again the traffic lights that skim thy swift
Unfractioned idiom, immaculate sigh of stars,
Beading thy path—condense eternity:
And we have seen night lifted in thine arms.

Under thy shadow by the piers I waited;
Only in darkness is thy shadow clear.
The City's fiery parcels all undone,
Already snow submerges an iron year...

O Sleepless as the river under thee,
Vaulting the sea, the prairies' dreaming sod,
Unto us lowliest sometime sweep, descend
And of the curveship lend a myth to God.

注释

1. **Brooklyn Bridge** 指纽约的布鲁克林大桥
2. **Terrific threshold of the prophet's pledge** 《圣经》中所预言的“地上天堂”的门槛

参考译诗

桥

从地上走去又走来，
在地上走上又走下。
——《约伯记》

致布鲁克林大桥

多少拂晓，因颤动的休息而受冻，
海鸥的翅膀俯冲忽又旋身向上

洒下骚乱的白环，在被锁住的
海水之上高高地建起自由神像——

然后，在完美的曲线中消失，
像幻景中的帆一般穿过
几页只待搁开归档的数字；——
直到电梯把我们从白昼降落……

我想到电影，场面壮观的技巧
大群人俯下身来面队闪闪的景象
从未发现真情，却在同一银幕上
匆匆地向另一些眼睛又做预言。

而你，跨越海湾，银色的步伐，
太阳好像跟着你走，你的脚步
却留下一些运动没有使用——
你的自由暗中把你自己留住！
从地道，小屋或阁楼上跑来，
一个疯子高速飞跑冲向栏杆，
一下歪倒，尖叫着，衬衣像气球
一个玩笑从无言的商队里跌落。

正午从桁梁的空隙漏入华尔街头
像乙炔灯把天空烧裂成齿状，
架在云头的吊杆整个下午转动……
你的巨缆吹静了北大西洋。

晦暗，就像犹太人的天堂，
你的奖赏……你授予的
无名爵位连时间都无法解除：
你显示了振荡的缓刑和赦免。

哦，狂想熔铸的竖琴和祭坛，
（单靠辛劳怎能调准你合奏的弦！）
先知所预言的可怕的门槛，
漂流者的祈祷，情人的哭泣——

汽车灯光又掠过你流畅的
不间断的语言，星星洁净的叹息
珠连起你的路径——凝聚的永恒
我们看到夜被你的手臂托起。

我在桥墩上，在你的影子下等待，
在暗处你的影子变得十分清晰。
城市燃烧的包裹全解开了
白雪已经淹没铁的岁月……

哦，你无眠，就像你身下的水流
穹盖着大海，和草原做着梦的土地，
有时你猛降到最卑微的我辈身上
用一种曲线性把神话借给上帝。

（赵毅衡　译）

思考题

1. What's the theme of this poem?
2. What's the symbolic meaning of the Brooklyn Bridge?

Theodore Roethke
西奥多·罗特克
(1908—1963)

Theodore Roethke was one of the most important poets during the middle decants of the 20th century. As the son of the most successful florist in Saginaw, Michigan, Roethke was able to further his education at Harvard after obtaining the B. A. (1929) and M.A. (1936) at the University of Michigan.

Roethke was a genius in writing poetry, but a reserved person in manner. His talent was first inspired by the beauty of his father's greenhouse, where every leaf and petal appeared significant to the boy as the embodiment of life, and meanwhile, as the symbol for something delicate and pleasant in this world. Nevertheless, outside the greenhouse, he found himself in torturing conflict with the ingrained values of conventional society. He had to make himself occupied in teaching and reading voraciously the books of the masters he admired: William Blake, William Butler Yeats, Walt Whitman and Emerson. His first book of poetry *Open House* appeared in 1941 with controversial comments. However, he did not give up but became a Pulitzer Prize winner for the poems of 8 volumes.

As a poet, the family greenhouse experience enabled Roethke to be a close observer of natural beauty. When composing, he was good at depicting the specific details of life and displaying the momentary aspiration of people. In his poems, metaphysical tension expresses itself in varied metaphors and fractured syntax, but he was, unlike most poets of his time, always optimistic in discussing such themes as life and death. He worked diligently to write poems in simple words and easy structure. As everyone can see, his early poems were written in a traditional style, while in the latter ones, some modern experimental skills can be largely traced.

Since the publication of his first book, Roethke succeeded through the publication of a chain of collections, until in 1963 his life was surprisingly interrupted by his accidental drowning in a friend's swimming pool.

The Lost Son, a book in memory of his father and the greenhouse childhood, was published in 1948. Two years later, the same theme was continued in another book *Praise to the End* (1951). The sincere pathos and affection carried in these two books were widely shared by his readers. Consequently, two years later, when Roethke's new collection of poems, *The Waking*, came out, the Pulitzer Prize was awarded to the writer. In 1957, *Words for the Wind* won him the Bollingen Prize.

In his honor, the Theodore Roethke Memorial Poetry Prize was established in 1967 and is awarded every three years. It is one of the most prestigious literary prizes in America.

My Papa's Waltz[1]

The whisky on your breath
Could make a small boy dizzy;
But I hung on like death[2]:
Such waltzing was not easy.

We romped[3] until the pans
Slid from the kitchen shelf;
My mother's countenance
Could not unfrown itself

The hand that held my wrist
Was battered on one knuckle[4];
At every step you missed
My right ear scraped a buckle[5].

You beat time on my head
With a palm caked hard by dirt,
Then waltzed me off to bed
Still clinging to your shirt.

注释

1. This poem was selected from *The Lost Son* (1948), a collection of the autobiographical poems about his childhood days together with his father.
2. **hung on like death** keep hold of you (the father) tightly
3. **romped** play together in a lively way; running; jumping
4. **battered on one knuckle** one knuckle of father's hands had been damaged to lose shape
5. **buckle** metal or plastic clasp with a hinged spike for fastening a belt or straps. The boy was very young and his ear could just reach the father's waist. When dancing with father and a step failed, the boy's ear would scrape the buckle of the father's belt. The father, a physical laborer, was rather clumsy in dancing but was filled with kindness toward children.

参考译诗

爸爸的华尔兹

你呼出来的威士忌酒气
足以使小男孩目眩头昏；
我却死抓着你紧紧偎依
这样跳华尔兹可不轻松。

我们又蹦又跳直嬉闹到
厨房搁板的锅盆掉下来；
妈妈的脸色可是不太妙
她额头紧蹙双眉展不开。

那只紧握着我手腕的手
有一根砸坏关节的指头；
每当你踏错一个舞步后
我右耳就蹭蹭你皮带扣。

你沾满泥土硬块的手掌
在我脑袋上敲打着节拍；

跳着华尔兹送我去上床
我仍抓着你衬衣不松开。

（李海云　译，李正栓　校）

思考题

1. What's the main idea of the poem?
2. What's the rhyme scheme?
3. Why does"my right ear scraped a buckle" mean?
4. Learn the first stanza by heart.

Langston Hughes
朗斯顿·休斯
(1902–1967)

Langston Hughes was the first prominent Black writer in American literary history. He contributed to the treasure house of literature over 60 books; out of them 12 are collections of poems. Besides, he was also a master in novel writing and composer of plays for children.

Hughes was born in a black family in Joplin, Missouri. From a very young age, he was not without racial pride and dignity: being proud of the music, history and legend of black culture. In 1921, Hughes enrolled at Columbia University and published his first poem *The Negro Speaks of Rivers*. Nevertheless, bored by formal education, Hughes left the university one year later for Africa and Europe, first as a sailor, then as a cook and busboy. The story is always told that one day in 1926, when Hughes, who'd returned to the States years before, was waiting a table in a restaurant, he served a guest, instead of the menu, with several poems, for he had recognized the man to be a very popular poet of the time, Vachel Lindsay. As a result, encouragement fell on his prepared head and Hughes got the good fortune to collect his poems into the book *The Wearing Blues*, and had it published in the same year. Good fortune was continued in the next year when another book *Fine Clothes to the Jew* followed suit. After finishing college education in 1929, Hughes began to support himself by his pen. He worked diligently and tried nearly every literary form and style: poetry, fiction, drama and essays for newspapers.

Hughes was the first writer who brought the stories of Black people in the Harlem area into American literature and initiated a new trend in Black literature. This resulted in the later famous literary and artistic movement known as the "Harlem Renaissance" of the 1920's and Hughes became the spokesman of Black writers.

As a Black lyric poet, Hughes took great advantage of the rhythms of jazz and the blues and, in addition, developed subjects from Black life and racial themes. In his poems readers of the 1920s were satisfied to find primitivism combined with classical technique. Hughes reached the summit of his achievements when he was honored with the informal title of "Poet Laureate of Harlem".

Hughes' poems were characterized by short lines and simple stanza patterns, but with strong rhythms of jazz and strict rhyme schemes derived from blues songs. Two principal themes of the poetry are constantly passionate presentation of Black life by applying rhythms and refrains from jazz and blues, and poems of racial protest.

Besides what is mentioned above, the other collections of Hughes include *Dear Lovely Death* (1931), *The Negro Mother* (1931), *Dream Keeper* (1932), *The New Song* (1938), *Shakespeare in Harlem* (1942), and *Ask Your Mama* (1961).

Harlem

What happens to a dream deferred?

Does it dry up
like a raisinin the sun?
Or festerlike a sore—
And then run?
Does it stink like rotten meat?
Or crust and sugar over—
like a syrupy sweet?

Maybe it just sags
like a heavy load.

...Or does it explode?

参考译诗

哈莱姆

如果梦想的实现延宕会怎样？

它会干涸吗？
就像阳光下的葡萄干？
或者溃烂像疮伤
而后脓汁流淌？
它会像腐肉发出恶臭吗？
或者结痂被敷上一层糖
像甜蜜的糖果？

或许它只会下垂
像沉重的负担。

或者它会蓄势爆发？

（张青梅　译）

思考题

1. What do you know about Harlem and Harlem Renaissance?
2. What are the possibilities of deferred dreams?
3. Which is the most impressive line?

I, Too, Sing America

I am the darker brother.
They send me to eat in the kitchen
When company comes,
But I laugh,

And eat well,
And grow strong.

Tomorrow,
I'll be at the table
When company comes.
Nobody'll dare
Say to me,
"Eat in the kitchen,"
Then.

Besides,
They'll see how beautiful I am
And be ashamed—

I, too, am America.

参考译诗

我，也歌唱美国

我，也歌唱美国。

我是黑皮肤兄弟，
来客人时，
他们让我躲到厨房吃饭。
我却大笑，
吃得好，
长得好。

明天，
来客人时，

我会坐上桌。
那时，
没人敢
对我说，
“厨房去！”

而且，
他们会看到我多么漂亮，
他们会为此自惭形秽。

我，也是美国人。

（张青梅　译）

思考题

1. The poem is a response to Whitman's *I Hear America Singing*. Is it a positive or negative response?
2. What makes the speaker bold enough to refuse to eat in the kitchen?
3. Learn the poem by heart.

The Negro Speaks of Rivers

I've known rivers:
I've known rivers ancient as the world and older than
　　The flow of human blood in human veins.

My soul has grown deep like the rivers.
I bathed in the Euphrates[1] when dawns were young.
I built my hut near the Congo[2] and it lulled me to sleep.
I looked upon the Nile[3] and raised the pyramids above it.
I heard the singing of the Mississippi[4] when Abe Lincoln[5]

Went down to New Orleans, and I've seen its
Muddy bosom turn all golden in the sunset.

I've known rivers:
Ancient, dusky rivers.

My soul has grown deep like the rivers.

注释

1. **the Euphrates** 幼发拉底河
2. **the Congo** 刚果河
3. **the Nile** 尼罗河
4. **the Mississippi** 密西西比河
5. **Abe Lincoln** Abraham Lincoln (1809–1865), the 16th president of the United States

参考译诗

黑人说河

我了解河：
我了解那像世界一样古老的河，
　　那比人类血脉里流淌的血液还古老的河。

我的灵魂已变得像河一样深沉。
我在曙色微现时分畅游于幼发拉底河中。
我搭小屋在刚果河畔，河水诱我沉沉入梦。
我仰望尼罗河水，视野中金字塔高于尼罗河。
我听到密西西比河在歌唱，伴着亚伯·林肯
　　顺流而下到新奥尔良，我看到
　　她泥泞的胸膛在落日里金光闪耀。

我了解河：
那古老、朦胧的河。

我的灵魂已变得像河一样深沉。

（李海云　译，李正栓　校）

思考题

1. Why does the poet talk about the names of rivers?
2. What do "ancient, dusky rivers" imply?

Robert Lowell
罗伯特·洛威尔
（1917–1977）

Robert Lowell, related through his father to the poets James Russell Lowell (his great-grand-uncle) and Amy Lowell (his cousin), was born in Boston and grew up there as a rebel in the family tradition. He enlisted at Harvard College in 1935, but after a unsatisfied freshman year there, he completed his formal education at Kenyon College in Ohio in 1940. After graduation, Lowell secured a position at Louisiana State University, where he worked with some New Critics, developed a Southern accent, and converted to Catholicism, though he retained an earlier interest in Puritan philosophy.

When World War Ⅱ broke out, Lowell's offer to enlist in the American navy was twice rejected because of his poor eyesight. But in 1943, when he was called by the army, he declared himself a conscientious objector to the country's participation in the war and was thus sentenced to one year in jail. Next year, his first volume of poems *Land of Unlikeness* was published and he was well accepted as one of the important poets of the time.

For a long time, Lowell suffered from severe mental disease. With the suggestion of a doctor, he attempted to relieve the symptoms through writing about his inner feelings and succeeded. This resulted in more original poems.

Lowell contributed most of his early poems to the rebelling against the social conventions of New England and to the description of his conversion to Catholicism. Poems of this period were scrupulously created with ironies, symbols and obscurity. With the publication of *Life Studies* in 1959, Lowell became more inclined for meditation and self-examination, which inaugurated an autobiographical project later called "confessional". Themes of this period also shifted from trivial private affairs to social problems as nihilist youth, to the deterioration of social morality, and to the spiritual sufferings of modern people. As a matter of fact, Lowell was once so radical in social activities that he was arrested for participating in a Pentagon March to protest against the Vietnam War.

As a poet, his style varied rapidly but the subjects were tended more and more towards a steady description of human internal world.

The Complete Works of Lowell contains more than the works talked above. His first book was closely followed by another volume of poems *Lord Weary's Castle* (1946), which brought him the Pulitzer Prize. Then the honor was succeeded by the publication of *The Mills of the Kavanaughs* (1951). His masterpiece *Life Studies* appeared in 1959, after that the major achievements of the 60s and 70s include *For the Union Dead* (1964), *History* (1973), and *Day by Day* in 1977.

Katherine's Dream

(From Lord Weary's Castle)
It must have been a Friday[1]. I could hear
the top-floor typist's thunder[2] and the beer
That you had brought in cases hurt my head;
I'd sent the pillows flying from my bed,
I hugged my knees together and I gasped.
The dangling telephone receiver rasped[3]
Like someone in a dream who cannot stop
For breath or logic till his victim drop
to darkness and the sheets. I must have slept,
But still could hear my father who had kept
Your guilty presents but cut off my hair.
He whispers that he really doesn't care
If I am your kept woman[4] all my life,
Or ruin your two children and your wife;
But my dishonor makes him drink. Of course
I'll tell the court the truth for his divorce.
I walk through snow into St.Patrick's yard[5].

Black nuns with glasses smile and stand on guard
Before a bulkhead[6] in a bank of snow,
Whose charred doors open, as good people go
Inside by twos to the confessor. One
Must have a friend to enter there, but none
Is friendless in this crowd, and the nuns smile.
I stand aside and marvel; for a while
The winter sun is pleasant and it warms
My heart with love for others, but the swarms
Of penitents[7] have dwindles. I begin
To cry and ask God's pardon for our sin.
Where are you? You were with me and are gone.
All the forgiven couples hurry on
To dinner and their nights, and none will stop.
I run about in circles till I drop
Against a padlocked[8] bulkhead in a yard
Where faces redden and the snow is hard.

注释

1. **Friday** It indicates a weekend, the frequent occasion for a mistress girl to meet her lover.
2. **thunder** the loud noise of a typewriter. The exaggeration suggests that the girl was quite annoyed by something.
3. **rasped** made unpleasant grating sound. My receiver had been thrown away, yet, the speaking of the other end is going on through the line.
4. **kept woman** mistress; an unlawful sexual partner of a married man
5. **St. Patrick's yard** the yard of St. Patrick's church
6. **a bulkhead** a wall at the end of a building
7. **penitents** 忏悔者，悔罪者
8. **padlocked** locked

参考译诗

凯瑟琳之梦

（从韦利勋爵的城堡）
那一定是星期五。我能听到
楼顶打字机的轰鸣，还有
你用箱子装来的啤酒弄伤了我的头；
我把枕头扔下床，
紧抱双膝喘着气，
悬摆着的电话听筒里传来的刺耳声
像是有人梦呓般地喋喋不休
不停下喘口气或顾不上推敲直说得他的牺牲品跌进
黑暗和床单之间。我一定是睡着了，
可仍听得见父亲的数落声，他留着
你罪孽的礼物却剪去了我的头发。
他低声说他真的不在乎
是否我一辈子做你的情妇
或毁掉你的两个孩子和太太，
但我丢人的行为却让他开始酗酒。当然
我会向法庭说明他离婚的真相。
我踏着积雪走进圣帕特立克教堂的庭院，
戴眼镜的黑衣修女们微笑着守卫在
白雪堆积的防水壁前，
它烧焦的门全都开着，那些好人们
成双结队走进去向神父忏悔。每人
要有一个朋友作陪，但大家
个个都有朋友陪。修女们在微笑。
我站在一旁惊呀不已；有一阵子
冬日的阳光令人愉悦，像对别人一样
它用爱温暖了我的心，可是
忏悔的人越来越少。我开始

哭着恳求上帝饶恕我们的罪孽。
可上帝，你在哪里？你本来与我同在现在却走了。
所有被宽恕的伴侣们匆匆前去
吃晚餐度夜晚，没人停下来。
我一圈圈地奔跑直到
跌倒在院中一面挂锁的防水壁门前
那里有一张张发红的脸和已变硬的雪。

（李海云 译，李正栓 校）

思考题

1. What is the speaker's trouble? What is her dream?
2. What is the poet's intention in this poem?

John Ashbery
约翰·阿什贝利
（1927–Present）

John Ashbery was born in Rochester, New York, on July 28, 1927. He is the author of more than twenty books of poetry, and he has won nearly every major American award for poetry. His collection *A Wave* won the Lenore Marshall Poetry Prize; *Self-Portrait in a Convex Mirror* received the Pulitzer Prize for Poetry, the National Book Critics Circle Award, and the National Book Award; and *Some Trees* was selected by W. H. Auden for the Yale Younger Poets Series.

Ashbery has stated that he wishes his work to be accessible to as many people as possible, and not to be a private dialogue with himself. At the same time, he once joked that some critics still view him as "a harebrained, homegrown surrealist whose poetry defies even the rules and logic of Surrealism."

Mark Ford compared Ashbery's poetry to Walt Whitman's. "Like Whitman's, it is essentially a means of involving the reader in the poem on what Whitman calls 'equal terms'..." Nicholas Jenkins concluded in the *New York Times Book Review* that Ashbery's poetry "appeals not because it offers wisdom in a packaged form, but because the elusiveness and mysterious promise of his lines remind us that we always have a future and a condition of meaningfulness to start out toward." In 2008, the Library of America published *John Ashbery: Collected Poems, 1956–1987*, the first collection of a living poet ever published by the series. "No figure looms so large in American poetry over the past 50 years as John Ashbery," Langdon Hammer, chairman of the English Department at Yale University, wrote in 2008. "No American poet has had a larger, more diverse vocabulary, not Whitman, not Pound." Stephen Burt, a poet and Harvard professor of English, has compared Ashbery to T. S. Eliot, calling Ashbery "the last figure whom half the English-language poets alive thought a great model, and the other half thought incomprehensible."

Ashbery served as the poet laureate of New York State from 2001 to 2003. A former Chancellor of the Academy of American Poets, Ashbery is currently the

Charles P. Stevenson, Jr., Professor of Languages and Literature at Bard College. He divides his time between New York City and Hudson, New York.

Some Trees

These are amazing: each
Joining a neighbor, as though speech
Were a still performance.
Arranging by chance

To meet as far this morning
From the world as agreeing
With it, you and I
Are suddenly what the trees try

To tell us we are:
That their merely being there
Means something; that soon
We may touch, love, explain.

And glad not to have invented
Such comeliness, we are surrounded:
A silence already filled with noises,
A canvas on which emerges

A chorus of smiles, a winter morning.
Placed in a puzzling light, and moving,
Our days put on such reticence
These accents seem their own defense.

参考译诗

一 些 树

这些树令人惊奇：每一棵
都与邻树相连，似乎言语
是一次静止的表演。
偶然地做出这样的安排

今晨我们相会
远离这个世界，似乎
心有默契，你和我
突然变成这些树

想告诉我们的那个样子：
仅仅它们在这里的存在
就有某种意味；不久
我们就会抚摸，相爱，解释。

高兴的是我们从未发明
这样的美，我们被包围：
一种寂静已充满喧嚣
一幅油画，里面涌出

一支微笑的合唱曲，一个冬天的早晨。
安置在令人迷惑的光中，移动，
我们的岁月裹在这样的沉默中
似乎用这些话音就能自卫。

（马永波　译）

思考题

1. What is the main idea of this poem?
2. What do the trees tell us?
3. Learn the stanza you like best by heart.

David Lehman
大卫·莱曼
(1948–Present)

David Lehman is one of the foremost editors, literary critics, and anthologists of contemporary American literature. He is also one of the most accomplished American poets. He is the author of numerous collections of poetry, including *Yeshiva Boys* (2009), *When a Woman Loves a Man* (2005); and *The Evening Sun* (2002) and *The Daily Mirror: A Journal in Poetry* (1998), two collections of poems culled from Lehman's five-year long project of writing a poem a day. Lehman has also written collaborative books of poetry, including *Poetry Forum* (2007), with Judith Hall; and *Jim and Dave Defeat the Masked Man* (2005), a collection of sestinas he wrote with the poet James Cummins.

Lehman inaugurated *The Best American Poetry* series in 1988. As series editor, he has earned high acclaim for his pivotal role in garnering contemporary American poetry a larger audience. In an early interview about the series with Judith Moore, Lehman noted "I want the books to have a lot to commend them beyond the poems themselves. The 75 poems are of course the center of the book, but we want also to have a foreword by me that can provide a context, that gives an idea of what happened in poetry this year, and an essay in which the guest editor propounds his or her criteria." Lehman's work as an editor also includes such volumes as *The Best American Erotic Poems* (2008), *The Oxford Book of American Poetry* (2006), *A.R. Ammons: Selected Poems* (2006), *Great American Prose Poems: From Poe to the Present* (2003), and *Ecstatic Occasions, Expedient Forms* (1996). He was the director of the University of Michigan Press's *Poets on Poetry* and the *Under Discussion* series from 1994 to 2006.

Lehman's poems appeared in Chinese in the bilingual anthology *Contemporary American Poetry*, published through a partnership between the NEA and the Chinese government. Lehman's work has been translated into sixteen languages, including Spanish, French, German, Danish, Russian, Polish, Korean and Japanese.

In an interview published in *Smithsonian* Magazine, Lehman discusses the artistry of the great lyricists: "The best song lyrics seem to me so artful, so brilliant, so warm and humorous, with both passion and wit, that my admiration is matched only by my envy...these lyricists needed to work within boundaries, to get complicated emotions across and fit the lyrics to the music, and to the mood thereof. That takes genius."

When a Woman Loves a Man

When she says Margarita[1] she means Daiquiri[2].
When she says quixotic[3] she means mercurial[4].
And when she says, "I'll never speak to you again,"
she means, "Put your arms around me from behind
as I stand disconsolate at the window."

He's supposed to know that.

When a man loves a woman he is in New York and she is in Virginia
or he is in Boston, writing, and she is in New York, reading,
or she is wearing a sweater and sunglasses in Balboa Park and he
    is raking leaves in Ithaca
or he is driving to East Hampton and she is standing disconsolate
    at the window overlooking the bay
where a regatta[5] of many-colored sails is going on
while he is stuck in traffic on the Long Island Expressway.

When a woman loves a man it is one-ten in the morning,
she is asleep he is watching the ball scores and eating pretzels[6]
    drinking lemonade
and two hours later he wakes up and staggers into bed

where she remains asleep and very warm.

When she says tomorrow she means in three or four weeks.
When she says, "We're talking about me now,"
he stops talking. Her best friend comes over and says,
"Did somebody die?"

When a woman loves a man, they have gone
to swim naked in the stream
on a glorious July day
with the sound of the waterfall like a chuckle
of water rushing over smooth rocks,
and there is nothing alien in the universe.

Ripe apples fall about them.
What else can they do but eat?

When he says, "Ours is a transitional era[7]."
"That's very original of you," she replies,
dry as the Martini he is sipping.

They fight all the time
It's fun
What do I owe you?
Let's start with an apology
Ok, I'm sorry, you dickhead[8].
A sign is held up saying "Laughter."
It's a silent picture.
"I've been fucked without a kiss," she says,
"and you can quote me on that,"
which sounds great in an English accent.

One year they broke up seven times and threatened to do it
    another nine times.

When a woman loves a man, she wants him to meet her at the
    airport in a foreign country with a jeep.
When a man loves a woman he's there. He doesn't complain that
    she's two hours late
and there's nothing in the refrigerator.

When a woman loves a man, she wants to stay awake.
She's like a child crying
at nightfall because she didn't want the day to end.

When a man loves a woman, he watches her sleep, thinking:
as midnight to the moon is sleep to the beloved.
A thousand fireflies wink at him.
The frogs sound like the string section
of the orchestra warming up.
The stars dangle down like earrings the shape of grapes.

注释

1. **Margarita** 玛格丽塔酒，由墨西哥龙舌兰酒、酸橙或柠檬汁以及橙味酒混合调制而成
2. **Daiquiri** 得其利，一种鸡尾酒
3. **quixotic** 堂吉诃德式的；愚侠的；不切实际的；幻想的
4. **mercurial** （指人）反复无常的；（指人或性质）灵活的，易变的
5. **regatta** 划船比赛，赛艇会
6. **pretzels** 椒盐脆饼干
7. **transitional era** 过渡时期。it implies that their relationship is not firm and smooth.
8. **dickhead** (slang) If someone calls a man dickhead, he is saying that he is very stupid.

参考译诗

当女人爱上男人

她说要玛格丽塔酒，意思是想喝要得其利。
她说喜欢堂吉诃德式的，其实是墨丘利式的。
她说："再也不理你了，"
她想说的是："看我闷闷不乐站在窗前，
你该伸出手臂从身后拥抱我。"

他该知道这些。

当男人爱上女人他在纽约而她在弗吉尼亚
或者他在波士顿，在写作，而她在纽约，在读书，
或者她在巴尔博亚公园，穿着毛衫戴着太阳镜
而他却在伊萨卡清扫落叶
或者他正开车前往东汉普顿而她却站在窗前
　　郁郁寡欢地俯瞰海湾
那里千帆竞发色彩斑斓
而他却塞车在长岛的高速路上无法动弹。

当女人爱上男人，在凌晨一点十分
她在熟睡他在看球赛吃着饼干
喝着柠檬水
过了两小时后他醒了晃晃悠悠爬上床
她仍在睡梦中那么温暖

她说明天其实是指三四个星期以后
她说："现在说说我的事吧，"
他缄口不言。她的好闺密来了会问：
"有人离世了吗？"

当女人爱上男人，他们一起去过
小溪裸泳
那是阳光灿烂的七月
潺潺的水流的像咯咯的笑声
冲刷着光洁的石头
只有他们两人在整个宇宙中。

熟透的苹果掉下来落向他们
除了吃掉还能做什么？

当他说："咱俩的关系还不稳定，"
"你说得很独到，"她回答，
语气冷冷的一如他啜饮的马提尼。

他们一直在吵闹
真有趣
我欠你什么？
让我们开始道歉
好吧，对不起，你个白痴。
一个信号"笑"被举了起来。
画面沉默。
"你和我做爱没吻我，"她说，
"你可以不断提醒我这事，"
英国口音听起来很悦耳。

有一年他们闹分手七次威胁对方要分手九次。

当女人爱上男人，她要他开着吉普车
去很远的机场接她。
当男人爱上女人他会去接她。他不会抱怨
她晚了俩小时，也不抱怨

冰箱里空空如也。

当女人爱上男人，她想一直不睡，
她像孩子一样在黄昏哭泣
因为她不想让这一天结束。

当男人爱上女人，他会看她酣睡，心想：
睡眠对于爱人来说，就像午夜对于月亮。
无数的萤火虫在对他眨眼。
像乐队的弦乐手们在热身
青蛙叫声一片。
星星向下低垂恰似葡萄形状的耳坠。

（张青梅　译）

思考题

1. The poem describes what men and women do when they fall in love. Where do they differ?
2. What do the following lines imply?

    Ripe apples fall about them.
    What else can they do but eat?

3. Learn the last two stanzas by heart.

参考文献

Abrams, M. H. ed. 1979. *The Norton Anthology of English Literature*. New York: W. W. Norton & Company.

Gottesman, Ronald et al. 1979. *The Norton Anthology of American Literature*. New York: W. W. Norton & Company.

桂扬清，吴翔林. 1991. 英美文学选读[M]. 北京：中国对外翻译出版公司.

胡家峦. 1995. 英语诗歌精品[M]. 北京：北京大学出版社.

胡家峦. 2008. 英美诗歌名篇详注[M]. 北京：中国人民大学出版社.

凯・赖安. 2011. 当代美国诗选[M]. 北京：人民文学出版社.

林以亮. 1989. 美国诗选[M]. 北京：生活・读书・新知三联书店.

陶　洁. 2008. 美国诗歌选读[M]. 北京：北京大学出版社.

吴伟仁. 1988. 英国文学史及选读[M]. 北京：外语教学与研究出版社.

吴伟仁. 1988. 美国文学史及选读[M]. 北京：外语教学与研究出版社.

赵毅衡. 1985. 美国现代诗选[M]. 北京：外国文学出版社.

清华大学出版社 高等学校英语专业系列教材

高级英语视听说教程学生用书（第二版）上 作者：戴劲、刘晶 等
定价：22.00 书号：978-7-302-22869-1

高级英语视听说教程学生用书（第二版）下 作者：戴劲、刘晶 等
定价：29.80 书号：978-7-302-22870-7

高级英语视听说教程教师用书（第二版）全一册 作者：戴劲、刘晶 等
定价：49.80 书号：978-7-302-22868-4

中级英语视听说教程学生用书（第二版）上 作者：王祥兵、刘晶 等
定价：17.80 书号：978-7-302-23420-3

中级英语视听说教程学生用书（第二版）下 作者：王祥兵、刘晶 等
定价：18.00 书号：978-7-302-23421-0

中级英语视听说教程教师用书（第二版）全一册 作者：王祥兵、刘晶 等
定价：34.80 书号：978-7-302-23422-7

英语写作实践教程（第二版） 作者：李贵苍 等
定价：32.00 书号：978-7-302-29921-9

《高级英汉翻译理论与实践》（第三版） 作者：叶子南
定价：35.00 书号：978-7-302-32813-1

汉英比较翻译教程（第二版） 作者：魏志成
定价：39.90 书号：978-7-302-29526-6

汉英比较翻译教程练习（第二版） 作者：魏志成、余军
定价：18.00 书号：978-7-302-31904-7

英汉比较翻译教程（第二版） 作者：魏志成
定价：38.50 书号：978-7-302-29015-5

英汉比较翻译教程练习（第二版） 作者：魏志成、余军
定价：20.00 书号：978-7-302-31610-7

英汉互译入门教程 作者：许建平
定价：22.00 书号：978-7-302-19772-0

英汉互译实践与技巧（第四版） 作者：许建平
定价：39.80 书号：978-7-302-29029-2

英汉互译实践与技巧（第四版）教学参考书 作者：许建平
定价：42.00 书号：978-7-302-29028-5

《英汉互译实践与技巧》辅导备考教程 作者：许建平
定价：39.90 书号：978-7-302-32898-8

英汉语篇翻译（第三版） 作者：李运兴
定价：35.00 书号：978-7-302-26652-5

高级汉英语篇翻译（修订版） 作者：居祖纯
定价：22.00 书号：978-7-302-27569-5

美国文学学习指南（第二版）——美国文学史及选读综合练习 作者：李正栓 等
定价：33.00 书号：978-7-302-12462-7

英国文学学习指南（第二版）——英国文学史及选读综合练习 作者：李正栓 等
定价：42.00 书号：978-7-302-12218-0

英美诗歌教程（第二版） 作者：李正栓 等
定价：48.00 书号：978-7-302 -37600-2

英美文学赏析教程（散文与诗歌） 作者：罗选民 等
定价：20.00 书号：978-7-302-05404-7

英美文学赏析教程（第二版）：小说卷 作者：罗选民 等
定价：55.00 书号：978-7-302-37154-0

新编简明英语语言学概论 作者：马琰 王峰
定价：待定 书号：978-7-302-37533-3

实用大学英语语法新编 作者：曾亚军 等
定价：58.00 书号：978-7-302-36900-4